孫子兵法

THE ART OF WAR

• AND OTHER EASTERN CLASSICS •

SUN TZU

PAGE CLASSICS

ISBN: 978-1-64833-801-4

The Art of War
The Tao Te Ching
Confucian Analects

Published by Page Publications 2024

Printed in China

Contents

SUN TZŬ ON THE ART OF WAR

THE OLDEST MILITARY TREATISE IN THE WORLD

Translated from the Chinese with Introduction and Critical Notes

LIONEL GILES, M.A.

Assistant in the Department of Oriental Printed Books and MSS. in the British Museum

1910

To my brother
Captain Valentine Giles, R.G.
in the hope that
a work 2400 years old
may yet contain lessons worth consideration
by the soldier of today
this translation
is affectionately dedicated.

Contents

Preface by Lionel Giles

The seventh volume of *Mémoires concernant l'histoire, les sciences, les arts, les mœurs, les usages, &c., des Chinois* is devoted to the Art of War, and contains, amongst other treatises, "Les Treize Articles de Sun-tse," translated from the Chinese by a Jesuit Father, Joseph Amiot. Père Amiot appears to have enjoyed no small reputation as a sinologue in his day, and the field of his labours was certainly extensive. But his so-called translation of the Sun Tzŭ, if placed side by side with the original, is seen at once to be little better than an imposture. It contains a great deal that Sun Tzŭ did not write, and very little indeed of what he did. Here is a fair specimen, taken from the opening sentences of chapter 5:—

> *De l'habileté dans le gouvernement des Troupes.* Sun-tse dit : Ayez les noms de tous les Officiers tant généraux que subalternes; inscrivez-les dans un catalogue à part, avec la note des talents & de la capacité de chacun d'eux, afin de pouvoir les employer avec avantage lorsque l'occasion en sera venue. Faites en sorte que tous ceux que vous devez commander soient persuadés que votre principale attention est de les préserver de tout dommage. Les troupes que vous ferez avancer contre l'ennemi doivent être comme des pierres que vous lanceriez contre des œufs. De vous à l'ennemi il ne doit y avoir d'autre différence que celle du fort au faible, du vide au plein. Attaquez à découvert, mais soyez vainqueur en secret. Voilà en peu de mots en quoi consiste

l'habileté & toute la perfection même du gouvernement des troupes.

Throughout the nineteenth century, which saw a wonderful development in the study of Chinese literature, no translator ventured to tackle Sun Tzŭ, although his work was known to be highly valued in China as by far the oldest and best compendium of military science. It was not until the year 1905 that the first English translation, by Capt. E.F. Calthrop. R.F.A., appeared at Tokyo under the title "Sonshi"(the Japanese form of Sun Tzŭ). Unfortunately, it was evident that the translator's knowledge of Chinese was far too scanty to fit him to grapple with the manifold difficulties of Sun Tzŭ. He himself plainly acknowledges that without the aid of two Japanese gentlemen "the accompanying translation would have been impossible." We can only wonder, then, that with their help it should have been so excessively bad. It is not merely a question of downright blunders, from which none can hope to be wholly exempt. Omissions were frequent; hard passages were wilfully distorted or slurred over. Such offences are less pardonable. They would not be tolerated in any edition of a Greek or Latin classic, and a similar standard of honesty ought to be insisted upon in translations from Chinese.

From blemishes of this nature, at least, I believe that the present translation is free. It was not undertaken out of any inflated estimate of my own powers; but I could not help feeling that Sun Tzŭ deserved a better fate than had befallen him, and I knew that, at any rate, I could hardly fail to improve on the work of my predecessors. Towards the end of 1908, a new and revised edition of Capt. Calthrop's translation was published in London, this time, however, without any allusion to his Japanese collaborators. My first three chapters were then already in the printer's hands, so that the criticisms of Capt. Calthrop therein contained must be understood as referring to his earlier edition. This is on the whole an improvement on the other, thought there still remains much that cannot pass muster. Some of the grosser blunders have been rectified and lacunae filled up, but on the other hand a certain number of new mistakes appear. The very first sentence of the introduction is startlingly inaccurate; and later on, while mention is made of "an army of Japanese commentators" on Sun Tzŭ (who are these, by the way?), not a word is vouchsafed about the Chinese commentators, who nevertheless, I venture to assert, form a much more numerous and infinitely more important "army."

A few special features of the present volume may now be noticed. In the first place, the text has been cut up into numbered paragraphs, both in order to facilitate cross-reference and for the convenience of students generally. The division follows broadly that of Sun Hsing-yen's edition; but I have sometimes found it desirable to join two or more of his paragraphs into one. In quoting from other works, Chinese writers seldom give more than the bare title by way of reference, and the task of research is apt to be seriously hampered in consequence. With a view to obviating this difficulty so far as Sun Tzŭ is concerned, I have also appended a complete concordance of Chinese characters, following in this the admirable example of Legge, though an alphabetical arrangement has been preferred to the distribution under radicals which he adopted. Another feature borrowed from "The Chinese Classics" is the printing of text, translation and notes on the same page; the notes, however, are inserted, according to the Chinese method, immediately after the passages to which they refer. From the mass of native commentary my aim has been to extract the cream only, adding the Chinese text here and there when it seemed to present points of literary interest. Though constituting in itself an important branch of Chinese literature, very little commentary of this kind has hitherto been made directly accessible by translation.

I may say in conclusion that, owing to the printing off of my sheets as they were completed, the work has not had the benefit of a final revision. On a review of the whole, without modifying the substance of my criticisms, I might have been inclined in a few instances to temper their asperity. Having chosen to wield a bludgeon, however, I shall not cry out if in return I am visited with more than a rap over the knuckles. Indeed, I have been at some pains to put a sword into the hands of future opponents by scrupulously giving either text or reference for every passage translated. A scathing review, even from the pen of the Shanghai critic who despises "mere translations," would not, I must confess, be altogether unwelcome. For, after all, the worst fate I shall have to dread is that which befell the ingenious paradoxes of George in *The Vicar of Wakefield*.

Introduction

Sun Tzŭ and his Book

Ssŭ-ma Ch'ien gives the following biography of Sun Tzŭ:

> Sun Tzŭ Wu was a native of the Ch'i State. His *Art of War* brought him to the notice of Ho Lü, King of Wu. Ho Lü said to him:
>
> "I have carefully perused your thirteen chapters. May I submit your theory of managing soldiers to a slight test?"
>
> Sun Tzŭ replied: "You may."
>
> Ho Lü asked: "May the test be applied to women?"
>
> The answer was again in the affirmative, so arrangements were made to bring on hundred eighty ladies out of the Palace. Sun Tzŭ divided them into two companies, and placed one of the King's favourite concubines at the head of each. He then bade them all take spears in their hands, and addressed them thus: "I presume you know the difference between front and back, right hand and left hand?"
>
> The girls replied: Yes.
>
> Sun Tzŭ went on: "When I say "Eyes front," you must look straight ahead. When I say "Left turn," you must face towards your left hand. When I say "Right turn," you must face towards your right hand. When I say "About turn," you must face right round towards your back."

Again the girls assented. The words of command having been thus explained, he set up the halberds and battle-axes in order to begin the drill. Then, to the sound of drums, he gave the order "Right turn." But the girls only burst out laughing. Sun Tzŭ said: "If words of command are not clear and distinct, if orders are not thoroughly understood, then the general is to blame."

So he started drilling them again, and this time gave the order "Left turn," whereupon the girls once more burst into fits of laughter. Sun Tzŭ: "If words of command are not clear and distinct, if orders are not thoroughly understood, the general is to blame. But if his orders *are* clear, and the soldiers nevertheless disobey, then it is the fault of their officers."

So saying, he ordered the leaders of the two companies to be beheaded. Now the king of Wu was watching the scene from the top of a raised pavilion; and when he saw that his favourite concubines were about to be executed, he was greatly alarmed and hurriedly sent down the following message: "We are now quite satisfied as to our general's ability to handle troops. If we are bereft of these two concubines, our meat and drink will lose their savor. It is our wish that they shall not be beheaded."

Sun Tzŭ replied: "Having once received His Majesty's commission to be the general of his forces, there are certain commands of His Majesty which, acting in that capacity, I am unable to accept."

Accordingly, he had the two leaders beheaded, and straightway installed the pair next in order as leaders in their place. When this had been done, the drum was sounded for the drill once more; and the girls went through all the evolutions,

> turning to the right or to the left, marching ahead or wheeling back, kneeling or standing, with perfect accuracy and precision, not venturing to utter a sound. Then Sun Tzŭ sent a messenger to the King saying: "Your soldiers, Sire, are now properly drilled and disciplined, and ready for your majesty's inspection. They can be put to any use that their sovereign may desire; bid them go through fire and water, and they will not disobey."
>
> But the King replied: "Let our general cease drilling and return to camp. As for us, We have no wish to come down and inspect the troops."
>
> Thereupon Sun Tzŭ said: "The King is only fond of words, and cannot translate them into deeds."
>
> After that, Ho Lü saw that Sun Tzŭ was one who knew how to handle an army, and finally appointed him general. In the west, he defeated the Ch'u State and forced his way into Ying, the capital; to the north he put fear into the States of Ch'i and Chin, and spread his fame abroad amongst the feudal princes. And Sun Tzŭ shared in the might of the King.

About Sun Tzŭ himself this is all that Ssŭ-ma Ch'ien has to tell us in this chapter. But he proceeds to give a biography of his descendant, Sun Pin, born about a hundred years after his famous ancestor's death, and also the outstanding military genius of his time. The historian speaks of him too as Sun Tzŭ, and in his preface we read: "Sun Tzŭ had his feet cut off and yet continued to discuss the art of war." It seems likely, then, that "Pin" was a nickname bestowed on him after his mutilation, unless the story was invented in order to account for the name. The crowning incident of his career, the crushing defeat of his treacherous rival P'ang Chüan, will be found briefly related in Chapter V. § 19 of *The Art of War*.

To return to the elder Sun Tzŭ. He is mentioned in two other passages of the *Shih Chi*:—

> In the third year of his reign [512 B.C.] Ho Lü, king of Wu, took the field with Tzŭ-hsü [i.e. Wu Yüan] and Po P'ei, and attacked Ch'u. He captured the town of Shu and slew the two prince's sons who had formerly been generals of Wu. He was then meditating a descent on Ying [the capital]; but the general Sun Wu said: "The army is exhausted. It is not yet possible. We must wait'.... [After further successful fighting,] "in the ninth year [506 B.C.], King Ho Lü addressed Wu Tzŭ-hsü and Sun Wu, saying: "Formerly, you declared that it was not yet possible for us to enter Ying. Is the time ripe now?" The two men replied: "Ch'u's general Tzŭ-ch'ang, is grasping and covetous, and the princes of T'ang and Ts'ai both have a grudge against him. If Your Majesty has resolved to make a grand attack, you must win over T'ang and Ts'ai, and then you may succeed." Ho Lü followed this advice, [beat Ch'u in five pitched battles and marched into Ying.]

This is the latest date at which anything is recorded of Sun Wu. He does not appear to have survived his patron, who died from the effects of a wound in 496. In another chapter there occurs this passage:

> From this time onward, a number of famous soldiers arose, one after the other: Kao-fan, who was employed by the Chin State; Wang-tzŭ, in the service of Ch'i; and Sun Wu, in the service of Wu. These men developed and threw light upon the principles of war.

It is obvious enough that Ssŭ-ma Ch'ien at least had no doubt about the reality of Sun Wu as an historical personage; and with one exception, to be noticed presently, he is by far the most important authority on the period in question. It will not be necessary, therefore, to say much of such a work as the *Wu Yüeh Ch'un Ch'iu*, which is supposed to have been written by Chao Yeh of the 1st century A.D. The attribution is somewhat doubtful; but even if it were otherwise, his account would be of little value, based as it is on the *Shih Chi* and expanded with romantic details. The story of Sun Tzŭ will be found, for what it is worth, in chapter 2. The only new points in it worth noting are: (1) Sun Tzŭ was first recommended to Ho Lü by Wu Tzŭ-hsü. (2) He is called a native of Wu. (3) He had previously lived a retired life, and his contemporaries were unaware of his ability.

The following passage occurs in the Huai-nan Tzŭ: "When sovereign and ministers show perversity of mind, it is impossible even for a Sun Tzŭ to encounter the foe." Assuming that this work is genuine (and hitherto no doubt has been cast upon it), we have here the earliest direct reference for Sun Tzŭ, for Huai-nan Tzŭ died in 122 B.C., many years before the *Shih Chi* was given to the world.

Liu Hsiang (80-9 B.C.) says: "The reason why Sun Tzŭ at the head of 30,000 men beat Ch'u with 200,000 is that the latter were undisciplined."

Têng Ming-shih informs us that the surname "Sun" was bestowed on Sun Wu's grandfather by Duke Ching of Ch'i [547-490 B.C.]. Sun Wu's father Sun P'ing, rose to be a Minister of State in Ch'i, and Sun Wu himself, whose style was Ch'ang-ch'ing, fled to Wu on account of the rebellion which was being fomented by the kindred of T'ien Pao. He had three sons, of whom the second, named Ming, was the father of Sun Pin. According to this account then, Pin was the grandson of Wu, which, considering that Sun Pin's victory over Wei was gained in 341 B.C., may be dismissed as chronologically impossible. Whence these data were obtained by Têng Ming-shih I do not know, but of course no reliance whatever can be placed in them.

An interesting document which has survived from the close of the Han period is the short preface written by the Great Ts'ao Ts'ao, or Wei Wu Ti, for his edition of Sun Tzŭ. I shall give it in full:—

> I have heard that the ancients used bows and arrows to their advantage. The *Lun Yü* says: "There must be a sufficiency of military strength." The *Shu Ching* mentions "the army" among the "eight objects of government." The *I Ching* says: "'army' indicates firmness and justice; the experienced leader will have good fortune." The *Shih Ching* says: "The King rose majestic in his wrath, and he marshalled his troops." The Yellow Emperor, T'ang the Completer and Wu Wang all used spears and battle-axes in order to succour their generation. The *Ssŭ-ma Fa* says: "If one man slay another of set purpose, he himself may rightfully be slain." He who relies solely on warlike measures shall be exterminated; he who relies solely on peaceful measures shall perish. Instances of this are Fu Ch'ai on the one hand and Yen Wang on the other. In military matters, the Sage's rule is normally to keep the peace, and to move his forces only when occasion requires. He will not use armed force unless driven to it by necessity.
>
> Many books have I read on the subject of war and fighting; but the work composed by Sun Wu is the profoundest of them all. [Sun Tzŭ was a native of the Ch'i state, his personal name was Wu. He wrote the *Art of War* in 13 chapters for Ho Lü, King of Wu. Its principles were tested on women, and he was subsequently made a general. He led an army westwards, crushed the Ch'u state and entered Ying the capital. In the north, he kept Ch'i and Chin in awe. A hundred years and more after his time, Sun Pin lived. He was a descendant of Wu.] In his treatment of deliberation and planning, the importance of rapidity in taking the field, clearness of conception, and depth of design, Sun Tzŭ

> stands beyond the reach of carping criticism. My contemporaries, however, have failed to grasp the full meaning of his instructions, and while putting into practice the smaller details in which his work abounds, they have overlooked its essential purport. That is the motive which has led me to outline a rough explanation of the whole.

One thing to be noticed in the above is the explicit statement that the thirteen chapters were specially composed for King Ho Lü. This is supported by the internal evidence of I. § 15, in which it seems clear that some ruler is addressed.

In the bibliographic section of the *Han Shu*, there is an entry which has given rise to much discussion: "The works of Sun Tzŭ of Wu in 82 *p'ien* (or chapters), with diagrams in 9 *chüan*." It is evident that this cannot be merely the thirteen chapters known to Ssŭ-ma Ch'ien, or those we possess today. Chang Shou-chieh refers to an edition of Sun Tzŭ's *Art of War* of which the "thirteen chapters" formed the first *chüan*, adding that there were two other *chüan* besides. This has brought forth a theory, that the bulk of these 82 chapters consisted of other writings of Sun Tzŭ—we should call them apocryphal—similar to the *Wên Ta*, of which a specimen dealing with the Nine Situations is preserved in the *T'ung Tien*, and another in Ho Shin's commentary. It is suggested that before his interview with Ho Lü, Sun Tzŭ had only written the 13 chapters, but afterwards composed a sort of exegesis in the form of question and answer between himself and the King. Pi I-hsün, the author of the *Sun Tzŭ Hsü Lu*, backs this up with a quotation from the *Wu Yüeh Ch'un Ch'iu*: "The King of Wu summoned Sun Tzŭ, and asked him questions about the art of war. Each time he set forth a chapter of his work, the King could not find words enough to praise him." As he points out, if the whole work was expounded on the same scale as in the above-mentioned fragments, the total number of chapters could not fail to be considerable. Then the numerous other treatises attributed to Sun Tzŭ might be included. The fact that the *Han Chih* mentions no work of Sun Tzŭ except the 82 *p'ien*, whereas the Sui and T'ang bibliographies give the titles of others in addition to the "thirteen chapters," is good proof, Pi I-hsün thinks, that all of these were contained in the 82 *p'ien*. Without pinning our faith to the accuracy of details supplied by the *Wu Yüeh Ch'un Ch'iu*, or admitting the genuineness of any of the treatises cited by Pi I-hsün, we may see in this theory a probable solution of the mystery. Between Ssŭ-ma Ch'ien and Pan Ku there was plenty of time for a luxuriant crop of forgeries to have grown up under the magic name of Sun Tzŭ, and the 82 *p'ien* may very well represent a collected edition of these lumped together with the original work. It is also possible, though less likely, that some of them existed in the time of the earlier historian and were purposely ignored by him.

Tu Mu's conjecture seems to be based on a passage which states: "Wei Wu Ti strung together Sun Wu's *Art of War*," which in turn may have resulted from a misunderstanding of the final words of Ts'ao King's preface. This, as Sun Hsing-yen points out, is only a modest way of saying that he made an explanatory paraphrase, or in other words, wrote a commentary on it. On the whole, this theory has met with very little acceptance. Thus, the *Ssŭ K'u Ch'üan Shu* says: "The mention of the thirteen chapters in the *Shih Chi* shows that they were in existence before the *Han Chih*, and that latter accretions are not to be considered part of the original work. Tu Mu's assertion can certainly not be taken as proof."

There is every reason to suppose, then, that the thirteen chapters existed in the time of Ssŭ-ma Ch'ien practically as we have them now. That the work was then well known he tells us in so many words. "Sun Tzŭ's *Thirteen Chapters* and Wu Ch'i's *Art of War* are the two books that people commonly refer to on the subject of military matters. Both of them are widely distributed, so I will not discuss them here." But as we go further back, serious difficulties begin to arise. The salient fact which has to be faced is that the *Tso Chüan*, the greatest contemporary record, makes no mention whatsoever of Sun Wu, either as a general or as a writer. It is natural, in view of this awkward circumstance, that many scholars should not only cast doubt on the story of Sun Wu as given in the *Shih Chi*, but even show themselves frankly skeptical as to the existence of the man at all. The most powerful presentment of this side of the case is to be found in the following disposition by Yeh Shui-hsin:—

> It is stated in Ssŭ-ma Ch'ien's history that Sun Wu was a native of the Ch'i State, and employed by Wu; and that in the reign of Ho Lü he crushed Ch'u, entered Ying, and was a great general. But in Tso's Commentary no Sun Wu appears at all. It is true that Tso's Commentary need not contain absolutely everything that other histories contain. But Tso has not omitted to mention vulgar plebeians and hireling ruffians such as Ying K'ao-shu Ts'ao Kuei, Chu Chih-wu and Chüan She-chu. In the case of Sun Wu, whose fame and achievements were so brilliant, the omission is much more glaring. Again, details are given, in their due order, about his contemporaries Wu Yüan and the Minister P'ei. Is it credible that Sun Wu alone should have been passed over?
>
> In point of literary style, Sun Tzŭ's work belongs to the same school as *Kuan Tzŭ*, *Liu T'ao*, and the *Yüeh Yü* and may have been the production of some private scholar living towards the end of the "Spring and Autumn" or the beginning of the "Warring States" period. The story that his precepts were actually applied by the Wu State, is merely the outcome of big talk on the part of his followers.
>
> From the flourishing period of the Chou dynasty down to the time of the "Spring and Autumn," all military commanders were statesmen as well, and the class of professional

> generals, for conducting external campaigns, did not then exist. It was not until the period of the "Six States" that this custom changed. Now although Wu was an uncivilized State, it is conceivable that Tso should have left unrecorded the fact that Sun Wu was a great general and yet held no civil office? What we are told, therefore, about Jang-chu and Sun Wu, is not authentic matter, but the reckless fabrication of theorizing pundits. The story of Ho Lü's experiment on the women, in particular, is utterly preposterous and incredible.

Yeh Shui-hsin represents Ssŭ-ma Ch'ien as having said that Sun Wu crushed Ch'u and entered Ying. This is not quite correct. No doubt the impression left on the reader's mind is that he at least shared in these exploits. The fact may or may not be significant; but it is nowhere explicitly stated in the *Shih Chi* either that Sun Tzŭ was general on the occasion of the taking of Ying, or that he even went there at all. Moreover, as we know that Wu Yüan and Po P'ei both took part in the expedition, and also that its success was largely due to the dash and enterprise of Fu Kai, Ho Lü's younger brother, it is not easy to see how yet another general could have played a very prominent part in the same campaign.

Ch'ên Chên-sun of the Sung dynasty has the note:—

> Military writers look upon Sun Wu as the father of their art. But the fact that he does not appear in the *Tso Chüan*, although he is said to have served under Ho Lü King of Wu, makes it uncertain what period he really belonged to.

He also says:—

> The works of Sun Wu and Wu Ch'i may be of genuine antiquity.

It is noticeable that both Yeh Shui-hsin and Ch'ên Chên-sun, while rejecting the personality of Sun Wu as he figures in Ssŭ-ma Ch'ien's history, are inclined to accept the date traditionally assigned to the work which passes under his name. The author of the *Hsü Lu* fails to appreciate this distinction, and consequently his bitter attack on Ch'ên Chên-sun really misses its mark. He makes one of two points, however, which certainly tell in favour of the high antiquity of our "Thirteen chapters." "Sun Tzŭ," he says, "must have lived in the age of Ching Wang [519-476], because he is frequently plagiarized in subsequent works of the Chou, Ch'in and Han dynasties." The two most shameless offenders in this respect are Wu Ch'i and Huai-nan Tzŭ, both of them important historical personages in their day. The former lived only a century after the alleged date of Sun Tzŭ, and his death is known to have taken place in 381 B.C. It was to him, according to Liu Hsiang, that Tsêng Shên delivered the *Tso Chüan*, which had been entrusted to him by its author. Now the fact that quotations from the *Art of War*, acknowledged or otherwise, are to be found in so many authors of different epochs, establishes a very strong anterior to them all,—in other words, that Sun Tzŭ's treatise was already in existence towards the end of the 5th century B.C. Further proof of Sun Tzŭ's antiquity is furnished by the archaic or wholly obsolete meanings attaching to a number of the words he uses. A list of these, which might perhaps be extended, is given in the *Hsü Lu;* and though some of the interpretations are doubtful, the main argument is hardly affected thereby. Again, it must not be forgotten that Yeh Shui-hsin, a scholar and critic of the first rank, deliberately pronounces the style of the thirteen chapters to belong to the early part of the fifth century. Seeing that he is actually engaged in an attempt to disprove the existence of Sun Wu himself, we may be sure that he would not have hesitated to assign the work to a later date had he not honestly believed the contrary. And it is precisely on such a point that the judgment of an educated Chinaman will carry most weight. Other internal evidence is not far to seek. Thus in XIII. § 1, there is an unmistakable allusion to the ancient system of land-tenure which had already passed away by the time of Mencius, who was anxious to see it revived in a modified form. The only warfare Sun Tzŭ knows is that carried on between the various feudal princes, in which armored chariots play a large part. Their use seems to have entirely died out before the end of the Chou dynasty. He speaks as a man of Wu, a state which ceased to exist as early as 473 B.C. On this I shall touch presently.

But once refer the work to the 5th century or earlier, and the chances of its being other than a *bonâ fide* production are sensibly diminished. The great age of forgeries did not come until long after. That it should have been forged in the period immediately following 473 is particularly unlikely, for no one, as a rule, hastens to identify himself with a lost cause. As for Yeh Shui-hsin's theory, that the author was a literary recluse, that seems to me quite untenable. If one thing is more apparent than another after reading the maxims of Sun Tzŭ, it is that their essence has been distilled from a large store of personal observation and experience. They reflect the mind not only of a born strategist, gifted with a rare faculty of generalization, but also of a practical soldier closely acquainted with the military conditions of his time. To say nothing of the fact that these sayings have been accepted and endorsed by all the greatest captains of Chinese history, they offer a combination of freshness and sincerity, acuteness and common sense, which quite excludes the idea that they were artificially concocted in the study. If we admit, then, that the thirteen chapters were the genuine production of a military man living towards the end of the "*Ch'un Ch'iu*" period, are we not bound, in spite of the silence of the *Tso Chüan*, to accept Ssŭ-ma Ch'ien's account in its entirety? In view of his high repute as a sober historian, must we not hesitate to assume that the records he drew upon for Sun Wu's biography were false and untrustworthy? The answer, I fear, must be in the negative. There is still one grave, if not fatal, objection to the chronology involved in the story as told in the *Shih*

Chi, which, so far as I am aware, nobody has yet pointed out. There are two passages in Sun Tzŭ in which he alludes to contemporary affairs. The first in in VI. § 21:—

> Though according to my estimate the soldiers of Yüeh exceed our own in number, that shall advantage them nothing in the matter of victory. I say then that victory can be achieved.

The other is in XI. § 30:—

> Asked if an army can be made to imitate the *shuai-jan*, I should answer, Yes. For the men of Wu and the men of Yüeh are enemies; yet if they are crossing a river in the same boat and are caught by a storm, they will come to each other's assistance just as the left hand helps the right.

These two paragraphs are extremely valuable as evidence of the date of composition. They assign the work to the period of the struggle between Wu and Yüeh. So much has been observed by Pi I-hsün. But what has hitherto escaped notice is that they also seriously impair the credibility of Ssŭ-ma Ch'ien's narrative. As we have seen above, the first positive date given in connection with Sun Wu is 512 B.C. He is then spoken of as a general, acting as confidential adviser to Ho Lü, so that his alleged introduction to that monarch had already taken place, and of course the thirteen chapters must have been written earlier still. But at that time, and for several years after, down to the capture of Ying in 506, Ch'u and not Yüeh, was the great hereditary enemy of Wu. The two states, Ch'u and Wu, had been constantly at war for over half a century, whereas the first war between Wu and Yüeh was waged only in 510, and even then was no more than a short interlude sandwiched in the midst of the fierce struggle with Ch'u. Now Ch'u is not mentioned in the thirteen chapters at all. The natural inference is that they were written at a time when Yüeh had become the prime antagonist of Wu, that is, after Ch'u had suffered the great humiliation of 506. At this point, a table of dates may be found useful.

B.C.	
514	Accession of Ho Lü.
512	Ho Lü attacks Ch'u, but is dissuaded from entering Ying, the capital. Shih Chi mentions Sun Wu as general.
511	Another attack on Ch'u.
510	Wu makes a successful attack on Yüeh. This is the first war between the two states.
509 or 508	Ch'u invades Wu, but is signally defeated at Yü-chang.
506	Ho Lü attacks Ch'u with the aid of T'ang and Ts'ai. Decisive battle of Po-chü, and capture of Ying. Last mention of Sun Wu in Shih Chi.
505	Yüeh makes a raid on Wu in the absence of its army. Wu is beaten by Ch'in and evacuates Ying.
504	Ho Lü sends Fu Ch'ai to attack Ch'u.
497	Kou Chien becomes King of Yüeh.
496	Wu attacks Yüeh, but is defeated by Kou Chien at Tsui-li. Ho Lü is killed.
494	Fu Ch'ai defeats Kou Chien in the great battle of Fu-chaio, and enters the capital of Yüeh.
485 or 484	Kou Chien renders homage to Wu. Death of Wu Tzŭ-hsü.
482	Kou Chien invades Wu in the absence of Fu Ch'ai.

478 to 476	Further attacks by Yüeh on Wu.
475	Kou Chien lays siege to the capital of Wu.
473	Final defeat and extinction of Wu.

The sentence quoted above from VI. § 21 hardly strikes me as one that could have been written in the full flush of victory. It seems rather to imply that, for the moment at least, the tide had turned against Wu, and that she was getting the worst of the struggle. Hence we may conclude that our treatise was not in existence in 505, before which date Yüeh does not appear to have scored any notable success against Wu. Ho Lü died in 496, so that if the book was written for him, it must have been during the period 505-496, when there was a lull in the hostilities, Wu having presumably exhausted by its supreme effort against Ch'u. On the other hand, if we choose to disregard the tradition connecting Sun Wu's name with Ho Lü, it might equally well have seen the light between 496 and 494, or possibly in the period 482-473, when Yüeh was once again becoming a very serious menace. We may feel fairly certain that the author, whoever he may have been, was not a man of any great eminence in his own day. On this point the negative testimony of the *Tso Chüan* far outweighs any shred of authority still attaching to the *Shih Chi*, if once its other facts are discredited. Sun Hsing-yen, however, makes a feeble attempt to explain the omission of his name from the great commentary. It was Wu Tzŭ-hsü, he says, who got all the credit of Sun Wu's exploits, because the latter (being an alien) was not rewarded with an office in the State.

How then did the Sun Tzŭ legend originate? It may be that the growing celebrity of the book imparted by degrees a kind of factitious renown to its author. It was felt to be only right and proper that one so well versed in the science of war should have solid achievements to his credit as well. Now the capture of Ying was undoubtedly the greatest feat of arms in Ho Lü's reign; it made a deep and lasting impression on all the surrounding states, and raised Wu to the short-lived zenith of her power. Hence, what more natural, as time went on, than that the acknowledged master of strategy, Sun Wu, should be popularly identified with that campaign, at first perhaps only in the sense that his brain conceived and planned it; afterwards, that it was actually carried out by him in conjunction with Wu Yüan, Po P'ei and Fu Kai?

It is obvious that any attempt to reconstruct even the outline of Sun Tzŭ's life must be based almost wholly on conjecture. With this necessary proviso, I should say that he probably entered the service of Wu about the time of Ho Lü's accession, and gathered experience, though only in the capacity of a subordinate officer, during the intense military activity which marked the first half of the prince's reign. If he rose to be a general at all, he certainly was never on an equal footing with the three above mentioned. He was doubtless present at the investment and occupation of Ying, and witnessed Wu's sudden collapse in the following year. Yüeh's attack at this critical juncture, when her rival was embarrassed on every side, seems to have convinced him that this upstart kingdom was the great enemy against whom every effort would henceforth have to be directed. Sun Wu was thus a well-seasoned warrior when he sat down to write his famous book, which according to my reckoning must have appeared towards the end, rather than the beginning of Ho Lü's reign. The story of the women may possibly have grown out of some real incident occurring about the same time. As we hear no more of Sun Wu after this from any source, he is hardly likely to have survived his patron or to have taken part in the death-struggle with Yüeh, which began with the disaster at Tsui-li.

If these inferences are approximately correct, there is a certain irony in the fate which decreed that China's most illustrious man of peace should be contemporary with her greatest writer on war.

The Text of Sun Tzŭ

I have found it difficult to glean much about the history of Sun Tzŭ's text. The quotations that occur in early authors go to show that the "thirteen chapters" of which Ssŭ-ma Ch'ien speaks were essentially the same as those now extant. We have his word for it that they were widely circulated in his day, and can only regret that he refrained from discussing them on that account. Sun Hsing-yen says in his preface:—

> During the Ch'in and Han dynasties Sun Tzŭ's *Art of War* was in general use amongst military commanders, but they seem to have treated it as a work of mysterious import, and were unwilling to expound it for the benefit of posterity. Thus it came about that Wei Wu was the first to write a commentary on it.

As we have already seen, there is no reasonable ground to suppose that Ts'ao Kung tampered with the text. But the text itself is often so obscure, and the number of editions which appeared from that time onward so great, especially during the T'ang and Sung dynasties, that it would be surprising if numerous corruptions had not managed to creep in. Towards the middle of the Sung period, by which time all the chief commentaries on Sun Tzŭ were in existence, a certain Chi T'ien-pao published a work in 15 *chüan* entitled "Sun Tzŭ with the collected commentaries of ten writers." There was another text, with variant readings put forward by Chu

Fu of Ta-hsing, which also had supporters among the scholars of that period; but in the Ming editions, Sun Hsing-yen tells us, these readings were for some reason or other no longer put into circulation. Thus, until the end of the 18th century, the text in sole possession of the field was one derived from Chi T'ien-pao's edition, although no actual copy of that important work was known to have survived. That, therefore, is the text of Sun Tzŭ which appears in the War section of the great Imperial encyclopedia printed in 1726, the *Ku Chin T'u Shu Chi Ch'êng*. Another copy at my disposal of what is practically the same text, with slight variations, is that contained in the "Eleven philosophers of the Chou and Ch'in dynasties" [1758]. And the Chinese printed in Capt. Calthrop's first edition is evidently a similar version which has filtered through Japanese channels. So things remained until Sun Hsing-yen [1752-1818], a distinguished antiquarian and classical scholar, who claimed to be an actual descendant of Sun Wu, accidentally discovered a copy of Chi T'ien-pao's long-lost work, when on a visit to the library of the Hua-yin temple. Appended to it was the *I Shuo* of Chêng Yu-Hsien, mentioned in the *T'ung Chih*, and also believed to have perished. This is what Sun Hsing-yen designates as the "original edition (or text)"—a rather misleading name, for it cannot by any means claim to set before us the text of Sun Tzŭ in its pristine purity. Chi T'ien-pao was a careless compiler, and appears to have been content to reproduce the somewhat debased version current in his day, without troubling to collate it with the earliest editions then available. Fortunately, two versions of Sun Tzŭ, even older than the newly discovered work, were still extant, one buried in the *T'ung Tien*, Tu Yu's great treatise on the Constitution, the other similarly enshrined in the *T'ai P'ing Yü Lan* encyclopedia. In both the complete text is to be found, though split up into fragments, intermixed with other matter, and scattered piecemeal over a number of different sections. Considering that the *Yü Lan* takes us back to the year 983, and the *T'ung Tien* about 200 years further still, to the middle of the T'ang dynasty, the value of these early transcripts of Sun Tzŭ can hardly be overestimated. Yet the idea of utilizing them does not seem to have occurred to anyone until Sun Hsing-yen, acting under Government instructions, undertook a thorough recension of the text. This is his own account:—

> Because of the numerous mistakes in the text of Sun Tzŭ which his editors had handed down, the Government ordered that the ancient edition [of Chi T'ien-pao] should be used, and that the text should be revised and corrected throughout. It happened that Wu Nien-hu, the Governor Pi Kua, and Hsi, a graduate of the second degree, had all devoted themselves to this study, probably surpassing me therein. Accordingly, I have had the whole work cut on blocks as a textbook for military men.

The three individuals here referred to had evidently been occupied on the text of Sun Tzŭ prior to Sun Hsing-yen's commission, but we are left in doubt as to the work they really accomplished. At any rate, the new edition, when ultimately produced, appeared in the names of Sun Hsing-yen and only one co-editor Wu Jen-shi. They took the "original edition" as their basis, and by careful comparison with older versions, as well as the extant commentaries and other sources of information such as the *I Shuo*, succeeded in restoring a very large number of doubtful passages, and turned out, on the whole, what must be accepted as the closest approximation we are ever likely to get to Sun Tzŭ's original work. This is what will hereafter be denominated the "standard text."

The copy which I have used belongs to a reissue dated 1877. It is in 6 *pen*, forming part of a well-printed set of 23 early philosophical works in 83 *pen*. It opens with a preface by Sun Hsing-yen (largely quoted in this introduction), vindicating the traditional view of Sun Tzŭ's life and performances, and summing up in remarkably concise fashion the evidence in its favour. This is followed by Ts'ao Kung's preface to his edition, and the biography of Sun Tzŭ from the *Shih Chi*, both translated above. Then come, firstly, Chêng Yu-Hsien's *I Shuo*, with author's preface, and next, a short miscellany of historical and bibliographical information entitled *Sun Tzŭ Hsü Lu*, compiled by Pi I-hsün. As regards the body of the work, each separate sentence is followed by a note on the text, if required, and then by the various commentaries appertaining to it, arranged in chronological order. These we shall now proceed to discuss briefly, one by one.

The Commentators

Sun Tzŭ can boast an exceptionally long distinguished roll of commentators, which would do honour to any classic. Ou-yang Hsiu remarks on this fact, though he wrote before the tale was complete, and rather ingeniously explains it by saying that the artifices of war, being inexhaustible, must therefore be susceptible of treatment in a great variety of ways.

1 TS'AO TS'AO or Ts'ao Kung, afterwards known as Wei Wu Ti (A.D. 155-220). There is hardly any room for doubt that the earliest commentary on Sun Tzŭ actually came from the pen of this extraordinary man, whose biography in the *San Kuo Chih* reads like a romance. One of the greatest military geniuses that the world has seen, and Napoleonic in the scale of his operations, he was especially famed for the marvelous rapidity of his marches, which has found expression in the line "Talk of Ts'ao Ts'ao, and Ts'ao Ts'ao will appear." Ou-yang Hsiu says of him that he was a great captain who "measured his strength against Tung Cho, Lü Pu and the two Yüan, father and son, and vanquished them all; whereupon he divided the Empire of Han with Wu and Shu, and made himself king. It is recorded that whenever a council of war was held by Wei on the eve of a far-reaching campaign, he had all his calculations ready; those generals who made use of them did not lose one battle in ten; those who ran counter to them in any particular saw their armies incontinently beaten and put to flight." Ts'ao Kung's notes on

Sun Tzŭ, models of austere brevity, are so thoroughly characteristic of the stern commander known to history, that it is hard indeed to conceive of them as the work of a mere *littérateur*. Sometimes, indeed, owing to extreme compression, they are scarcely intelligible and stand no less in need of a commentary than the text itself.

2 MÊNG SHIH. The commentary which has come down to us under this name is comparatively meager, and nothing about the author is known. Even his personal name has not been recorded. Chi T'ien-pao's edition places him after Chia Lin, and Ch'ao Kung-wu also assigns him to the T'ang dynasty, but this is a mistake. In Sun Hsing-yen's preface, he appears as Mêng Shih of the Liang dynasty (502-557). Others would identify him with Mêng K'ang of the 3rd century. He is named in one work as the last of the "Five Commentators," the others being Wei Wu Ti, Tu Mu, Ch'ên Hao and Chia Lin.

3 LI CH'ÜAN of the 8th century was a well-known writer on military tactics. One of his works has been in constant use down to the present day. The *T'ung Chih* mentions "Lives of famous generals from the Chou to the T'ang dynasty" as written by him. According to Ch'ao Kung-wu and the *T'ien-i-ko* catalogue, he followed a variant of the text of Sun Tzŭ which differs considerably from those now extant. His notes are mostly short and to the point, and he frequently illustrates his remarks by anecdotes from Chinese history.

4 TU YU (died 812) did not publish a separate commentary on Sun Tzŭ, his notes being taken from the *T'ung Tien*, the encyclopedic treatise on the Constitution which was his life-work. They are largely repetitions of Ts'ao Kung and Mêng Shih, besides which it is believed that he drew on the ancient commentaries of Wang Ling and others. Owing to the peculiar arrangement of *T'ung Tien*, he has to explain each passage on its merits, apart from the context, and sometimes his own explanation does not agree with that of Ts'ao Kung, whom he always quotes first. Though not strictly to be reckoned as one of the "Ten Commentators," he was added to their number by Chi T'ien-pao, being wrongly placed after his grandson Tu Mu.

5 TU MU (803-852) is perhaps the best known as a poet—a bright star even in the glorious galaxy of the T'ang period. We learn from Ch'ao Kung-wu that although he had no practical experience of war, he was extremely fond of discussing the subject, and was moreover well read in the military history of the *Ch'un Ch'iu* and *Chan Kuo* eras. His notes, therefore, are well worth attention. They are very copious, and replete with historical parallels. The gist of Sun Tzŭ's work is thus summarized by him: "Practice benevolence and justice, but on the other hand make full use of artifice and measures of expediency." He further declared that all the military triumphs and disasters of the thousand years which had elapsed since Sun Tzŭ's death would, upon examination, be found to uphold and corroborate, in every particular, the maxims contained in his book. Tu Mu's somewhat spiteful charge against Ts'ao Kung has already been considered elsewhere.

6 CH'ÊN HAO appears to have been a contemporary of Tu Mu. Ch'ao Kung-wu says that he was impelled to write a new commentary on Sun Tzŭ because Ts'ao Kung's on the one hand was too obscure and subtle, and that of Tu Mu on the other too long-winded and diffuse. Ou-yang Hsiu, writing in the middle of the 11th century, calls Ts'ao Kung, Tu Mu and Ch'ên Hao the three chief commentators on Sun Tzŭ, and observes that Ch'ên Hao is continually attacking Tu Mu's shortcomings. His commentary, though not lacking in merit, must rank below those of his predecessors.

7 CHIA LIN is known to have lived under the T'ang dynasty, for his commentary on Sun Tzŭ is mentioned in the *T'ang Shu* and was afterwards republished by Chi Hsieh of the same dynasty together with those of Mêng Shih and Tu Yu. It is of somewhat scanty texture, and in point of quality, too, perhaps the least valuable of the eleven.

8 MEI YAO-CH'ÊN (1002-1060), commonly known by his "style" as Mei Shêng-yü, was, like Tu Mu, a poet of distinction. His commentary was published with a laudatory preface by the great Ou-yang Hsiu, from which we may cull the following:—

> Later scholars have misread Sun Tzŭ, distorting his words and trying to make them square with their own one-sided views. Thus, though commentators have not been lacking, only a few have proved equal to the task. My friend Shêng-yü has not fallen into this mistake. In attempting to provide a critical commentary for Sun Tzŭ's work, he does not lose sight of the fact that these sayings were intended for states engaged in internecine warfare; that the author is not concerned with the military conditions prevailing under the sovereigns of the three ancient dynasties, nor with the nine punitive measures prescribed to the Minister of War. Again, Sun Wu loved brevity of diction, but his meaning is always deep. Whether the subject be marching an army, or handling soldiers, or estimating the enemy, or controlling the forces of victory, it is always systematically treated; the sayings are bound together in strict logical sequence, though this has been obscured by commentators who have probably failed to grasp their meaning. In his own commentary, Mei Shêng-yü has brushed aside all the obstinate prejudices of these critics, and has tried to bring out the true meaning of Sun Tzŭ himself. In this way, the clouds of confusion have

> been dispersed and the sayings made clear. I am convinced that the present work deserves to be handed down side by side with the three great commentaries; and for a great deal that they find in the sayings, coming generations will have constant reason to thank my friend Shêng-yü.

Making some allowance for the exuberance of friendship, I am inclined to endorse this favourable judgment, and would certainly place him above Ch'ên Hao in order of merit.

9 WANG HSI, also of the Sung dynasty, is decidedly original in some of his interpretations, but much less judicious than Mei Yao-ch'ên, and on the whole not a very trustworthy guide. He is fond of comparing his own commentary with that of Ts'ao Kung, but the comparison is not often flattering to him. We learn from Ch'ao Kung-wu that Wang Hsi revised the ancient text of Sun Tzŭ, filling up lacunae and correcting mistakes. [45]

10 HO YEN-HSI of the Sung dynasty. The personal name of this commentator is given as above by Chéng Ch'iao in the *Tung Chih*, written about the middle of the twelfth century, but he appears simply as Ho Shih in the *Yü Hai*, and Ma Tuan-lin quotes Ch'ao Kung-wu as saying that his personal name is unknown. There seems to be no reason to doubt Chéng Ch'iao's statement, otherwise I should have been inclined to hazard a guess and identify him with one Ho Ch'ü-fei, the author of a short treatise on war, who lived in the latter part of the 11th century. Ho Shih's commentary, in the words of the *T'ien-i-ko* catalogue, "contains helpful additions" here and there, but is chiefly remarkable for the copious extracts taken, in adapted form, from the dynastic histories and other sources.

11 CHANG YÜ. The list closes with a commentator of no great originality perhaps, but gifted with admirable powers of lucid

> exposition. His commentator is based on that of Ts'ao Kung, whose terse sentences he contrives to expand and develop in masterly fashion. Without Chang Yü, it is safe to say that much of Ts'ao Kung's commentary would have remained cloaked in its pristine obscurity and therefore valueless. His work is not mentioned in the Sung history, the *T'ung K'ao*, or the *Yü Hai*, but it finds a niche in the *T'ung Chih*, which also names him as the author of the "Lives of Famous Generals."

It is rather remarkable that the last-named four should all have flourished within so short a space of time. Ch'ao Kung-wu accounts for it by saying: "During the early years of the Sung dynasty the Empire enjoyed a long spell of peace, and men ceased to practice the art of war. but when [Chao] Yüan-hao's rebellion came (1038-42) and the frontier generals were defeated time after time, the Court made strenuous inquiry for men skilled in war, and military topics became the vogue amongst all the high officials. Hence it is that the commentators of Sun Tzŭ in our dynasty belong mainly to that period.

Besides these eleven commentators, there are several others whose work has not come down to us. The *Sui Shu* mentions four, namely Wang Ling (often quoted by Tu Yu as Wang Tzŭ); Chang Tzŭ-shang; Chia Hsü of Wei; and Shên Yu of Wu. The *T'ang Shu* adds Sun Hao, and the *T'ung Chih* Hsiao Chi, while the *T'u Shu* mentions a Ming commentator, Huang Jun-yu. It is possible that some of these may have been merely collectors and editors of other commentaries, like Chi T'ien-pao and Chi Hsieh, mentioned above.

Appreciations of Sun Tzŭ

Sun Tzŭ has exercised a potent fascination over the minds of some of China's greatest men. Among the famous generals who are known to have studied his pages with enthusiasm may be mentioned Han Hsin (*d.* 196 B.C.), Fêng I (*d.* 34 A.D.), Lü Mêng (*d.* 219), and Yo Fei (1103-1141). The opinion of Ts'ao Kung, who disputes with Han Hsin the highest place in Chinese military annals, has already been recorded. Still more remarkable, in one way, is the testimony of purely literary men, such as Su Hsün (the father of Su Tung-p'o), who wrote several essays on military topics, all of which owe their chief inspiration to Sun Tzŭ. The following short passage by him is preserved in the *Yü Hai:* [54]—

> Sun Wu's saying, that in war one cannot make certain of conquering, is very different indeed from what other books tell us. Wu Ch'i was a man of the same stamp as Sun Wu: they both wrote books on war, and they are linked together in popular speech as "Sun and Wu." But Wu Ch'i's remarks on war are less weighty, his rules are rougher and more crudely stated, and there is not the same unity of plan as in Sun Tzŭ's work, where the style is terse, but the meaning fully brought out.

The following is an extract from the "Impartial Judgments in the Garden of Literature" by Chéng Hou:—

> Sun Tzŭ's thirteen chapters are not only the staple and base of all military men's training, but also compel the most careful attention of scholars and men of letters. His sayings are terse yet elegant, simple yet profound, perspicuous and eminently practical. Such works as the *Lun Yü*, the *I Ching* and the great Commentary, as well as the writings of Mencius, Hsun K'uang and Yang Chu, all fall below the level of Sun Tzŭ.

Chu Hsi, commenting on this, fully admits the first part of the criticism, although he dislikes the audacious comparison with the venerated classical works. Language of this sort, he says, "encourages a ruler's bent towards unrelenting warfare and reckless militarism."

Apologies for War

Accustomed as we are to think of China as the greatest peace-loving nation on earth, we are in some danger of forgetting that her experience of war in all its phases has also been such as no modern State can parallel. Her long military annals stretch back to a point at which they are lost in the mists of time. She had built the Great Wall and was maintaining a huge standing army along her frontier centuries before the first Roman legionary was seen on the Danube. What with the perpetual collisions of the ancient feudal States, the grim conflicts with Huns, Turks and other invaders after the centralization of government, the terrific upheavals which accompanied the overthrow of so many dynasties, besides the countless rebellions and minor disturbances that have flamed up and flickered out again one by one, it is hardly too much to say that the clash of arms has never ceased to resound in one portion or another of the Empire.

No less remarkable is the succession of illustrious captains to whom China can point with pride. As in all countries, the greatest are fond of emerging at the most fateful crises of her history. Thus, Po Ch'i stands out conspicuous in the period when Ch'in was entering upon her final struggle with the remaining independent states. The stormy years which followed the break-up of the Ch'in dynasty are illuminated by the transcendent genius of Han Hsin. When the House of Han in turn is tottering to its fall, the great and baleful figure of Ts'ao Ts'ao dominates the scene. And in the establishment of the T'ang dynasty, one of the mightiest tasks achieved by man, the superhuman energy of Li Shih-min (afterwards the Emperor T'ai Tsung) was seconded by the brilliant strategy of Li Ching. None of these generals need fear comparison with the greatest names in the military history of Europe.

In spite of all this, the great body of Chinese sentiment, from Lao Tzŭ downwards, and especially as reflected in the standard literature of Confucianism, has been consistently pacific and intensely opposed to militarism in any form. It is such an uncommon thing to find any of the literati defending warfare on principle, that I have thought it worth while to collect and translate a few passages in which the unorthodox view is upheld. The following, by Ssŭ-ma Ch'ien, shows that for all his ardent admiration of Confucius, he was yet no advocate of peace at any price:—

> Military weapons are the means used by the Sage to punish violence and cruelty, to give peace to troublous times, to remove difficulties and dangers, and to succour those who are in peril. Every animal with blood in its veins and horns on its head will fight when it is attacked. How much more so will man, who carries in his breast the faculties of love and hatred, joy and anger! When he is pleased, a feeling of affection springs up within him; when angry, his poisoned sting is brought into play. That is the natural law which governs his being.... What then shall be said of those scholars of our time, blind to all great issues, and without any appreciation of relative values, who can only bark out their stale formulas about "virtue" and "civilization," condemning the use of military weapons? They will surely bring our country to impotence and dishonour and the loss of her rightful heritage; or, at the very least, they will bring about invasion and rebellion, sacrifice of territory and general enfeeblement. Yet they obstinately refuse to modify the position they have taken up. The truth is that, just as in the family the

> teacher must not spare the rod, and punishments cannot be dispensed with in the State, so military chastisement can never be allowed to fall into abeyance in the Empire. All one can say is that this power will be exercised wisely by some, foolishly by others, and that among those who bear arms some will be loyal and others rebellious. [58]

The next piece is taken from Tu Mu's preface to his commentary on Sun Tzŭ:—

> War may be defined as punishment, which is one of the functions of government. It was the profession of Chung Yu and Jan Ch'iu, both disciples of Confucius. Nowadays, the holding of trials and hearing of litigation, the imprisonment of offenders and their execution by flogging in the market-place, are all done by officials. But the wielding of huge armies, the throwing down of fortified cities, the hauling of women and children into captivity, and the beheading of traitors—this is also work which is done by officials. The objects of the rack and of military weapons are essentially the same. There is no intrinsic difference between the punishment of flogging and cutting off heads in war. For the lesser infractions of law, which are easily dealt with, only a small amount of force need be employed: hence the use of military weapons and wholesale decapitation. In both cases, however, the end in view is to get rid of wicked people, and to give comfort and relief to the good....
>
> Chi-sun asked Jan Yu, saying: "Have you, Sir, acquired your military aptitude by study, or is it innate?" Jan Yu replied: "It has been acquired by study." "How can that be so," said Chi-sun, "seeing that you are a disciple of Confucius?" "It is a fact," replied Jan Yu; "I was taught by Confucius. It is fitting that the great Sage should exercise both civil and

> military functions, though to be sure my instruction in the art of fighting has not yet gone very far."
>
> Now, who the author was of this rigid distinction between the "civil" and the "military," and the limitation of each to a separate sphere of action, or in what year of which dynasty it was first introduced, is more than I can say. But, at any rate, it has come about that the members of the governing class are quite afraid of enlarging on military topics, or do so only in a shamefaced manner. If any are bold enough to discuss the subject, they are at once set down as eccentric individuals of coarse and brutal propensities. This is an extraordinary instance in which, through sheer lack of reasoning, men unhappily lose sight of fundamental principles.
>
> When the Duke of Chou was minister under Ch'êng Wang, he regulated ceremonies and made music, and venerated the arts of scholarship and learning; yet when the barbarians of the River Huai revolted, he sallied forth and chastised them. When Confucius held office under the Duke of Lu, and a meeting was convened at Chia-ku, he said: "If pacific negotiations are in progress, warlike preparations should have been made beforehand." He rebuked and shamed the Marquis of Ch'i, who cowered under him and dared not proceed to violence. How can it be said that these two great Sages had no knowledge of military matters?

We have seen that the great Chu Hsi held Sun Tzŭ in high esteem. He also appeals to the authority of the Classics:—

> Our Master Confucius, answering Duke Ling of Wei, said: "I have never studied matters connected with armies and battalions." Replying to K'ung Wen-tzu, he said: I have not been instructed about buff-coats and weapons." But if we

turn to the meeting at Chia-ku, we find that he used armed force against the men of Lai, so that the marquis of Ch'i was overawed. Again, when the inhabitants of Pi revolted; he ordered his officers to attack them, whereupon they were defeated and fled in confusion. He once uttered the words: "If I fight, I conquer." And Jan Yu also said: "The Sage exercises both civil and military functions." Can it be a fact that Confucius never studied or received instruction in the art of war? We can only say that he did not specially choose matters connected with armies and fighting to be the subject of his teaching.

Sun Hsing-yen, the editor of Sun Tzŭ, writes in similar strain:—

Confucius said: "I am unversed in military matters." He also said: "If I fight, I conquer." Confucius ordered ceremonies and regulated music. Now war constitutes one of the five classes of State ceremonial, [66] and must not be treated as an independent branch of study. Hence, the words "I am unversed in" must be taken to mean that there are things which even an inspired Teacher does not know. Those who have to lead an army and devise stratagems, must learn the art of war. But if one can command the services of a good general like Sun Tzŭ, who was employed by Wu Tzŭ-hsü, there is no need to learn it oneself. Hence the remark added by Confucius: "If I fight, I conquer."

The men of the present day, however, willfully interpret these words of Confucius in their narrowest sense, as though he meant that books on the art of war were not worth reading. With blind persistency, they adduce the example of Chao Kua, who pored over his father's books to no purpose, as a proof that all military theory is useless. Again, seeing that books on war have to do with such things as opportunism in designing plans, and the conversion of spies, they hold that the art is immoral and unworthy of a sage. These people ignore the fact that the studies of our scholars and the civil administration of our officials also require steady application and practice before efficiency is reached. The ancients were particularly chary of allowing mere novices to botch their work. Weapons are baneful and fighting perilous; and useless unless a general is in constant practice, he ought not to hazard other men's lives in battle. Hence it is essential that Sun Tzŭ's thirteen chapters should be studied.

Hsiang Liang used to instruct his nephew Chi in the art of war. Chi got a rough idea of the art in its general bearings, but would not pursue his studies to their proper outcome, the consequence being that he was finally defeated and overthrown. He did not realize that the tricks and artifices of war are beyond verbal computation. Duke Hsiang of Sung and King Yen of Hsu were brought to destruction by their misplaced humanity. The treacherous and underhand nature of war necessitates the use of guile and stratagem suited to the occasion. There is a case on record of Confucius himself having violated an extorted oath, and also of his having left the Sung State in disguise. Can we then recklessly arraign Sun Tzŭ for disregarding truth and honesty?

Bibliography

The following are the oldest Chinese treatises on war, after Sun Tzŭ. The notes on each have been drawn principally from the *Ssŭ k'u ch'üan shu chien ming mu lu*, ch. 9, fol. 22 sqq.

1 *Wu Tzŭ*, in 1 *chüan* or 6 chapters. By Wu Ch'i (*d*. 381 B.C.). A genuine work. See *Shih Chi*, ch. 65.

2 *Ssŭ-ma Fa*, in 1 *chüan* or 5 chapters. Wrongly attributed to Ssŭ-ma Jang-chü of the 6th century B.C. Its date, however, must be early, as the customs of the three ancient dynasties are constantly to be met within its pages. See *Shih Chi*, ch. 64.

The *Ssŭ K'u Ch'üan Shu* (ch. 99, f. 1) remarks that the oldest three treatises on war, *Sun Tzŭ*, *Wu Tzŭ* and *Ssŭ-ma Fa*, are, generally speaking, only concerned with things strictly military—the art of producing, collecting, training and drilling troops, and the correct theory with regard to measures of expediency, laying plans, transport of goods and the handling of soldiers—in strong contrast to later works, in which the science of war is usually blended with metaphysics, divination and magical arts in general.

3 *Liu T'ao*, in 6 *chüan*, or 60 chapters. Attributed to Lü Wang (or Lü Shang, also known as T'ai Kung) of the 12th century B.C. [74] But its style does not belong to the era of the Three Dynasties. Lu Tê-ming (550-625 A.D.) mentions the work, and enumerates the headings of the six sections so that the forgery cannot have been later than Sui dynasty.

4 *Wei Liao Tzŭ*, in 5 *chüan*. Attributed to Wei Liao (4th cent. B.C.), who studied under the famous Kuei-ku Tzŭ. The work appears to have been originally in 31 chapters, whereas the text we possess contains only 24. Its matter is sound enough in the main, though the strategical devices differ considerably from those of the Warring States period. It is been furnished with a commentary by the well-known Sung philosopher Chang Tsai.

5 *San Lüeh* in 3 *chüan*. Attributed to Huang-shih Kung, a legendary personage who is said to have bestowed it on Chang Liang (*d.* 187 B.C.) in an interview on a bridge. But here again, the style is not that of works dating from the Ch'in or Han period. The Han Emperor Kuang Wu [25-57 A.D.] apparently quotes from it in one of his proclamations; but the passage in question may have been inserted later on, in order to prove the genuineness of the work. We shall not be far out if we refer it to the Northern Sung period [420-478 A.D.], or somewhat earlier.

6 *Li Wei Kung Wên Tui*, in 3 sections. Written in the form of a dialogue between T'ai Tsung and his great general Li Ching, it is usually ascribed to the latter. Competent authorities consider it a forgery, though the author was evidently well versed in the art of war.

7 *Li Ching Ping Fa* (not to be confounded with the foregoing) is a short treatise in 8 chapters, preserved in the T'ung Tien, but not published separately. This fact explains its omission from the *Ssŭ K'u Ch'üan Shu*.

8 *Wu Ch'i Ching*, in 1 *chüan*. Attributed to the legendary minister Feng Hou, with exegetical notes by Kung-sun Hung of the Han dynasty (*d.* 121 B.C.), and said to have been eulogized by the celebrated general Ma Lung (*d.* 300 A.D.). Yet the earliest mention of it is in the *Sung Chih*. Although a forgery, the work is well put together.

Considering the high popular estimation in which Chu-ko Liang has always been held, it is not surprising to find more than one work on war ascribed to his pen. Such are (1) the *Shih Liu Ts'ê* (1 *chüan*), preserved in the *Yung Lo Ta Tien;* (2) *Chiang Yüan* (1 *chüan*); and (3) *Hsin Shu* (1 *chüan*), which steals wholesale from Sun Tzŭ. None of these has the slightest claim to be considered genuine.

Most of the large Chinese encyclopedias contain extensive sections devoted to the literature of war. The following references may be found useful:—

T'ung Tien (circa 800 A.D.), ch. 148-162.
T'ai P'ing Yü Lan (983), ch. 270-359.
Wên Hsien Tung K'ao (13th cent.), ch. 221.
Yü Hai (13th cent.), ch. 140, 141.
San Ts'ai T'u Hui (16th cent).
Kuang Po Wu Chih (1607), ch. 31, 32.
Ch'ien Ch'io Lei Shu (1632), ch. 75.
Yüan Chien Lei Han (1710), ch. 206-229.
Ku Chin T'u Shu Chi Ch'êng (1726), section XXX, esp. ch. 81-90.
Hsü Wen Hsien T'ung K'ao (1784), ch. 121-134.
Huang Ch'ao Ching Shih Wên Pien (1826), ch. 76, 77.

The bibliographical sections of certain historical works also deserve mention:—

Ch'ien Han Shu, ch. 30.
Sui Shu, ch. 32-35.
Chiu T'ang Shu, ch. 46, 47.
Hsin T'ang Shu, ch. 57,60.
Sung Shih, ch. 202-209.
T'ung Chih (circa 1150), ch. 68.

To these of course must be added the great Catalogue of the Imperial Library:—

Ssŭ K'u Ch'üan Shu Tsung Mu T'i Yao (1790), ch. 99, 100.

Chapter 1

Laying Plans

[Ts'ao Kung, in defining the meaning of the Chinese for the title of this chapter, says it refers to the deliberations in the temple selected by the general for his temporary use, or as we should say, in his tent. See paragraph 26.]

1 Sun Tzŭ said: The art of war is of vital importance to the State.

2 It is a matter of life and death, a road either to safety or to ruin. Hence it is a subject of inquiry which can on no account be neglected.

3 The art of war, then, is governed by five constant factors, to be taken into account in one's deliberations, when seeking to determine the conditions obtaining in the field.

4 These are: (1) The Moral Law; (2) Heaven; (3) Earth; (4) The Commander; (5) Method and discipline.

[It appears from what follows that Sun Tzŭ means by "Moral Law" a principle of harmony, not unlike the Tao of Lao Tzŭ in its moral aspect. One might be tempted to render it by "morale," were it not considered as an attribute of the *ruler* in paragraph 13.]

5, 6 *The Moral Law* causes the people to be in complete accord with their ruler, so that they will follow him regardless of their lives, undismayed by any danger.

[Tu Yu quotes Wang Tzŭ as saying: "Without constant practice, the officers will be nervous and undecided when mustering for battle; without constant practice, the general will be wavering and irresolute when the crisis is at hand."]

7 *Heaven* signifies night and day, cold and heat, times and seasons.

[The commentators, I think, make an unnecessary mystery of two words here. Mêng Shih refers to "the hard and the soft, waxing and waning" of Heaven. Wang Hsi, however, may be right in saying that what is meant is "the general economy of Heaven," including the five elements, the four seasons, wind and clouds, and other phenomena.]

8 *Earth* comprises distances, great and small; danger and security; open ground and narrow passes; the chances of life and death.

9 *The Commander* stands for the virtues of wisdom, sincerity, benevolence, courage and strictness.

[The five cardinal virtues of the Chinese are (1) humanity or benevolence; (2) uprightness of mind; (3) self-respect, self-control, or "proper feeling;" (4) wisdom; (5) sincerity or good faith. Here "wisdom" and "sincerity" are put before "humanity or benevolence," and the two military virtues of "courage" and "strictness" substituted for "uprightness of mind" and "self-respect, self-control, or 'proper feeling.'"]

10 By *Method and discipline* are to be understood the marshalling of the army in its proper subdivisions, the gradations of rank among the officers, the maintenance of roads by which supplies may reach the army, and the control of military expenditure.

11 These five heads should be familiar to every general: he who knows them will be victorious; he who knows them not will fail.

12 Therefore, in your deliberations, when seeking to determine the military conditions, let them be made the basis of a comparison, in this wise:—

13

(1) Which of the two sovereigns is imbued with the Moral law?

[I.e., "is in harmony with his subjects." See paragraph 5.]

(2) Which of the two generals has most ability?

(3) With whom lie the advantages derived from Heaven and Earth?

[See paragraphs 7, 8]

(4) On which side is discipline most rigorously enforced?

[Tu Mu alludes to the remarkable story of Ts'ao Ts'ao (A.D. 155-220), who was such a strict disciplinarian that once, in accordance with his own severe regulations against injury to standing crops, he condemned himself to death for having allowed his horse to shy into a field of corn! However, in lieu of losing his head, he was persuaded to satisfy his sense of justice by cutting off his hair. Ts'ao Ts'ao's own comment on the present passage is characteristically curt: "when you lay down a law, see that it is not disobeyed; if it is disobeyed the offender must be put to death."]

(5) Which army is the stronger?

[Morally as well as physically. As Mei Yao-ch'ên puts it, freely rendered, "*esprit de corps* and 'big battalions.'"]

(6) On which side are officers and men more highly trained?

[Tu Yu quotes Wang Tzŭ as saying: "Without constant practice, the officers will be nervous and undecided when mustering for battle; without constant practice, the general will be wavering and irresolute when the crisis is at hand."]

(7) In which army is there the greater constancy both in reward and punishment?

[On which side is there the most absolute certainty that merit will be properly rewarded and misdeeds summarily punished?]

14 By means of these seven considerations I can forecast victory or defeat.

15 The general that hearkens to my counsel and acts upon it, will conquer:—let such a one be retained in command! The general that hearkens not to my counsel nor acts upon it, will suffer defeat:—let such a one be dismissed!

[The form of this paragraph reminds us that Sun Tzŭ's treatise was composed expressly for the benefit of his patron Ho Lü, king of the Wu State.]

16 While heeding the profit of my counsel, avail yourself also of any helpful circumstances over and beyond the ordinary rules.

17 According as circumstances are favourable, one should modify one's plans.

[Sun Tzŭ, as a practical soldier, will have none of the "bookish theoric." He cautions us here not to pin our faith to abstract principles; "for," as Chang Yü puts it, "while the main laws of strategy can be stated clearly enough for the benefit of all and sundry, you must be guided by the actions of the enemy in attempting to secure a favourable position in actual warfare." On the eve of the battle of Waterloo, Lord Uxbridge, commanding the cavalry, went to the Duke of Wellington in order to learn what his plans and calculations were for the morrow, because, as he explained, he might suddenly find himself Commander-in-chief and would be unable to frame new plans in a critical moment. The Duke listened quietly and then said: "Who will attack the first tomorrow—I or Bonaparte?" "Bonaparte," replied Lord Uxbridge. "Well," continued the Duke, "Bonaparte has not given me any idea of his projects; and as my plans will depend upon his, how can you expect me to tell you what mine are?" [1]]

18 All warfare is based on deception.

[The truth of this pithy and profound saying will be admitted by every soldier. Col. Henderson tells us that Wellington, great in so many military qualities, was especially distinguished by "the extraordinary skill with which he concealed his movements and deceived both friend and foe."]

19 Hence, when able to attack, we must seem unable; when using our forces, we must seem inactive; when we are near, we must make the enemy believe we are far away; when far away, we must make him believe we are near.

20 Hold out baits to entice the enemy. Feign disorder, and crush him.

[All commentators, except Chang Yü, say, "When he is in disorder, crush him." It is more natural to suppose that Sun Tzŭ is still illustrating the uses of deception in war.]

21 If he is secure at all points, be prepared for him. If he is in superior strength, evade him.

22 If your opponent is of choleric temper, seek to irritate him. Pretend to be weak, that he may grow arrogant.

[Wang Tzŭ, quoted by Tu Yu, says that the good tactician plays with his adversary as a cat plays with a mouse, first feigning weakness and immobility, and then suddenly pouncing upon him.]

23 If he is taking his ease, give him no rest.

[This is probably the meaning though Mei Yao-ch'ên has the note: "while we are taking our ease, wait for the enemy to tire himself out." The *Yü Lan* has "Lure him on and tire him out."]

If his forces are united, separate them.

[Less plausible is the interpretation favoured by most of the commentators: "If sovereign and subject are in accord, put division between them."]

24 Attack him where he is unprepared, appear where you are not expected.

25 These military devices, leading to victory, must not be divulged beforehand.

26 Now the general who wins a battle makes many calculations in his temple ere the battle is fought.

[Chang Yü tells us that in ancient times it was customary for a temple to be set apart for the use of a general who was about to take the field, in order that he might there elaborate his plan of campaign.]

The general who loses a battle makes but few calculations beforehand. Thus do many calculations lead to victory, and few calculations to defeat: how much more no calculation at all! It is by attention to this point that I can foresee who is likely to win or lose.

Chapter 2
Waging War

[Ts'ao Kung has the note: "He who wishes to fight must first count the cost," which prepares us for the discovery that the subject of the chapter is not what we might expect from the title, but is primarily a consideration of ways and means.]

1 Sun Tzŭ said: In the operations of war, where there are in the field a thousand swift chariots, as many heavy chariots, and a hundred thousand mail-clad soldiers,

[The "swift chariots" were lightly built and, according to Chang Yü, used for the attack; the "heavy chariots" were heavier, and designed for purposes of defense. Li Ch'üan, it is true, says that the latter were light, but this seems hardly probable. It is interesting to note the analogies between early Chinese warfare and that of the Homeric Greeks. In each case, the war-chariot was the important factor, forming as it did the nucleus round which was grouped a certain number of foot-soldiers. With regard to the numbers given here, we are informed that each swift chariot was accompanied by 75 footmen, and each heavy chariot by 25 footmen, so that the whole army would be divided up into a thousand battalions, each consisting of two chariots and a hundred men.]

with provisions enough to carry them a thousand *li*,

[2.78 modern *li* go to a mile. The length may have varied slightly since Sun Tzŭ's time.]

the expenditure at home and at the front, including entertainment of guests, small items such as glue and paint, and sums spent on chariots and armour, will reach the total of a thousand ounces of silver per day. Such is the cost of raising an army of 100,000 men.

2 When you engage in actual fighting, if victory is long in coming, the men's weapons will grow dull and their ardour will be damped. If you lay siege to a town, you will exhaust your strength.

3 Again, if the campaign is protracted, the resources of the State will not be equal to the strain.

4 Now, when your weapons are dulled, your ardour damped, your strength exhausted and your treasure spent, other chieftains will spring up to take advantage of your extremity. Then no man, however wise, will be able to avert the consequences that must ensue.

5 Thus, though we have heard of stupid haste in war, cleverness has never been seen associated with long delays.

[This concise and difficult sentence is not well explained by any of the commentators. Ts'ao Kung, Li Ch'üan, Mêng Shih, Tu Yu, Tu Mu and Mei Yao-ch'ên have notes to the effect that a general, though naturally stupid, may nevertheless conquer through sheer force of rapidity. Ho Shih says: "Haste may be stupid, but at any rate it saves expenditure of energy and treasure; protracted operations may be very clever, but they bring calamity in their train." Wang Hsi evades the difficulty by remarking: "Lengthy operations mean an army growing old, wealth being expended, an empty exchequer and distress among the people; true cleverness insures against the occurrence of such calamities." Chang Yü says: "So long as victory can be attained, stupid haste is preferable to clever dilatoriness." Now Sun Tzŭ says nothing whatever, except possibly by implication, about ill-considered haste being better than ingenious but lengthy operations. What he does say is something much more guarded, namely that, while speed may sometimes be injudicious, tardiness can never be anything but foolish—if only because it means impoverishment to the nation. In considering the point raised here by Sun Tzŭ, the classic example of Fabius Cunctator will inevitably occur to the mind. That general deliberately measured the endurance of Rome against that of Hannibals's isolated army, because it seemed to him that the latter was more likely to suffer from a long campaign in a strange country. But it is quite a moot question whether his tactics would have proved successful in the long run. Their reversal it is true, led to Cannae; but this only establishes a negative presumption in their favour.]

6 There is no instance of a country having benefited from prolonged warfare.

7 It is only one who is thoroughly acquainted with the evils of war that can thoroughly understand the profitable way of carrying it on.

[That is, with rapidity. Only one who knows the disastrous effects of a long war can realize the supreme importance of rapidity in bringing it to a close. Only two commentators seem to favour this interpretation, but it fits well into the logic of the context, whereas the rendering, "He who does not know the evils of war cannot appreciate its benefits," is distinctly pointless.]

8 The skillful soldier does not raise a second levy, neither are his supply-waggons loaded more than twice.

[Once war is declared, he will not waste precious time in waiting for reinforcements, nor will he return his army back for fresh supplies, but crosses the enemy's frontier without delay. This may seem an audacious policy to recommend, but with all great strategists, from Julius Caesar to Napoleon Bonaparte, the value of time—that is, being a little ahead of your opponent—has counted for more than either numerical superiority or the nicest calculations with regard to commissariat.]

9 Bring war material with you from home, but forage on the enemy. Thus the army will have food enough for its needs.

[The Chinese word translated here as "war material" literally means "things to be used", and is meant in the widest sense. It includes all the impedimenta of an army, apart from provisions.]

10 Poverty of the State exchequer causes an army to be maintained by contributions from a distance. Contributing to maintain an army at a distance causes the people to be impoverished.

[The beginning of this sentence does not balance properly with the next, though obviously intended to do so. The arrangement, moreover, is so awkward that I cannot help suspecting some corruption in the text. It never seems to occur to Chinese commentators that an emendation may be necessary for the sense, and we get no help from them there. The Chinese words Sun Tzŭ used to indicate the cause of the people's impoverishment clearly have reference to some system by which the husbandmen sent their contributions of corn to the army direct. But why should it fall on them to maintain an army in this way, except because the State or Government is too poor to do so?]

11 On the other hand, the proximity of an army causes prices to go up; and high prices cause the people's substance to be drained away.

[Wang Hsi says high prices occur before the army has left its own territory. Ts'ao Kung understands it of an army that has already crossed the frontier.]

12 When their substance is drained away, the peasantry will be afflicted by heavy exactions.

13, 14 With this loss of substance and exhaustion of strength, the homes of the people will be stripped bare, and three-tenths of their incomes will be dissipated;

[Tu Mu and Wang Hsi agree that the people are not mulcted not of 3/10, but of 7/10, of their income. But this is hardly to be extracted from our text. Ho Shih has a characteristic tag: "The *people* being regarded as the essential part of the State, and *food* as the people's heaven, is it not right that those in authority should value and be careful of both?"]

while Government expenses for broken chariots, worn-out horses, breast-plates and helmets, bows and arrows, spears and shields, protective mantlets, draught-oxen and heavy waggons, will amount to four-tenths of its total revenue.

15 Hence a wise general makes a point of foraging on the enemy. One cartload of the enemy's provisions is equivalent to twenty of one's own, and likewise a single *picul* of his provender is equivalent to twenty from one's own store.

[Because twenty cartloads will be consumed in the process of transporting one cartload to the front. A *picul* is a unit of measure equal to 133.3 pounds (65.5 kilograms).]

16 Now in order to kill the enemy, our men must be roused to anger; that there may be advantage from defeating the enemy, they must have their rewards.

[Tu Mu says: "Rewards are necessary in order to make the soldiers see the advantage of beating the enemy; thus, when you capture spoils from the enemy, they must be used as rewards, so that all your men may have a keen desire to fight, each on his own account."]

17 Therefore in chariot fighting, when ten or more chariots have been taken, those should be rewarded who took the first. Our own flags should be substituted for those of the enemy, and the chariots mingled and used in conjunction with ours. The captured soldiers should be kindly treated and kept.

18 This is called, using the conquered foe to augment one's own strength.

19 In war, then, let your great object be victory, not lengthy campaigns.

[As Ho Shih remarks: "War is not a thing to be trifled with." Sun Tzŭ here reiterates the main lesson which this chapter is intended to enforce."]

20 Thus it may be known that the leader of armies is the arbiter of the people's fate, the man on whom it depends whether the nation shall be in peace or in peril.

Chapter 3
Attack by Stratagem

1 Sun Tzŭ said: In the practical art of war, the best thing of all is to take the enemy's country whole and intact; to shatter and destroy it is not so good. So, too, it is better to capture an army entire than to destroy it, to capture a regiment, a detachment or a company entire than to destroy them.

[The equivalent to an army corps, according to Ssŭ-ma Fa, consisted nominally of 12500 men; according to Ts'ao Kung, the equivalent of a regiment contained 500 men, the equivalent to a detachment consists from any number between 100 and 500, and the equivalent of a company contains from 5 to 100 men. For the last two, however, Chang Yü gives the exact figures of 100 and 5 respectively.]

2 Hence to fight and conquer in all your battles is not supreme excellence; supreme excellence consists in breaking the enemy's resistance without fighting.

[Here again, no modern strategist but will approve the words of the old Chinese general. Moltke's greatest triumph, the capitulation of the huge French army at Sedan, was won practically without bloodshed.]

3 Thus the highest form of generalship is to baulk the enemy's plans;

[Perhaps the word "balk" falls short of expressing the full force of the Chinese word, which implies not an attitude of defense, whereby one might be content to foil the enemy's stratagems one after another, but an active policy of counter-attack. Ho Shih puts this very clearly in his note: "When the enemy has made a plan of attack against us, we must anticipate him by delivering our own attack first."]

the next best is to prevent the junction of the enemy's forces;

[Isolating him from his allies. We must not forget that Sun Tzŭ, in speaking of hostilities, always has in mind the numerous states or principalities into which the China of his day was split up.]

the next in order is to attack the enemy's army in the field;

[When he is already at full strength.]

and the worst policy of all is to besiege walled cities.

4 The rule is, not to besiege walled cities if it can possibly be avoided.

[Another sound piece of military theory. Had the Boers acted upon it in 1899, and refrained from dissipating their strength before Kimberley, Mafeking, or even Ladysmith, it is more than probable that they would have been masters of the situation before the British were ready seriously to oppose them.]

The preparation of mantlets, movable shelters, and various implements of war, will take up three whole months;

[It is not quite clear what the Chinese word, here translated as "mantlets", described. Ts'ao Kung simply defines them as "large shields," but we get a better idea of them from Li Ch'üan, who says they were to protect the heads of those who were assaulting the city walls at close quarters. This seems to suggest a sort of Roman *testudo*, ready made. Tu Mu says they were wheeled vehicles used in repelling attacks, but this is denied by Ch'ên Hao. See *supra* II. 14. The name is also applied to turrets on city walls. Of the "movable shelters" we get a fairly clear description from several commentators. They were wooden missile-proof structures on four wheels, propelled from within, covered over with raw hides, and used in sieges to convey parties of men to and from the walls, for the purpose of filling up the encircling moat with earth. Tu Mu adds that they are now called "wooden donkeys."]

and the piling up of mounds over against the walls will take three months more.

[These were great mounds or ramparts of earth heaped up to the level of the enemy's walls in order to discover the weak points in the defense, and also to destroy the fortified turrets mentioned in the preceding note.]

5 The general, unable to control his irritation, will launch his men to the assault like swarming ants,

[This vivid simile of Ts'ao Kung is taken from the spectacle of an army of ants climbing a wall. The meaning is that the general, losing patience at the long delay, may make a premature attempt to storm the place before his engines of war are ready.]

with the result that one-third of his men are slain, while the town still remains untaken. Such are the disastrous effects of a siege.

[We are reminded of the terrible losses of the Japanese before Port Arthur, in the most recent siege which history has to record.]

6 Therefore the skillful leader subdues the enemy's troops without any fighting; he captures their cities without laying siege to them; he overthrows their kingdom without lengthy operations in the field.

[Chia Lin notes that he only overthrows the Government, but does no harm to individuals. The classical instance is Wu Wang, who after having put an end to the Yin dynasty was acclaimed "Father and mother of the people."]

7 With his forces intact he will dispute the mastery of the Empire, and thus, without losing a man, his triumph will be complete.

[Owing to the double meanings in the Chinese text, the latter part of the sentence is susceptible of quite a different meaning: "And thus, the weapon not being blunted by use, its keenness remains perfect."]

This is the method of attacking by stratagem.

8 It is the rule in war, if our forces are ten to the enemy's one, to surround him; if five to one, to attack him;

[Straightway, without waiting for any further advantage.] if twice as numerous, to divide our army into two.

[Tu Mu takes exception to the saying; and at first sight, indeed, it appears to violate a fundamental principle of war. Ts'ao Kung, however, gives a clue to Sun Tzŭ's meaning: "Being two to the enemy's one, we may use one part of our army in the regular way, and the other for some special diversion." Chang Yü thus further elucidates the point: "If our force is twice as numerous as that of the enemy, it should be split up into two divisions, one to meet the enemy in front, and one to fall upon his rear; if he replies to the frontal attack, he may be crushed from behind; if to the rearward attack, he may be crushed in front." This is what is meant by saying that 'one part may be used in the regular way, and the other for some special diversion.' Tu Mu does not understand that dividing one's army is simply an irregular, just as concentrating it is the regular, strategical method, and he is too hasty in calling this a mistake."]

9 If equally matched, we can offer battle;

[Li Ch'üan, followed by Ho Shih, gives the following paraphrase: "If attackers and attacked are equally matched in strength, only the able general will fight."]

if slightly inferior in numbers, we can avoid the enemy;

[The meaning, "we can *watch* the enemy," is certainly a great improvement on the above; but unfortunately there appears to be no very good authority for the variant. Chang Yü reminds us that the saying only applies if the other factors are equal; a small difference in numbers is often more than counterbalanced by superior energy and discipline.]

if quite unequal in every way, we can flee from him.

10 Hence, though an obstinate fight may be made by a small force, in the end it must be captured by the larger force.

11 Now the general is the bulwark of the State: if the bulwark is complete at all points; the State will be strong; if the bulwark is defective, the State will be weak.

[As Li Ch'üan tersely puts it: "Gap indicates deficiency; if the general's ability is not perfect (i.e. if he is not thoroughly versed in his profession), his army will lack strength."]

12 There are three ways in which a ruler can bring misfortune upon his army:—

13 (1) By commanding the army to advance or to retreat, being ignorant of the fact that it cannot obey. This is called hobbling the army.

[Li Ch'üan adds the comment: "It is like tying together the legs of a thoroughbred, so that it is unable to gallop." One would naturally think of "the ruler" in this passage as being at home, and trying to direct the movements of his army from a distance. But the commentators understand just the reverse, and quote the saying of T'ai Kung: "A kingdom should not be governed from without, and army should not be directed from within." Of course it is true that, during an engagement, or when in close touch with the enemy, the general should not be in the thick of his own troops, but a little distance apart. Otherwise, he will be liable to misjudge the position as a whole, and give wrong orders.]

14 (2) By attempting to govern an army in the same way as he administers a kingdom, being ignorant of the conditions which obtain in an army. This causes restlessness in the soldier's minds.

[Ts'ao Kung's note is, freely translated: "The military sphere and the civil sphere are wholly distinct; you can't handle an army in kid gloves." And Chang Yü says: "Humanity and justice are the principles on which to govern a state, but not an army; opportunism and flexibility, on the other hand, are military rather than civil virtues to assimilate the governing of an army"—to that of a State, understood.]

15 (3) By employing the officers of his army without discrimination,

[That is, he is not careful to use the right man in the right place.]

through ignorance of the military principle of adaptation to circumstances. This shakes the confidence of the soldiers.

[I follow Mei Yao-ch'ên here. The other commentators refer not to the ruler, as in §§ 13, 14, but to the officers he employs. Thus Tu Yu says: "If a general is ignorant of the principle of adaptability, he must not be entrusted with a position of authority." Tu Mu quotes: "The skillful employer of men will employ the wise man, the brave man, the covetous man, and the stupid man. For the wise man delights in establishing his merit, the brave man likes to show his courage in action, the covetous man is quick at seizing advantages, and the stupid man has no fear of death."]

16 But when the army is restless and distrustful, trouble is sure to come from the other feudal princes. This is simply bringing anarchy into the army, and flinging victory away.

17 Thus we may know that there are five essentials for victory:

(1) He will win who knows when to fight and when not to fight.

[Chang Yü says: If he can fight, he advances and takes the offensive; if he cannot fight, he retreats and remains on the defensive. He will invariably conquer who knows whether it is right to take the offensive or the defensive.]

(2) He will win who knows how to handle both superior and inferior forces.

[This is not merely the general's ability to estimate numbers correctly, as Li Ch'üan and others make out. Chang Yü expounds the saying more satisfactorily: "By applying the art of war, it is possible with a lesser force to defeat a greater, and *vice versa*. The secret lies in an eye for locality, and in not letting the right moment slip. Thus Wu Tzŭ says: 'With a superior force, make for easy ground; with an inferior one, make for difficult ground.'"]

(3) He will win whose army is animated by the same spirit throughout all its ranks.

(4) He will win who, prepared himself, waits to take the enemy unprepared.

(5) He will win who has military capacity and is not interfered with by the sovereign.

[Tu Yu quotes Wang Tzŭ as saying: "It is the sovereign's function to give broad instructions, but to decide on battle it is the function of the general." It is needless to dilate on the military disasters which have been caused by undue interference with operations in the field on the part of the home government. Napoleon undoubtedly owed much of his extraordinary success to the fact that he was not hampered by central authority.]

Victory lies in the knowledge of these five points.

[Literally, "These five things are knowledge of the principle of victory."]

18 Hence the saying: If you know the enemy and know yourself, you need not fear the result of a hundred battles. If you know yourself but not the enemy, for every victory gained you will also suffer a defeat.

[Li Ch'üan cites the case of Fu Chien, prince of Ch'in, who in 383 A.D. marched with a vast army against the Chin Emperor. When warned not to despise an enemy who could command the services of such men as Hsieh An and Huan Ch'ung, he boastfully replied: "I have the population of eight provinces at my back, infantry and horsemen to the number of one million; why, they could dam up the Yangtsze River itself by merely throwing their whips into the stream. What danger have I to fear?" Nevertheless, his forces were soon after disastrously routed at the Fei River, and he was obliged to beat a hasty retreat.]

If you know neither the enemy nor yourself, you will succumb in every battle.

[Chang Yü said: "Knowing the enemy enables you to take the offensive, knowing yourself enables you to stand on the defensive." He adds: "Attack is the secret of defense; defense is the planning of an attack." It would be hard to find a better epitome of the root-principle of war.]

Chapter 4
Tactical Dispositions

[Ts'ao Kung explains the Chinese meaning of the words for the title of this chapter: "marching and countermarching on the part of the two armies with a view to discovering each other's condition." Tu Mu says: "It is through the dispositions of an army that its condition may be discovered. Conceal your dispositions, and your condition will remain secret, which leads to victory; show your dispositions, and your condition will become patent, which leads to defeat." Wang Hsi remarks that the good general can "secure success by modifying his tactics to meet those of the enemy."]

1 Sun Tzŭ said: The good fighters of old first put themselves beyond the possibility of defeat, and then waited for an opportunity of defeating the enemy.

2 To secure ourselves against defeat lies in our own hands, but the opportunity of defeating the enemy is provided by the enemy himself.

[That is, of course, by a mistake on the enemy's part.]

3 Thus the good fighter is able to secure himself against defeat,

[Chang Yü says this is done, "By concealing the disposition of his troops, covering up his tracks, and taking unremitting precautions."]

but cannot make certain of defeating the enemy.

4 Hence the saying: One may *know* how to conquer without being able to *do* it.

5 Security against defeat implies defensive tactics; ability to defeat the enemy means taking the offensive.

[I retain the sense found in a similar passage in §§ 1-3, in spite of the fact that the commentators are all against me. The meaning they give, "He who cannot conquer takes the defensive," is plausible enough.]

6 Standing on the defensive indicates insufficient strength; attacking, a superabundance of strength.

7 The general who is skilled in defense hides in the most secret recesses of the earth;

[Literally, "hides under the ninth earth," which is a metaphor indicating the utmost secrecy and concealment, so that the enemy may not know his whereabouts."]

he who is skilled in attack flashes forth from the topmost heights of heaven.

[Another metaphor, implying that he falls on his adversary like a thunderbolt, against which there is no time to prepare. This is the opinion of most of the commentators.]

Thus on the one hand we have ability to protect ourselves; on the other, a victory that is complete.

8 To see victory only when it is within the ken of the common herd is not the acme of excellence.

[As Ts'ao Kung remarks, "the thing is to see the plant before it has germinated," to foresee the event before the action has begun. Li Ch'üan alludes to the story of Han Hsin who, when about to attack the vastly superior army of Chao, which was strongly entrenched in the city of Ch'eng-an, said to his officers: "Gentlemen, we are going to annihilate the enemy, and shall meet again at dinner." The officers hardly took his words seriously, and gave a very dubious assent. But Han Hsin had already worked out in his mind the details of a clever stratagem, whereby, as he foresaw, he was able to capture the city and inflict a crushing defeat on his adversary."]

9 Neither is it the acme of excellence if you fight and conquer and the whole Empire says, "Well done!"

[True excellence being, as Tu Mu says: "To plan secretly, to move surreptitiously, to foil the enemy's intentions and balk his schemes, so that at last the day may be won without shedding a drop of blood." Sun Tzŭ reserves his approbation for things that

10 To lift an autumn hair is no sign of great strength;

["Autumn hair" is explained as the fur of a hare, which is finest in autumn, when it begins to grow afresh. The phrase is a very common one in Chinese writers.]

to see sun and moon is no sign of sharp sight; to hear the noise of thunder is no sign of a quick ear.

[Ho Shih gives as real instances of strength, sharp sight and quick hearing: Wu Huo, who could lift a tripod weighing 250 stone; Li Chu, who at a distance of a hundred paces could see objects no bigger than a mustard seed; and Shih K'uang, a blind musician who could hear the footsteps of a mosquito.]

11 What the ancients called a clever fighter is one who not only wins, but excels in winning with ease.

[The last half is literally "one who, conquering, excels in easy conquering." Mei Yao-ch'ên says: "He who only sees the obvious, wins his battles with difficulty; he who looks below the surface of things, wins with ease."]

12 Hence his victories bring him neither reputation for wisdom nor credit for courage.

[Tu Mu explains this very well: "Inasmuch as his victories are gained over circumstances that have not come to light, the world as large knows nothing of them, and he wins no reputation for wisdom; inasmuch as the hostile state submits before there has been any bloodshed, he receives no credit for courage."]

13 He wins his battles by making no mistakes.

[Ch'ên Hao says: "He plans no superfluous marches, he devises no futile attacks." The connection of ideas is thus explained by Chang Yü: "One who seeks to conquer by sheer strength, clever though he may be at winning pitched battles, is also liable on occasion to be vanquished; whereas he who can look into the future and discern conditions that are not yet manifest, will never make a blunder and therefore invariably win."]

Making no mistakes is what establishes the certainty of victory, for it means conquering an enemy that is already defeated.

14 Hence the skillful fighter puts himself into a position which makes defeat impossible, and does not miss the moment for defeating the enemy.

[A "counsel of perfection" as Tu Mu truly observes. "Position" need not be confined to the actual ground occupied by the troops. It includes all the arrangements and preparations which a wise general will make to increase the safety of his army.]

15 Thus it is that in war the victorious strategist only seeks battle after the victory has been won, whereas he who is destined to defeat first fights and afterwards looks for victory.

[Ho Shih thus expounds the paradox: "In warfare, first lay plans which will ensure victory, and then lead your army to battle; if you will not begin with stratagem but rely on brute strength alone, victory will no longer be assured."]

16 The consummate leader cultivates the moral law, and strictly adheres to method and discipline; thus it is in his power to control success.

17 In respect of military method, we have, firstly, Measurement; secondly, Estimation of quantity; thirdly, Calculation; fourthly, Balancing of chances; fifthly, Victory.

18 Measurement owes its existence to Earth; Estimation of quantity to Measurement; Calculation to Estimation of quantity; Balancing of chances to Calculation; and Victory to Balancing of chances.

[It is not easy to distinguish the four terms very clearly in the Chinese. The first seems to be surveying and measurement of the ground, which enable us to form an estimate of the enemy's strength, and to make calculations based on the data thus obtained; we are thus led to a general weighing-up, or comparison of the enemy's chances with our own; if the latter turn the scale, then victory ensues. The chief difficulty lies in third term, which in the Chinese some commentators take as a calculation of *numbers*, thereby making it nearly synonymous with the second term. Perhaps the second term should be thought of as a consideration of the enemy's general position or condition, while the third term is the estimate of his numerical strength. On the other hand, Tu Mu says: "The question of relative strength having been settled, we can bring the varied resources of cunning into play." Ho Shih seconds this interpretation, but weakens it. However, it points to the third term as being a calculation of numbers.]

19 A victorious army opposed to a routed one, is as a pound's weight placed in the scale against a single grain.

[Literally, "a victorious army is like an *i* (20 oz.) weighed against a *shu* (1/24 oz.); a routed army is a *shu* weighed against an *i*." The point is simply the enormous advantage which a disciplined force, flushed with victory, has over one demoralized by defeat. Legge, in his note on Mencius, I. 2. ix. 2, makes the *i* to be 24 Chinese ounces, and corrects Chu Hsi's statement that it equaled 20 oz. only. But Li Ch'üan of the T'ang dynasty here gives the same figure as Chu Hsi.]

20 The onrush of a conquering force is like the bursting of pent-up waters into a chasm a thousand fathoms deep. So much for tactical dispositions.

Chapter 5
Energy

1 Sun Tzŭ said: The control of a large force is the same principle as the control of a few men: it is merely a question of dividing up their numbers.

[That is, cutting up the army into regiments, companies, etc., with subordinate officers in command of each. Tu Mu reminds us of Han Hsin's famous reply to the first Han Emperor, who once said to him: "How large an army do you think I could lead?" "Not more than 100,000 men, your Majesty." "And you?" asked the Emperor. "Oh!" he answered, "the more the better."]

2 Fighting with a large army under your command is nowise different from fighting with a small one: it is merely a question of instituting signs and signals.

3 To ensure that your whole host may withstand the brunt of the enemy's attack and remain unshaken—this is effected by manœuvers direct and indirect.

[We now come to one of the most interesting parts of Sun Tzŭ's treatise, the discussion of the *chéng* and the *ch'i*." As it is by no means easy to grasp the full significance of these two terms, or to render them consistently by good English equivalents; it may be as well to tabulate some of the commentators' remarks on the subject before proceeding further. Li Ch'üan: "Facing the enemy is *chéng*, making lateral diversion is *ch'i*. Chia Lin: "In presence of the enemy, your troops should be arrayed in normal fashion, but in order to secure victory abnormal manœuvers must be employed." Mei Yao-ch'ên: "*Ch'i* is active, *chéng* is passive; passivity means waiting for an opportunity, activity brings the victory itself." Ho Shih: "We must cause the enemy to regard our straightforward attack as one that is secretly designed, and vice versa; thus *chéng* may also be *ch'i*, and *ch'i* may also be *chéng*." He instances the famous exploit of Han Hsin, who when marching ostensibly against Lin-chin (now Chao-i in Shensi), suddenly threw a large force across the Yellow River in wooden tubs, utterly disconcerting his opponent. (Ch'ien Han Shu, ch. 3.) Here, we are told, the march on Lin-chin was *chéng*, and the surprise manœuver was *ch'i*." Chang Yü gives the following summary of opinions on the words: "Military writers do not agree with regard to the meaning of *ch'i* and *chéng*. Wei Liao Tzŭ (4th cent. B.C.) says: 'Direct warfare favours frontal attacks, indirect warfare attacks from the rear.' Ts'ao Kung says: 'Going straight out to join battle is a direct operation; appearing on the enemy's rear is an indirect manœuver.' Li Wei-kung (6th and 7th cent. A.D.) says: 'In war, to march straight ahead is *chéng*; turning movements, on the other hand, are *ch'i*.' These writers simply regard *chéng* as *chéng*, and *ch'i* as *ch'i*; they do not note that the two are mutually interchangeable and run into each other like the two sides of a circle (see infra, § 11). A comment on the T'ang Emperor T'ai Tsung goes to the root of the matter: 'A *ch'i* manœuver may be *chéng*, if we make the enemy look upon it as *chéng*; then our real attack will be *ch'i*, and vice versa. The whole secret lies in confusing the enemy, so that he cannot fathom our real intent.'" To put it perhaps a little more clearly: any attack or other operation is *chéng*, on which the enemy has had his attention fixed; whereas that is *ch'i*," which takes him by surprise or comes from an unexpected quarter. If the enemy perceives a movement which is meant to be *ch'i*," it immediately becomes *chéng*."]

4 That the impact of your army may be like a grindstone dashed against an egg—this is effected by the science of weak points and strong.

5 In all fighting, the direct method may be used for joining battle, but indirect methods will be needed in order to secure victory.

[Chang Yü says: "Steadily develop indirect tactics, either by pounding the enemy's flanks or falling on his rear." A brilliant example of "indirect tactics" which decided the fortunes of a campaign was Lord Roberts' night march round the Peiwar Kotal in the second Afghan war. [1]]

6 Indirect tactics, efficiently applied, are inexhaustible as Heaven and Earth, unending as the flow of rivers and streams; like the sun and moon, they end but to begin anew; like the four seasons, they pass away but to return once more.

[Tu Yu and Chang Yu understand this of the permutations of *ch'i* and *chéng*. But at present Sun Tzŭ is not speaking of *chéng* at all, unless, indeed, we suppose with Chêng Yu-Hsien that a clause relating to it has fallen out of the text. Of course, as has already been pointed out, the two are so inextricably interwoven in all military operations, that they cannot really be considered apart. Here we simply have an expression, in figurative language, of the almost infinite resource of a great leader.]

7 There are not more than five musical notes, yet the combinations of these five give rise to more melodies than can ever be heard.

8 There are not more than five primary colours (blue, yellow, red, white, and black), yet in combination they produce more hues than can ever be seen.

9 There are not more than five cardinal tastes (sour, acrid, salt, sweet, bitter), yet combinations of them yield more flavours than can ever be tasted.

10 In battle, there are not more than two methods of attack—the direct and the indirect; yet these two in combination give rise to an endless series of manœuvers.

11 The direct and the indirect lead on to each other in turn. It is like moving in a circle—you never come to an end. Who can exhaust the possibilities of their combination?

12 The onset of troops is like the rush of a torrent which will even roll stones along in its course.

13 The quality of decision is like the well-timed swoop of a falcon which enables it to strike and destroy its victim.

[The Chinese here is tricky and a certain key word in the context it is used defies the best efforts of the translator. Tu Mu defines this word as "the measurement or estimation of distance." But this meaning does not quite fit the illustrative simile in §. 15. Applying this definition to the falcon, it seems to me to denote that instinct of *self-restraint* which keeps the bird from swooping on its quarry until the right moment, together with the power of judging when the right moment has arrived. The analogous quality in soldiers is the highly important one of being able to reserve their fire until the very instant at which it will be most effective. When the "Victory" went into action at Trafalgar at hardly more than drifting pace, she was for several minutes exposed to a storm of shot and shell before replying with a single gun. Nelson coolly waited until he was within close range, when the broadside he brought to bear worked fearful havoc on the enemy's nearest ships.]

14 Therefore the good fighter will be terrible in his onset, and prompt in his decision.

[The word "decision" would have reference to the measurement of distance mentioned above, letting the enemy get near before striking. But I cannot help thinking that Sun Tzŭ meant to use the word in a figurative sense comparable to our own idiom "short and sharp." Cf. Wang Hsi's note, which after describing the falcon's mode of attack, proceeds: "This is just how the 'psychological moment' should be seized in war."]

15 Energy may be likened to the bending of a crossbow; decision, to the releasing of the trigger.

[None of the commentators seem to grasp the real point of the simile of energy and the force stored up in the bent cross-bow until released by the finger on the trigger.]

16 Amid the turmoil and tumult of battle, there may be seeming disorder and yet no real disorder at all; amid confusion and chaos, your array may be without head or tail, yet it will be proof against defeat.

[Mei Yao-ch'ên says: "The subdivisions of the army having been previously fixed, and the various signals agreed upon, the separating and joining, the dispersing and collecting which will take place in the course of a battle, may give the appearance of disorder when no real disorder is possible. Your formation may be without head or tail, your dispositions all topsy-turvy, and yet a rout of your forces quite out of the question."]

17 Simulated disorder postulates perfect discipline; simulated fear postulates courage; simulated weakness postulates strength.

[In order to make the translation intelligible, it is necessary to tone down the sharply paradoxical form of the original. Ts'ao Kung throws out a hint of the meaning in his brief note: "These things all serve to destroy formation and conceal one's condition." But Tu Mu is the first to put it quite plainly: "If you wish to feign confusion in order to lure the enemy on, you must first have perfect discipline; if you wish to display timidity in order to entrap the enemy, you must have extreme courage; if you wish to parade your weakness in order to make the enemy over-confident, you must have exceeding strength."]

18 Hiding order beneath the cloak of disorder is simply a question of subdivision;

[See *supra*, § 1.]

concealing courage under a show of timidity presupposes a fund of latent energy;

[The commentators strongly understand a certain Chinese word here differently than anywhere else in this chapter. Thus Tu Mu says: "seeing that we are favourably circumstanced and yet make no move, the enemy will believe that we are really afraid."]

masking strength with weakness is to be effected by tactical dispositions.

[Chang Yü relates the following anecdote of Kao Tsu, the first Han Emperor: "Wishing to crush the Hsiung-nu, he sent out spies to report on their condition. But the Hsiung-nu, forewarned, carefully concealed all their able-bodied men and well-fed horses, and only allowed infirm soldiers and emaciated cattle to be seen. The result was that spies one and all recommended the Emperor to deliver his attack. Lou Ching alone opposed them, saying: 'When two countries go to war, they are naturally inclined to make an ostentatious display of their strength. Yet our spies have seen nothing but old age and infirmity. This is surely some *ruse* on the part of the enemy, and it would be unwise for us to attack.' The Emperor, however, disregarding this advice, fell into the trap and found himself surrounded at Po-teng."]

19 Thus one who is skillful at keeping the enemy on the move maintains deceitful appearances, according to which the enemy will act.

[Ts'ao Kung's note is "Make a display of weakness and want." Tu Mu says: "If our force happens to be superior to the enemy's, weakness may be simulated in order to lure him on; but if inferior, he must be led to believe that we are strong, in order that he may keep off. In fact, all the enemy's movements should be determined by the signs that we choose to give him." Note the following anecdote of Sun Pin, a descendent of Sun Wu: In 341 B.C., the Ch'i State being at war with Wei, sent T'ien Chi and Sun Pin against the general P'ang Chüan, who happened to be a deadly personal enemy of the later. Sun Pin said: "The Ch'i State has a reputation for cowardice, and therefore our adversary despises us. Let us turn this circumstance to account." Accordingly, when the army had crossed the border into Wei territory, he gave orders to show 100,000 fires on the first night, 50,000 on the next, and the night after only 20,000. P'ang Chüan pursued them hotly, saying to himself: "I knew these men of Ch'i were cowards: their numbers have already fallen away by more than half.' In his retreat, Sun Pin came to a narrow defile, which he calculated that his pursuers would reach after dark. Here he had a tree stripped of its bark, and inscribed upon it the words: "Under this tree shall P'ang Chüan die." Then, as night began to fall, he placed a strong body of archers in ambush near by, with orders to shoot directly if they saw a light. Later on, P'ang Chüan arrived at the spot, and noticing the tree, struck a light in order to read what was written on it. His body was immediately riddled by a volley of arrows, and his whole army thrown into confusion. (The above is Tu Mu's version of the story; the *Shih Chi*, less dramatically but probably with more historical truth, makes P'ang Chüan cut his own throat with an exclamation of despair, after the rout of his army.)]

He sacrifices something, that the enemy may snatch at it.

20 By holding out baits, he keeps him on the march; then with a body of picked men he lies in wait for him.

[With an emendation suggested by Li Ching, this then reads, "He lies in wait with the main body of his troops."]

21 The clever combatant looks to the effect of combined energy, and does not require too much from individuals.

[Tu Mu says: "He first of all considers the power of his army in the bulk; afterwards he takes individual talent into account, and uses each men according to his capabilities. He does not demand perfection from the untalented."]

Hence his ability to pick out the right men and utilise combined energy.

22 When he utilizes combined energy, his fighting men become as it were like unto rolling logs or stones. For it is the nature of a log or stone to remain motionless on level ground, and to move when on a slope; if four-cornered, to come to a standstill, but if round-shaped, to go rolling down.

[Ts'au Kung calls this "the use of natural or inherent power."]

23 Thus the energy developed by good fighting men is as the momentum of a round stone rolled down a mountain thousands of feet in height. So much on the subject of energy.

[The chief lesson of this chapter, in Tu Mu's opinion, is the paramount importance in war of rapid evolutions and sudden rushes. "Great results," he adds, "can thus be achieved with small forces."]

[1] "Forty-one Years in India," chapter 46.

Chapter 6
Weak Points and Strong

[Chang Yü attempts to explain the sequence of chapters as follows: "Chapter IV, on Tactical Dispositions, treated of the offensive and the defensive; chapter V, on Energy, dealt with direct and indirect methods. The good general acquaints himself first with the theory of attack and defense, and then turns his attention to direct and indirect methods. He studies the art of varying and combining these two methods before proceeding to the subject of weak and strong points. For the use of direct or indirect methods arises out of attack and defense, and the perception of weak and strong points depends again on the above methods. Hence the present chapter comes immediately after the chapter on Energy."]

1 Sun Tzŭ said: Whoever is first in the field and awaits the coming of the enemy, will be fresh for the fight; whoever is second in the field and has to hasten to battle, will arrive exhausted.

2 Therefore the clever combatant imposes his will on the enemy, but does not allow the enemy's will to be imposed on him.

[One mark of a great soldier is that he fight on his own terms or fights not at all. [1]]

3 By holding out advantages to him, he can cause the enemy to approach of his own accord; or, by inflicting damage, he can make it impossible for the enemy to draw near.

[In the first case, he will entice him with a bait; in the second, he will strike at some important point which the enemy will have to defend.]

4 If the enemy is taking his ease, he can harass him;

[This passage may be cited as evidence against Mei Yao- Ch'en's interpretation of I. § 23.]

if well supplied with food, he can starve him out; if quietly encamped, he can force him to move.

5 Appear at points which the enemy must hasten to defend; march swiftly to places where you are not expected.

6 An army may march great distances without distress, if it marches through country where the enemy is not.

[Ts'ao Kung sums up very well: "Emerge from the void [q.d. like "a bolt from the blue"], strike at vulnerable points, shun places that are defended, attack in unexpected quarters."]

7 You can be sure of succeeding in your attacks if you only attack places which are undefended.

[Wang Hsi explains "undefended places" as "weak points; that is to say, where the general is lacking in capacity, or the soldiers in spirit; where the walls are not strong enough, or the precautions not strict enough; where relief comes too late, or provisions are too scanty, or the defenders are variance amongst themselves."]

You can ensure the safety of your defense if you only hold positions that cannot be attacked.

[*I.e.*, where there are none of the weak points mentioned above. There is rather a nice point involved in the interpretation of this later clause. Tu Mu, Ch'ên Hao, and Mei Yao-ch'ên assume the meaning to be: "In order to make your defense quite safe, you must defend *even* those places that are not likely to be attacked;" and Tu Mu adds: "How much more, then, those that will be attacked." Taken thus, however, the clause balances less well with the preceding—always a consideration in the highly antithetical style which is natural to the Chinese. Chang Yü, therefore, seems to come nearer the mark in saying: "He who is skilled in attack flashes forth from the topmost heights of heaven [see IV. § 7], making it impossible for the enemy to guard against him. This being so, the places that I shall attack are precisely those that the enemy cannot defend.... He who is skilled in defense hides in the most secret recesses of the earth, making it impossible for the enemy to estimate his whereabouts. This being so, the places that I shall hold are precisely those that the enemy cannot attack."]

8 Hence that general is skillful in attack whose opponent does not know what to defend; and he is skillful in defense whose opponent does not know what to attack.

[An aphorism which puts the whole art of war in a nutshell.]

9 O divine art of subtlety and secrecy! Through you we learn to be invisible, through you inaudible;

[Literally, "without form or sound," but it is said of course with reference to the enemy.]

and hence we can hold the enemy's fate in our hands.

10 You may advance and be absolutely irresistible, if you make for the enemy's weak points; you may retire and be safe from pursuit if your movements are more rapid than those of the enemy.

11 If we wish to fight, the enemy can be forced to an engagement even though he be sheltered behind a high rampart and a deep ditch. All we need do is attack some other place that he will be obliged to relieve.

[Tu Mu says: "If the enemy is the invading party, we can cut his line of communications and occupy the roads by which he will have to return; if we are the invaders, we may direct our attack against the sovereign himself." It is clear that Sun Tzŭ, unlike certain generals in the late Boer war, was no believer in frontal attacks.]

12 If we do not wish to fight, we can prevent the enemy from engaging us even though the lines of our encampment be merely traced out on the ground. All we need do is to throw something odd and unaccountable in his way.

[This extremely concise expression is intelligibly paraphrased by Chia Lin: "even though we have constructed neither wall nor ditch." Li Ch'üan says: "we puzzle him by strange and unusual dispositions;" and Tu Mu finally clinches the meaning by three illustrative anecdotes—one of Chu-ko Liang, who when occupying Yang-p'ing and about to be attacked by Ssŭ-ma I, suddenly struck his colors, stopped the beating of the drums, and flung open the city gates, showing only a few men engaged in sweeping and sprinkling the ground. This unexpected proceeding had the intended effect; for Ssŭ-ma I, suspecting an ambush, actually drew off his army and retreated. What Sun Tzŭ is advocating here, therefore, is nothing more nor less than the timely use of "bluff."]

13 By discovering the enemy's dispositions and remaining invisible ourselves, we can keep our forces concentrated, while the enemy's must be divided.

[The conclusion is perhaps not very obvious, but Chang Yü (after Mei Yao-ch'ên) rightly explains it thus: "If the enemy's dispositions are visible, we can make for him in one body; whereas, our own dispositions being kept secret, the enemy will be obliged to divide his forces in order to guard against attack from every quarter."]

14 We can form a single united body, while the enemy must split up into fractions. Hence there will be a whole pitted against separate parts of a whole, which means that we shall be many to the enemy's few.

15 And if we are able thus to attack an inferior force with a superior one, our opponents will be in dire straits.

16 The spot where we intend to fight must not be made known; for then the enemy will have to prepare against a possible attack at several different points;

[Sheridan once explained the reason of General Grant's victories by saying that "while his opponents were kept fully employed wondering what he was going to do, *he* was thinking most of what he was going to do himself."]

and his forces being thus distributed in many directions, the numbers we shall have to face at any given point will be proportionately few.

17 For should the enemy strengthen his van, he will weaken his rear; should he strengthen his rear, he will weaken his van; should he strengthen his left, he will weaken his right; should he strengthen his right, he will weaken his left. If he sends reinforcements everywhere, he will everywhere be weak.

[In Frederick the Great's *Instructions to his Generals* we read: "A defensive war is apt to betray us into too frequent detachment. Those generals who have had but little experience attempt to protect every point, while those who are better acquainted with their profession, having only the capital object in view, guard against a decisive blow, and acquiesce in small misfortunes to avoid greater."]

18 Numerical weakness comes from having to prepare against possible attacks; numerical strength, from compelling our adversary to make these preparations against us.

[The highest generalship, in Col. Henderson's words, is "to compel the enemy to disperse his army, and then to concentrate superior force against each fraction in turn."]

19 Knowing the place and the time of the coming battle, we may concentrate from the greatest distances in order to fight.

[What Sun Tzŭ evidently has in mind is that nice calculation of distances and that masterly employment of strategy which enable a general to divide his army for the purpose of a long and rapid march, and afterwards to effect a junction at precisely the right spot and the right hour in order to confront the enemy in overwhelming strength. Among many such successful junctions which military history records, one of the most dramatic and decisive was the appearance of Blucher just at the critical moment on the field of Waterloo.]

20 But if neither time nor place be known, then the left wing will be impotent to succour the right, the right equally impotent to succour the left, the van unable to relieve the rear, or the rear to support the van. How much more so if the furthest portions of the army are anything under a hundred *li* apart, and even the nearest are separated by several *li*!

[The Chinese of this last sentence is a little lacking in precision, but the mental picture we are required to draw is probably that of an army advancing towards a given rendezvous in separate columns, each of which has orders to be there on a fixed date. If the general allows the various detachments to proceed at haphazard, without precise instructions as to the time and place of meeting, the enemy will be able to annihilate the army in detail. Chang Yü's note may be worth quoting here: "If we do not know the place where our opponents mean to concentrate or the day on which they will join battle, our unity will be forfeited through our preparations for defense, and the positions we hold will be insecure. Suddenly happening upon a powerful foe, we shall be brought to battle in a flurried condition, and no mutual support will be possible between wings, vanguard or rear, especially if there is any great distance between the foremost and hindmost divisions of the army."]

21 Though according to my estimate the soldiers of Yüeh exceed our own in number, that shall advantage them nothing in the matter of victory. I say then that victory can be achieved.

[Alas for these brave words! The long feud between the two states ended in 473 B.C. with the total defeat of Wu by Kou Chien and its incorporation in Yüeh. This was doubtless long after Sun Tzŭ's death. With his present assertion compare IV. § 4. Chang Yü is the only one to point out the seeming discrepancy, which he thus goes on to explain: "In the chapter on Tactical Dispositions it is said, 'One may *know* how to conquer without being able to *do* it,' whereas here we have the statement that 'victory' can be achieved.' The explanation is, that in the former chapter, where the offensive and defensive are under discussion, it is said that if the enemy is fully prepared, one cannot make certain of beating him. But the present passage refers particularly to the soldiers of Yüeh who, according to Sun Tzŭ's calculations, will be kept in ignorance of the time and place of the impending struggle. That is why he says here that victory can be achieved."]

22 Though the enemy be stronger in numbers, we may prevent him from fighting. Scheme so as to discover his plans and the likelihood of their success.

[An alternative reading offered by Chia Lin is: "Know beforehand all plans conducive to our success and to the enemy's failure."

23 Rouse him, and learn the principle of his activity or inactivity.

[Chang Yü tells us that by noting the joy or anger shown by the enemy on being thus disturbed, we shall be able to conclude whether his policy is to lie low or the reverse. He instances the action of Cho-ku Liang, who sent the scornful present of a woman's head-dress to Ssŭ-ma I, in order to goad him out of his Fabian tactics.]

Force him to reveal himself, so as to find out his vulnerable spots.

24 Carefully compare the opposing army with your own, so that you may know where strength is superabundant and where it is deficient.

[Cf. IV. § 6.]

25 In making tactical dispositions, the highest pitch you can attain is to conceal them;

[The piquancy of the paradox evaporates in translation. Concealment is perhaps not so much actual invisibility (see *supra* § 9) as "showing no sign" of what you mean to do, of the plans that are formed in your brain.]

conceal your dispositions, and you will be safe from the prying of the subtlest spies, from the machinations of the wisest brains.

[Tu Mu explains: "Though the enemy may have clever and capable officers, they will not be able to lay any plans against us."]

26 How victory may be produced for them out of the enemy's own tactics—that is what the multitude cannot comprehend.

27 All men can see the tactics whereby I conquer, but what none can see is the strategy out of which victory is evolved.

[*i.e.*, everybody can see superficially how a battle is won; what they cannot see is the long series of plans and combinations which has preceded the battle.]

28 Do not repeat the tactics which have gained you one victory, but let your methods be regulated by the infinite variety of circumstances.

[As Wang Hsi sagely remarks: "There is but one root-principle underlying victory, but the tactics which lead up to it are infinite in number." With this compare Col. Henderson: "The rules of strategy are few and simple. They may be learned in a week. They may be taught by familiar illustrations or a dozen diagrams. But such knowledge will no more teach a man to lead an army like Napoleon than a knowledge of grammar will teach him to write like Gibbon."]

29 Military tactics are like unto water; for water in its natural course runs away from high places and hastens downwards.

30 So in war, the way is to avoid what is strong and to strike at what is weak.

[Like water, taking the line of least resistance.]

31 Water shapes its course according to the nature of the ground over which it flows; the soldier works out his victory in relation to the foe whom he is facing.

32 Therefore, just as water retains no constant shape, so in warfare there are no constant conditions.

33 He who can modify his tactics in relation to his opponent and thereby succeed in winning, may be called a heaven-born captain.

34 The five elements (water, fire, wood, metal, earth) are not always equally predominant;

[That is, as Wang Hsi says: "they predominate alternately."]

the four seasons make way for each other in turn.

[Literally, "have no invariable seat."]

There are short days and long; the moon has its periods of waning and waxing.

[Cf. V. § 6. The purport of the passage is simply to illustrate the want of fixity in war by the changes constantly taking place in Nature. The comparison is not very happy, however, because the regularity of the phenomena which Sun Tzŭ mentions is by no means paralleled in war.]

[1] See Col. Henderson's biography of Stonewall Jackson, 1902 ed., vol. II, p. 490.

Chapter 7

Manœuvering

1 Sun Tzŭ said: In war, the general receives his commands from the sovereign.

2 Having collected an army and concentrated his forces, he must blend and harmonise the different elements thereof before pitching his camp.

["Chang Yü says: "the establishment of harmony and confidence between the higher and lower ranks before venturing into the field;" and he quotes a saying of Wu Tzŭ (chap. 1 ad init.): "Without harmony in the State, no military expedition can be undertaken; without harmony in the army, no battle array can be formed." In an historical romance Sun Tzŭ is represented as saying to Wu Yüan: "As a general rule, those who are waging war should get rid of all the domestic troubles before proceeding to attack the external foe."]

3 After that, comes tactical manœuvering, than which there is nothing more difficult.

[I have departed slightly from the traditional interpretation of Ts'ao Kung, who says: "From the time of receiving the sovereign's instructions until our encampment over against the enemy, the tactics to be pursued are most difficult." It seems to me that the tactics or manœuvers can hardly be said to begin until the army has sallied forth and encamped, and Ch'ien Hao's note gives color to this view: "For levying, concentrating, harmonizing and entrenching an army, there are plenty of old rules which will serve. The real difficulty comes when we engage in tactical operations." Tu Yu also observes that "the great difficulty is to be beforehand with the enemy in seizing favourable position."]

The difficulty of tactical manœuvering consists in turning the devious into the direct, and misfortune into gain.

[This sentence contains one of those highly condensed and somewhat enigmatical expressions of which Sun Tzŭ is so fond. This is how it is explained by Ts'ao Kung: "Make it appear that you are a long way off, then cover the distance rapidly and arrive on the scene before your opponent." Tu Mu says: "Hoodwink the enemy, so that he may be remiss and leisurely while you are dashing along with utmost speed." Ho Shih gives a slightly different turn: "Although you may have difficult ground to traverse and natural obstacles to encounter this is a drawback which can be turned into actual advantage by celerity of movement." Signal examples of this saying are afforded by the two famous passages across the Alps—that of Hannibal, which laid Italy at his mercy, and that of Napoleon two thousand years later, which resulted in the great victory of Marengo.]

4 Thus, to take a long and circuitous route, after enticing the enemy out of the way, and though starting after him, to contrive to reach the goal before him, shows knowledge of the artifice of *deviation*.

[Tu Mu cites the famous march of Chao Shê in 270 B.C. to relieve the town of O-yü, which was closely invested by a Ch'in army. The King of Chao first consulted Lien P'o on the advisability of attempting a relief, but the latter thought the distance too great, and the intervening country too rugged and difficult. His Majesty then turned to Chao Shê, who fully admitted the hazardous nature of the march, but finally said: "We shall be like two rats fighting in a whole—and the pluckier one will win!" So he left the capital with his army, but had only gone a distance of 30 *li* when he stopped and began throwing up entrenchments. For 28 days he continued strengthening his fortifications, and took care that spies should carry the intelligence to the enemy. The Ch'in general was overjoyed, and attributed his adversary's tardiness to the fact that the beleaguered city was in the Han State, and thus not actually part of Chao territory. But the spies had no sooner departed than Chao Shê began a forced march lasting for two days and one night, and arrive on the scene of action with such astonishing rapidity that he was able to occupy a commanding position on the "North hill" before the enemy had got wind of his movements. A crushing defeat followed for the Ch'in forces, who were obliged to raise the siege of O-yü in all haste and retreat across the border.]

5 Manœuvering with an army is advantageous; with an undisciplined multitude, most dangerous.

[I adopt the reading of the *T'ung Tien*, Chêng Yu-Hsien and the *T'u Shu*, since they appear to apply the exact nuance required in order to make sense. The commentators using the standard text take this line to mean that manœuvers may be profitable, or they may be dangerous: it all depends on the ability of the general.]

6 If you set a fully equipped army in march in order to snatch an advantage, the chances are that you will be too late. On the other hand, to detach a flying column for the purpose involves the sacrifice of its baggage and stores.

[Some of the Chinese text is unintelligible to the Chinese commentators, who paraphrase the sentence. I submit my own rendering without much enthusiasm, being convinced that there is some deep-seated corruption in the text. On the whole, it is clear that Sun Tzŭ does not approve of a lengthy march being undertaken without supplies. Cf. infra, § 11.]

7 Thus, if you order your men to roll up their buff-coats, and make forced marches without halting day or night, covering double the usual distance at a stretch,

[The ordinary day's march, according to Tu Mu, was 30 *li*; but on one occasion, when pursuing Liu Pei, Ts'ao Ts'ao is said to have covered the incredible distance of 300 *li* within twenty-four hours.]

doing a hundred *li* in order to wrest an advantage, the leaders of all your three divisions will fall into the hands of the enemy.

8 The stronger men will be in front, the jaded ones will fall behind, and on this plan only one-tenth of your army will reach its destination.

[The moral is, as Ts'ao Kung and others point out: Don't march a hundred *li* to gain a tactical advantage, either with or without impedimenta. Manœuvers of this description should be confined to short distances. Stonewall Jackson said: "The hardships of forced marches are often more painful than the dangers of battle." He did not often call upon his troops for extraordinary exertions. It was only when he intended a surprise, or when a rapid retreat was imperative, that he sacrificed everything for speed. [1]]

9 If you march fifty *li* in order to outmanœuver the enemy, you will lose the leader of your first division, and only half your force will reach the goal.

[Literally, "the leader of the first division will be *torn away*."]

10 If you march thirty *li* with the same object, two-thirds of your army will arrive.

[In the *T'ung Tien* is added: "From this we may know the difficulty of manœuvering."]

11 We may take it then that an army without its baggage-train is lost; without provisions it is lost; without bases of supply it is lost.

[I think Sun Tzŭ meant "stores accumulated in dépôts." But Tu Yu says "fodder and the like," Chang Yü says "Goods in general," and Wang Hsi says "fuel, salt, foodstuffs, etc."]

12 We cannot enter into alliances until we are acquainted with the designs of our neighbours.

13 We are not fit to lead an army on the march unless we are familiar with the face of the country—its mountains and forests, its pitfalls and precipices, its marshes and swamps.

14 We shall be unable to turn natural advantages to account unless we make use of local guides.

[§§. 12-14 are repeated in chap. XI. § 52.]

15 In war, practise dissimulation, and you will succeed.

[In the tactics of Turenne, deception of the enemy, especially as to the numerical strength of his troops, took a very prominent position. [2]]

Move only if there is a real advantage to be gained.

16 Whether to concentrate or to divide your troops, must be decided by circumstances.

17 Let your rapidity be that of the wind,

[The simile is doubly appropriate, because the wind is not only swift but, as Mei Yao-ch'ên points out, "invisible and leaves no tracks."]

your compactness that of the forest.

[Mêng Shih comes nearer to the mark in his note: "When slowly marching, order and ranks must be preserved"—so as to guard against surprise attacks. But natural forest do not grow in rows, whereas they do generally possess the quality of density or compactness.]

18 In raiding and plundering be like fire,

[Cf. *Shih Ching*, IV. 3. iv. 6: "Fierce as a blazing fire which no man can check."]

in immovability like a mountain.

[That is, when holding a position from which the enemy is trying to dislodge you, or perhaps, as Tu Yu says, when he is trying to entice you into a trap.]

19 Let your plans be dark and impenetrable as night, and when you move, fall like a thunderbolt.

[Tu Yu quotes a saying of T'ai Kung which has passed into a proverb: "You cannot shut your ears to the thunder or your eyes to the lighting—so rapid are they." Likewise, an attack should be made so quickly that it cannot be parried.]

20 When you plunder a countryside, let the spoil be divided amongst your men;

[Sun Tzŭ wishes to lessen the abuses of indiscriminate plundering by insisting that all booty shall be thrown into a common stock, which may afterwards be fairly divided amongst all.]

when you capture new territory, cut it up into allotments for the benefit of the soldiery.

[Ch'ên Hao says "quarter your soldiers on the land, and let them sow and plant it." It is by acting on this principle, and harvesting the lands they invaded, that the Chinese have succeeded in carrying out some of their most memorable and triumphant expeditions, such as that of Pan Ch'ao who penetrated to the Caspian, and in more recent years, those of Fu-k'ang-an and Tso Tsung-t'ang.]

21 Ponder and deliberate before you make a move.

[Chang Yü quotes Wei Liao Tzŭ as saying that we must not break camp until we have gained the resisting power of the enemy and the cleverness of the opposing general. Cf. the "seven comparisons" in I. § 13.]

22 He will conquer who has learnt the artifice of deviation.

[See *supra*, §§ 3, 4.]

Such is the art of manœuvering.

[With these words, the chapter would naturally come to an end. But there now follows a long appendix in the shape of an extract from an earlier book on War, now lost, but apparently extant at the time when Sun Tzŭ wrote. The style of this fragment is not noticeably different from that of Sun Tzŭ himself, but no commentator raises a doubt as to its genuineness.]

23 The Book of Army Management says:

[It is perhaps significant that none of the earlier commentators give us any information about this work. Mei Yao- Ch'en calls it "an ancient military classic," and Wang Hsi, "an old book on war." Considering the enormous amount of fighting that had gone on for centuries before Sun Tzŭ's time between the various kingdoms and principalities of China, it is not in itself improbable that a collection of military maxims should have been made and written down at some earlier period.]

On the field of battle,

[Implied, though not actually in the Chinese.]

the spoken word does not carry far enough: hence the institution of gongs and drums. Nor can ordinary objects be seen clearly enough: hence the institution of banners and flags.

24 Gongs and drums, banners and flags, are means whereby the ears and eyes of the host may be focussed on one particular point.

[Chang Yü says: "If sight and hearing converge simultaneously on the same object, the evolutions of as many as a million soldiers will be like those of a single man."!]

25 The host thus forming a single united body, is it impossible either for the brave to advance alone, or for the cowardly to retreat alone.

[Chüang Yu quotes a saying: "Equally guilty are those who advance against orders and those who retreat against orders." Tu Mu tells a story in this connection of Wu Ch'i, when he was fighting against the Ch'in State. Before the battle had begun, one of his soldiers, a man of matchless daring, sallied forth by himself, captured two heads from the enemy, and returned to camp. Wu Ch'i had the man instantly executed, whereupon an officer ventured to remonstrate, saying: "This man was a good soldier, and ought not to have been beheaded." Wu Ch'i replied: "I fully believe he was a good soldier, but I had him beheaded because he acted without orders."]

This is the art of handling large masses of men.

26 In night-fighting, then, make much use of signal-fires and drums, and in fighting by day, of flags and banners, as a means of influencing the ears and eyes of your army.

[Ch'ên Hao alludes to Li Kuang-pi's night ride to Ho-yang at the head of 500 mounted men; they made such an imposing display with torches, that though the rebel leader Shih Ssŭ-ming had a large army, he did not dare to dispute their passage.]

27 A whole army may be robbed of its spirit;

["In war," says Chang Yü, "if a spirit of anger can be made to pervade all ranks of an army at one and the same time, its onset will be irresistible. Now the spirit of the enemy's soldiers will be keenest when they have newly arrived on the scene, and it is therefore our cue not to fight at once, but to wait until their ardor and enthusiasm have worn off, and then strike. It is in this way that they may be robbed of their keen spirit." Li Ch'üan and others tell an anecdote (to be found in the *Tso Chüan*, year 10, § 1) of Ts'ao Kuei, a protege of Duke Chüang of Lu. The latter State was attacked by Ch'i, and the duke was about to join battle at Ch'ang-cho, after the first roll of the enemy's drums, when Ts'ao said: "Not just yet." Only after their drums had beaten for the third time, did he give the word for attack. Then they fought, and the men of Ch'i were utterly defeated. Questioned afterwards by the Duke as to the meaning of his delay, Ts'ao Kuei replied: "In battle, a courageous spirit is everything. Now the first roll of the drum tends to create this spirit, but with the second it is already on the wane, and after the third it is gone altogether. I attacked when their spirit was gone and ours was at its height. Hence our victory." Wu Tzŭ (chap. 4) puts "spirit" first among the "four important influences" in war, and continues: "The value of a whole army—a mighty host of a million men—is dependent on one man alone: such is the influence of spirit!"]

a commander-in-chief may be robbed of his presence of mind.

[Chang Yü says: "Presence of mind is the general's most important asset. It is the quality which enables him to discipline disorder and to inspire courage into the panic-stricken." The great general Li Ching

(A.D. 571-649) has a saying: "Attacking does not merely consist in assaulting walled cities or striking at an army in battle array; it must include the art of assailing the enemy's mental equilibrium."]

28 Now a soldier's spirit is keenest in the morning;

[Always provided, I suppose, that he has had breakfast. At the battle of the Trebia, the Romans were foolishly allowed to fight fasting, whereas Hannibal's men had breakfasted at their leisure. See Livy, XXI, liv. 8, lv. 1 and 8.]

by noonday it has begun to flag; and in the evening, his mind is bent only on returning to camp.

29 A clever general, therefore, avoids an army when its spirit is keen, but attacks it when it is sluggish and inclined to return. This is the art of studying moods.

30 Disciplined and calm, to await the appearance of disorder and hubbub amongst the enemy:—this is the art of retaining self-possession.

31 To be near the goal while the enemy is still far from it, to wait at ease while the enemy is toiling and struggling, to be well-fed while the enemy is famished:—this is the art of husbanding one's strength.

32 To refrain from intercepting an enemy whose banners are in perfect order, to refrain from attacking an army drawn up in calm and confident array:—this is the art of studying circumstances.

33 It is a military axiom not to advance uphill against the enemy, nor to oppose him when he comes downhill.

34 Do not pursue an enemy who simulates flight; do not attack soldiers whose temper is keen.

35 Do not swallow a bait offered by the enemy.

[Li Ch'üan and Tu Mu, with extraordinary inability to see a metaphor, take these words quite literally of food and drink that have been poisoned by the enemy. Ch'ên Hao and Chang Yü carefully point out that the saying has a wider application.]

Do not interfere with an army that is returning home.

[The commentators explain this rather singular piece of advice by saying that a man whose heart is set on returning home will fight to the death against any attempt to bar his way, and is therefore too dangerous an opponent to be tackled. Chang Yü quotes the words of Han Hsin: "Invincible is the soldier who hath his desire and returneth homewards." A marvelous tale is told of Ts'ao Ts'ao's courage and resource in ch. 1 of the *San Kuo Chi*, In 198 A.D., he was besieging Chang Hsiu in Jang, when Liu Piao sent reinforcements with a view to cutting off Ts'ao's retreat. The latter was obliged to draw off his troops, only to find himself hemmed in between two enemies, who were guarding each outlet of a narrow pass in which he had engaged himself. In this desperate plight Ts'ao waited until nightfall, when he bored a tunnel into the mountain side and laid an ambush in it. As soon as the whole army had passed by, the hidden troops fell on his rear, while Ts'ao himself turned and met his pursuers in front, so that they were thrown into confusion and annihilated. Ts'ao Ts'ao said afterwards: "The brigands tried to check my army in its retreat and brought me to battle in a desperate position: hence I knew how to overcome them."]

36 When you surround an army, leave an outlet free.

[This does not mean that the enemy is to be allowed to escape. The object, as Tu Mu puts it, is "to make him believe that there is a road to safety, and thus prevent his fighting with the courage of despair." Tu Mu adds pleasantly: "After that, you may crush him."]

Do not press a desperate foe too hard.

[Ch'ên Hao quotes the saying: "Birds and beasts when brought to bay will use their claws and teeth." Chang Yü says: "If your adversary has burned his boats and destroyed his cooking-pots, and is ready to stake all on the issue of a battle, he must not be pushed to extremities." Ho Shih illustrates the meaning by a story taken from the life of Yen-ch'ing. That general, together with his colleague Tu

Chung-wei was surrounded by a vastly superior army of Khitans in the year 945 A.D. The country was bare and desert-like, and the little Chinese force was soon in dire straits for want of water. The wells they bored ran dry, and the men were reduced to squeezing lumps of mud and sucking out the moisture. Their ranks thinned rapidly, until at last Fu Yen-ch'ing exclaimed: "We are desperate men. Far better to die for our country than to go with fettered hands into captivity!" A strong gale happened to be blowing from the northeast and darkening the air with dense clouds of sandy dust. To Chung-wei was for waiting until this had abated before deciding on a final attack; but luckily another officer, Li Shou-chéng by name, was quicker to see an opportunity, and said: "They are many and we are few, but in the midst of this sandstorm our numbers will not be discernible; victory will go to the strenuous fighter, and the wind will be our best ally." Accordingly, Fu Yen-ch'ing made a sudden and wholly unexpected onslaught with his cavalry, routed the barbarians and succeeded in breaking through to safety.]

37 Such is the art of warfare.

[1] See Col. Henderson, op. cit. vol. I. p. 426.

[2] For a number of maxims on this head, see "Marshal Turenne" (Longmans, 1907), p. 29.

Chapter 8
Variation of Tactics

[The heading means literally "The Nine Variations," but as Sun Tzŭ does not appear to enumerate these, and as, indeed, he has already told us (V §§ 6-11) that such deflections from the ordinary course are practically innumerable, we have little option but to follow Wang Hsi, who says that "Nine" stands for an indefinitely large number. "All it means is that in warfare we ought to vary our tactics to the utmost degree… I do not know what Ts'ao Kung makes these Nine Variations out to be, but it has been suggested that they are connected with the Nine Situations" - of chapt. XI. This is the view adopted by Chang Yü. The only other alternative is to suppose that something has been lost—a supposition to which the unusual shortness of the chapter lends some weight.]

1 Sun Tzŭ said: In war, the general receives his commands from the sovereign, collects his army and concentrates his forces.

[Repeated from VII. § 1, where it is certainly more in place. It may have been interpolated here merely in order to supply a beginning to the chapter.]

2 When in difficult country, do not encamp. In country where high roads intersect, join hands with your allies. Do not linger in dangerously isolated positions.

[The last situation is not one of the Nine Situations as given in the beginning of chap. XI, but occurs later on (ibid. § 43. q.v.). Chang Yü defines this situation as being situated across the frontier, in hostile territory. Li Ch'üan says it is "country in which there are no springs or wells, flocks or herds, vegetables or firewood;" Chia Lin, "one of gorges, chasms and precipices, without a road by which to advance."]

In hemmed-in situations, you must resort to stratagem. In a desperate position, you must fight.

3 There are roads which must not be followed,

["Especially those leading through narrow defiles," says Li Ch'üan, "where an ambush is to be feared."]

armies which must be not attacked,

[More correctly, perhaps, "there are times when an army must not be attacked." Ch'ên Hao says: "When you see your way to obtain a rival advantage, but are powerless to inflict a real defeat, refrain from attacking, for fear of overtaxing your men's strength."]

towns which must not be besieged,

[Cf. III. § 4 Ts'ao Kung gives an interesting illustration from his own experience. When invading the territory of Hsu-chou, he ignored the city of Hua-pi, which lay directly in his path, and pressed on into the heart of the country. This excellent strategy was rewarded by the subsequent capture of no fewer than fourteen important district cities. Chang Yü says: "No town should be attacked which, if taken, cannot be held, or if left alone, will not cause any trouble." Hsun Ying, when urged to attack Pi-yang, replied: "The city is small and well-fortified; even if I succeed intaking it, it will be no great feat of arms; whereas if I fail, I shall make myself a laughing-stock." In the seventeenth century, sieges still formed a large proportion of war. It was Turenne who directed attention to the importance of marches, countermarches and manœuvers. He said: "It is a great mistake to waste men in taking a town when the same expenditure of soldiers will gain a province." [1]]

positions which must not be contested, commands of the sovereign which must not be obeyed.

[This is a hard saying for the Chinese, with their reverence for authority, and Wei Liao Tzŭ (quoted by Tu Mu) is moved to exclaim:

"Weapons are baleful instruments, strife is antagonistic to virtue, a military commander is the negation of civil order!" The unpalatable fact remains, however, that even Imperial wishes must be subordinated to military necessity.]

4 The general who thoroughly understands the advantages that accompany variation of tactics knows how to handle his troops.

5 The general who does not understand these, may be well acquainted with the configuration of the country, yet he will not be able to turn his knowledge to practical account.

[Literally, "get the advantage of the ground," which means not only securing good positions, but availing oneself of natural advantages in every possible way. Chang Yü says: "Every kind of ground is characterized by certain natural features, and also gives scope for a certain variability of plan. How it is possible to turn these natural features to account unless topographical knowledge is supplemented by versatility of mind?"]

6 So, the student of war who is unversed in the art of war of varying his plans, even though he be acquainted with the Five Advantages, will fail to make the best use of his men.

[Chia Lin tells us that these imply five obvious and generally advantageous lines of action, namely: "if a certain road is short, it must be followed; if an army is isolated, it must be attacked; if a town is in a parlous condition, it must be besieged; if a position can be stormed, it must be attempted; and if consistent with military operations, the ruler's commands must be obeyed." But there are circumstances which sometimes forbid a general to use these advantages. For instance, "a certain road may be the shortest way for him, but if he knows that it abounds in natural obstacles, or that the enemy has laid an ambush on it, he will not follow that road. A hostile force may be open to attack, but if he knows that it is hard-pressed and likely to fight with desperation, he will refrain from striking," and so on.]

7 Hence in the wise leader's plans, considerations of advantage and of disadvantage will be blended together.

["Whether in an advantageous position or a disadvantageous one," says Ts'ao Kung, "the opposite state should be always present to your mind."]

8 If our expectation of advantage be tempered in this way, we may succeed in accomplishing the essential part of our schemes.

[Tu Mu says: "If we wish to wrest an advantage from the enemy, we must not fix our minds on that alone, but allow for the possibility of the enemy also doing some harm to us, and let this enter as a factor into our calculations."]

9 If, on the other hand, in the midst of difficulties we are always ready to seize an advantage, we may extricate ourselves from misfortune.

[Tu Mu says: "If I wish to extricate myself from a dangerous position, I must consider not only the enemy's ability to injure me, but also my own ability to gain an advantage over the enemy. If in my counsels these two considerations are properly blended, I shall succeed in liberating myself.... For instance; if I am surrounded by the enemy and only think of effecting an escape, the nervelessness of my policy will incite my adversary to pursue and crush me; it would be far better to encourage my men to deliver a bold counter-attack, and use the advantage thus gained to free myself from the enemy's toils." See the story of Ts'ao Ts'ao, VII. § 35, note.]

10 Reduce the hostile chiefs by inflicting damage on them;

[Chia Lin enumerates several ways of inflicting this injury, some of which would only occur to the Oriental mind:—"Entice away the enemy's best and wisest men, so that he may be left without counselors. Introduce traitors into his country, that the government policy may be rendered futile. Foment intrigue and deceit, and thus sow dissension between the ruler and his ministers. By means of every artful contrivance, cause deterioration amongst his men and waste of his treasure. Corrupt his morals by insidious gifts leading him into excess. Disturb and unsettle his mind by presenting him with lovely women." Chang Yü (after Wang Hsi) makes a different interpretation of Sun Tzŭ here: "Get the enemy into a position where he must suffer injury, and he will submit of his own accord."]

and make trouble for them,

[Tu Mu, in this phrase, in his interpretation indicates that trouble should be made for the enemy affecting their "possessions," or, as we might say, "assets," which he considers to be "a large army, a rich exchequer, harmony amongst the soldiers, punctual fulfillment of commands." These give us a whip-hand over the enemy.]

and keep them constantly engaged;

[Literally, "make servants of them." Tu Yu says "prevent them from having any rest."]

hold out specious allurements, and make them rush to any given point.

[Mêng Shih's note contains an excellent example of the idiomatic use of: "cause them to forget *pien* (the reasons for acting otherwise than on their first impulse), and hasten in our direction."]

11 The art of war teaches us to rely not on the likelihood of the enemy's not coming, but on our own readiness to receive him; not on the chance of his not attacking, but rather on the fact that we have made our position unassailable.

12 There are five dangerous faults which may affect a general:

(1) Recklessness, which leads to destruction;

["Bravery without forethought," as Ts'ao Kung analyzes it, which causes a man to fight blindly and desperately like a mad bull. Such an opponent, says Chang Yü, "must not be encountered with brute force, but may be lured into an ambush and slain." Cf. Wu Tzŭ, chap. IV. ad init.: "In estimating the character of a general, men are wont to pay exclusive attention to his courage, forgetting that courage is only one out of many qualities which a general should possess. The merely brave man is prone to fight recklessly; and he who fights recklessly, without any perception of what is expedient, must be condemned." Ssŭ-ma Fa, too, makes the incisive remark: "Simply going to one's death does not bring about victory."]

(2) cowardice, which leads to capture;

[Ts'ao Kung defines the Chinese word translated here as "cowardice" as being of the man "whom timidity prevents from advancing to seize an advantage," and Wang Hsi adds "who is quick to flee at the sight of danger." Mêng Shih gives the closer paraphrase "he who is bent on returning alive," this is, the man who will never take a risk. But, as Sun Tzŭ knew, nothing is to be achieved in war unless you are willing to take risks. T'ai Kung said: "He who lets an advantage slip will subsequently bring upon himself real disaster." In 404 A.D., Liu Yu pursued the rebel Huan Hsuan up the Yangtsze and fought a naval battle with him at the island of Ch'eng-hung. The loyal troops numbered only a few thousands, while their opponents were in great force. But Huan Hsuan, fearing the fate which was in store for him should be be overcome, had a light boat made fast to the side of his war-junk, so that he might escape, if necessary, at a moment's notice. The natural result was that the fighting spirit of his soldiers was utterly quenched, and when the loyalists made an attack from windward with fireships, all striving with the utmost ardor to be first in the fray, Huan Hsuan's forces were routed, had to burn all their baggage and fled for two days and nights without stopping. Chang Yü tells a somewhat similar story of Chao Ying-ch'i, a general of the Chin State who during a battle with the army of Ch'u in 597 B.C. had a boat kept in readiness for him on the river, wishing in case of defeat to be the first to get across.]

(3) a hasty temper, which can be provoked by insults;

[Tu Mu tells us that Yao Hsing, when opposed in 357 A.D. by Huang Mei, Teng Ch'iang and others shut himself up behind his walls and refused to fight. Teng Ch'iang said: "Our adversary is of a choleric temper and easily provoked; let us make constant sallies and break down his walls, then he will grow angry and come out. Once we can bring his force to battle, it is doomed to be our prey." This plan was acted upon, Yao Hsiang came out to fight, was lured as far as San-Yüan by the enemy's pretended flight and finally attacked and slain.]

(4) a delicacy of honour which is sensitive to shame;

This need not be taken to mean that a sense of honour is really a defect in a general. What Sun Tzŭ condemns is rather an exaggerated sensitiveness to slanderous reports, the thin-skinned man who is stung by opprobrium, however undeserved. Mei Yao-ch'ên truly observes, though somewhat paradoxically: "The seeker after glory should be careless of public opinion."]

(5) over-solicitude for his men, which exposes him to worry and trouble.

[Here again, Sun Tzŭ does not mean that the general is to be careless of the welfare of his troops. All he wishes to emphasize is the danger of sacrificing any important military advantage to the immediate comfort of his men. This is a shortsighted policy, because in the long run the troops will suffer more from the defeat, or, at best, the prolongation of the war, which will be the consequence. A mistaken feeling of pity will often induce a general to relieve a beleaguered city, or to reinforce a hard-pressed detachment, contrary to his military instincts. It is now generally admitted that our repeated efforts to relieve Ladysmith in the South African War were so many strategical blunders which defeated their own purpose. And in the end, relief came through the very man who started out with the distinct resolve no longer to subordinate the interests of the whole to sentiment in favour of a part. An old soldier of one of our generals who failed most conspicuously in this war, tried once, I remember, to defend him to me on the ground that he was always "so good to his men." By this plea, had he but known it, he was only condemning him out of Sun Tzŭ's mouth.]

13 These are the five besetting sins of a general, ruinous to the conduct of war.

14 When an army is overthrown and its leader slain, the cause will surely be found among these five dangerous faults. Let them be a subject of meditation.

[1] "Marshal Turenne," p. 50.

Chapter 9

The Army on the March

1 Sun Tzŭ said: We come now to the question of encamping the army, and observing signs of the enemy. Pass quickly over mountains, and keep in the neighbourhood of valleys.

[The idea is, not to linger among barren uplands, but to keep close to supplies of water and grass. Cf. Wu Tzŭ, ch. 3: "Abide not in natural ovens," i.e. "the openings of valleys.' Chang Yü tells the following anecdote: Wu-tu Ch'iang was a robber captain in the time of the Later Han, and Ma Yüan was sent to exterminate his gang. Ch'iang having found a refuge in the hills, Ma Yüan made no attempt to force a battle, but seized all the favourable positions commanding supplies of water and forage. Ch'iang was soon in such a desperate plight for want of provisions that he was forced to make a total surrender. He did not know the advantage of keeping in the neighbourhood of valleys."]

2 Camp in high places,

[Not on high hills, but on knolls or hillocks elevated above the surrounding country.]

facing the sun.

[Tu Mu takes this to mean 'facing south," and Ch'ên Hao "facing east." Cf. infra, §§ 11, 13.

Do not climb heights in order to fight. So much for mountain warfare.

3 After crossing a river, you should get far away from it.

["In order to tempt the enemy to cross after you," according to Ts'ao Kung, and also, says Chang Yü, "in order not to be impeded in your evolutions." The *T'ung Tien* reads, "If *the enemy* crosses a river," etc. But in view of the next sentence, this is almost certainly an interpolation.]

4 When an invading force crosses a river in its onward march, do not advance to meet it in mid-stream. It will be best to let half the army get across, and then deliver your attack.

[Li Ch'üan alludes to the great victory won by Han Hsin over Lung Chu at the Wei River. Turning to the *Ch'ien Han Shu*, ch. 34, fol. 6 verso, we find the battle described as follows: "The two armies were drawn up on opposite sides of the river. In the night, Han Hsin ordered his men to take some ten thousand sacks filled with sand and construct a dam higher up. Then, leading half his army across, he attacked Lung Chu; but after a time, pretending to have failed in his attempt, he hastily withdrew to the other bank. Lung Chu was much elated by this unlooked-for success, and exclaiming: "I felt sure that Han Hsin was really a coward!" he pursued him and began crossing the river in his turn. Han Hsin now sent a party to cut open the sandbags, thus releasing a great volume of water, which swept down and prevented the greater portion of Lung Chu's army from getting across. He then turned upon the force which had been cut off, and annihilated it, Lung Chu himself being amongst the slain. The rest of the army, on the further bank, also scattered and fled in all directions.]

5 If you are anxious to fight, you should not go to meet the invader near a river which he has to cross.

[For fear of preventing his crossing.]

6 Moor your craft higher up than the enemy, and facing the sun.

[See *supra*, § 2. The repetition of these words in connection with water is very awkward. Chang Yü has the note: "Said either of troops marshalled on the river-bank, or of boats anchored in the stream itself;

in either case it is essential to be higher than the enemy and facing the sun." The other commentators are not at all explicit.]

Do not move up-stream to meet the enemy.

[Tu Mu says: "As water flows downwards, we must not pitch our camp on the lower reaches of a river, for fear the enemy should open the sluices and sweep us away in a flood. Chu-ko Wu-hou has remarked that 'in river warfare we must not advance against the stream,' which is as much as to say that our fleet must not be anchored below that of the enemy, for then they would be able to take advantage of the current and make short work of us." There is also the danger, noted by other commentators, that the enemy may throw poison on the water to be carried down to us.]

So much for river warfare.

7 In crossing salt-marshes, your sole concern should be to get over them quickly, without any delay.

[Because of the lack of fresh water, the poor quality of the herbage, and last but not least, because they are low, flat, and exposed to attack.]

8 If forced to fight in a salt-marsh, you should have water and grass near you, and get your back to a clump of trees.

[Li Ch'üan remarks that the ground is less likely to be treacherous where there are trees, while Tu Mu says that they will serve to protect the rear.]

So much for operations in salt-marshes.

9 In dry, level country, take up an easily accessible position with rising ground to your right and on your rear,

[Tu Mu quotes T'ai Kung as saying: 'An army should have a stream or a marsh on its left, and a hill or tumulus on its right."]

so that the danger may be in front, and safety lie behind. So much for campaigning in flat country.

10 These are the four useful branches of military knowledge

[Those, namely, concerned with (1) mountains, (2) rivers, (3) marshes, and (4) plains. Compare Napoleon's "Military Maxims," no. 1.]

which enabled the Yellow Emperor to vanquish four several sovereigns.

[Regarding the "Yellow Emperor": Mei Yao-ch'ên asks, with some plausibility, whether there is an error in the text as nothing is known of Huang Ti having conquered four other Emperors. The *Shih Chi* (ch. 1 ad init.) speaks only of his victories over Yen Ti and Ch'ih Yu. In the *Liu T'ao* it is mentioned that he "fought seventy battles and pacified the Empire." Ts'ao Kung's explanation is, that the Yellow Emperor was the first to institute the feudal system of vassals princes, each of whom (to the number of four) originally bore the title of Emperor. Li Ch'üan tells us that the art of war originated under Huang Ti, who received it from his Minister Feng Hou.]

11 All armies prefer high ground to low,

["High Ground," says Mei Yao-ch'ên, "is not only more agreeable and salubrious, but more convenient from a military point of view; low ground is not only damp and unhealthy, but also disadvantageous for fighting."]

and sunny places to dark.

12 If you are careful of your men,

[Ts'ao Kung says: "Make for fresh water and pasture, where you can turn out your animals to graze."]

and camp on hard ground, the army will be free from disease of every kind,

[Chang Yü says: "The dryness of the climate will prevent the outbreak of illness."]

and this will spell victory.

13 When you come to a hill or a bank, occupy the sunny side, with the slope on your right rear. Thus you will at once act for the benefit of your soldiers and utilise the natural advantages of the ground.

14 When, in consequence of heavy rains up-country, a river which you wish to ford is swollen and flecked with foam, you must wait until it subsides.

15 Country in which there are precipitous cliffs with torrents running between, deep natural hollows,

The latter defined as "places enclosed on every side by steep banks, with pools of water at the bottom."]

confined places,

[Defined as "natural pens or prisons" or "places surrounded by precipices on three sides—easy to get into but hard to get out of."]

tangled thickets,

[Defined as "places covered with such dense undergrowth that spears cannot be used."]

quagmires

[Defined as "low-lying places, so heavy with mud as to be impassable for chariots and horsemen."]

and crevasses,

[Defined by Mei Yao-ch'ên as "a narrow difficult way between beetling cliffs." Tu Mu's note is "ground covered with trees and rocks, and intersected by numerous ravines and pitfalls." This is very vague, but Chia Lin explains it clearly enough as a defile or narrow pass, and Chang Yü takes much the same view. On the whole, the weight of the commentators certainly inclines to the rendering "defile." But the ordinary meaning of the Chinese in one place is "a crack or fissure" and the fact that the meaning of the Chinese elsewhere in the sentence indicates something in the nature of a defile, make me think that Sun Tzŭ is here speaking of crevasses.]

should be left with all possible speed and not approached.

16 While we keep away from such places, we should get the enemy to approach them; while we face them, we should let the enemy have them on his rear.

17 If in the neighbourhood of your camp there should be any hilly country, ponds surrounded by aquatic grass, hollow basins filled with reeds, or woods with thick undergrowth, they must be carefully routed out and searched; for these are places where men in ambush or insidious spies are likely to be lurking.

[Chang Yü has the note: "We must also be on our guard against traitors who may lie in close covert, secretly spying out our weaknesses and overhearing our instructions."]

18 When the enemy is close at hand and remains quiet, he is relying on the natural strength of his position.

[Here begin Sun Tzŭ's remarks on the reading of signs, much of which is so good that it could almost be included in a modern manual like Gen. Baden-Powell's "Aids to Scouting."]

19 When he keeps aloof and tries to provoke a battle, he is anxious for the other side to advance.

[Probably because we are in a strong position from which he wishes to dislodge us. "If he came close up to us, says Tu Mu, "and tried to force a battle, he would seem to despise us, and there would be less probability of our responding to the challenge."]

20 If his place of encampment is easy of access, he is tendering a bait.

21 Movement amongst the trees of a forest shows that the enemy is advancing.

[Ts'ao Kung explains this as "felling trees to clear a passage," and Chang Yü says: "Every man sends out scouts to climb high places and observe the enemy. If a scout sees that the trees of a forest are moving and shaking, he may know that they are being cut down to clear a passage for the enemy's march."]

The appearance of a number of screens in the midst of thick grass means that the enemy wants to make us suspicious.

[Tu Yu's explanation, borrowed from Ts'ao Kung's, is as follows: "The presence of a number of screens or sheds in the midst of thick vegetation is a sure sign that the enemy has fled and, fearing pursuit, has constructed these hiding-places in order to make us suspect an ambush." It appears that these "screens" were hastily knotted together out of any long grass which the retreating enemy happened to come across.]

22 The rising of birds in their flight is the sign of an ambuscade.

[Chang Yü's explanation is doubtless right: "When birds that are flying along in a straight line suddenly shoot upwards, it means that soldiers are in ambush at the spot beneath."]

Startled beasts indicate that a sudden attack is coming.

23 When there is dust rising in a high column, it is the sign of chariots advancing; when the dust is low, but spread over a wide area, it betokens the approach of infantry.

["High and sharp," or rising to a peak, is of course somewhat exaggerated as applied to dust. The commentators explain the phenomenon by saying that horses and chariots, being heavier than men, raise more dust, and also follow one another in the same wheel-track, whereas foot-soldiers would be marching in ranks, many abreast. According to Chang Yü, "every army on the march must have scouts some way in advance, who on sighting dust raised by the enemy, will gallop back and report it to the commander-in-chief." Cf. Gen. Baden-Powell: "As you move along, say, in a hostile country, your eyes should be looking afar for the enemy or any signs of him: figures, dust rising, birds getting up, glitter of arms, etc." [1]]

When it branches out in different directions, it shows that parties have been sent to collect firewood. A few clouds of dust moving to and fro signify that the army is encamping.

[Chang Yü says: "In apportioning the defenses for a cantonment, light horse will be sent out to survey the position and ascertain the weak and strong points all along its circumference. Hence the small quantity of dust and its motion."]

24 Humble words and increased preparations are signs that the enemy is about to advance.

["As though they stood in great fear of us," says Tu Mu. "Their object is to make us contemptuous and careless, after which they will attack us." Chang Yü alludes to the story of T'ien Tan of the Ch'i-mo against the Yen forces, led by Ch'i Chieh. In ch. 82 of the *Shih Chi* we read: "T'ien Tan openly said: 'My only fear is that the Yen army may cut off the noses of their Ch'i prisoners and place them in the front rank to fight against us; that would be the undoing of our city." The other side being informed of this speech, at once acted on the suggestion; but those within the city were enraged at seeing their fellow-countrymen thus mutilated, and fearing only lest they should fall into the enemy's hands, were nerved to defend themselves more obstinately than ever. Once again T'ien Tan sent back converted spies who reported these words to the enemy: "What I dread most is that the men of Yen may dig up the ancestral tombs outside the town, and by inflicting this indignity on our forefathers cause us to become faint-hearted." Forthwith the besiegers dug up all the graves and burned the corpses lying in them. And the inhabitants of Chi-mo, witnessing the outrage from the city-walls, wept passionately and were all impatient to go out and fight, their fury being increased tenfold. T'ien Tan knew then that his soldiers were ready for any enterprise. But instead of a sword, he himself took a mattock in his hands, and ordered others to be distributed amongst his best warriors, while the ranks were filled up with their wives and concubines. He then served out all the remaining rations and bade his men eat their fill. The regular soldiers were told to keep out of sight, and the walls were manned with the old and weaker men and with women. This done, envoys were dispatched to the enemy's camp to arrange terms of surrender, whereupon the Yen army began shouting for joy. T'ien Tan also collected 20,000 ounces of silver from the people, and got the wealthy citizens of Chi-mo to send it to the Yen general with the prayer that, when the town capitulated, he would not allow their homes to be plundered or their women to be maltreated. Ch'i Chieh, in high good humor, granted their prayer; but his army now became increasingly slack and careless. Meanwhile, T'ien Tan got together a thousand oxen, decked them with pieces of red silk, painted their bodies, dragon-like, with colored stripes, and fastened sharp blades on their horns and well-greased rushes on their tails. When night came on, he lighted the ends of the rushes, and drove the oxen through a number of holes which he had pierced in the walls, backing them up with a force of 5000 picked warriors. The animals, maddened with pain, dashed furiously into the enemy's camp where they caused the utmost confusion and dismay; for their tails acted as torches, showing up the hideous pattern on their bodies, and the weapons on their horns killed or wounded any with whom they came into contact. In the meantime, the band of 5000 had crept up with gags in their mouths, and now threw themselves on the enemy. At the same moment a frightful din arose in the city itself, all those that remained behind making as much noise as possible by banging drums and hammering on bronze vessels, until heaven and earth were convulsed by the uproar. Terror-stricken, the Yen army fled in disorder, hotly pursued by the men of Ch'i, who succeeded in slaying their general Ch'i Chien.... The result of the battle was the ultimate recovery of some seventy cities which had belonged to the Ch'i State.]

Violent language and driving forward as if to the attack are signs that he will retreat.

25 When the light chariots come out first and take up a position on the wings, it is a sign that the enemy is forming for battle.

26 Peace proposals unaccompanied by a sworn covenant indicate a plot.

[The reading here is uncertain. Li Ch'üan indicates "a treaty confirmed by oaths and hostages." Wang Hsi and Chang Yü, on the other hand, simply say "without reason," "on a frivolous pretext."]

27 When there is much running about

[Every man hastening to his proper place under his own regimental banner.]

and the soldiers fall into rank, it means that the critical moment has come.

28 When some are seen advancing and some retreating, it is a lure.

29 When the soldiers stand leaning on their spears, they are faint from want of food.

30 If those who are sent to draw water begin by drinking themselves, the army is suffering from thirst.

[As Tu Mu remarks: "One may know the condition of a whole army from the behavior of a single man."]

31 If the enemy sees an advantage to be gained and makes no effort to secure it, the soldiers are exhausted.

32 If birds gather on any spot, it is unoccupied.

[A useful fact to bear in mind when, for instance, as Ch'ên Hao says, the enemy has secretly abandoned his camp.]

Clamour by night betokens nervousness.

33 If there is disturbance in the camp, the general's authority is weak. If the banners and flags are shifted about, sedition is afoot. If the officers are angry, it means that the men are weary.

[Tu Mu understands the sentence differently: "If all the officers of an army are angry with their general, it means that they are broken with fatigue" owing to the exertions which he has demanded from them.]

34 When an army feeds its horses with grain and kills its cattle for food,

[In the ordinary course of things, the men would be fed on grain and the horses chiefly on grass.]

and when the men do not hang their cooking-pots over the camp-fires, showing that they will not return to their tents, you may know that they are determined to fight to the death.

[I may quote here the illustrative passage from the *Hou Han Shu*, ch. 71, given in abbreviated form by the *P'ei Wen Yun Fu*: "The rebel Wang Kuo of Liang was besieging the town of Ch'ên- ts'ang, and Huang-fu Sung, who was in supreme command, and Tung Cho were sent out against him. The latter pressed for hasty measures, but Sung turned a deaf ear to his counsel. At last the rebels were utterly worn out, and began to throw down their weapons of their own accord. Sung was not advancing to the attack, but Cho said: 'It is a principle of war not to pursue desperate men and not to press a retreating host.' Sung answered: 'That does not apply here. What I am about to attack is a jaded army, not a retreating host; with disciplined troops I am falling on a disorganized multitude, not a band of desperate men.' Thereupon he advances to the attack unsupported by his colleague, and routed the enemy, Wang Kuo being slain."]

35 The sight of men whispering together in small knots or speaking in subdued tones points to disaffection amongst the rank and file.

36 Too frequent rewards signify that the enemy is at the end of his resources;

[Because, when an army is hard pressed, as Tu Mu says, there is always a fear of mutiny, and lavish rewards are given to keep the men in good temper.]

too many punishments betray a condition of dire distress.

[Because in such case discipline becomes relaxed, and unwonted severity is necessary to keep the men to their duty.]

37 To begin by bluster, but afterwards to take fright at the enemy's numbers, shows a supreme lack of intelligence.

[I follow the interpretation of Ts'ao Kung, also adopted by Li Ch'üan, Tu Mu, and Chang Yü. Another possible meaning set forth by Tu Yu, Chia Lin, Mei Tao-ch'ên and Wang Hsi, is: "The general who is first tyrannical towards his men, and then in terror lest they should mutiny, etc." This would connect the sentence with what went before about rewards and punishments.]

38 When envoys are sent with compliments in their mouths, it is a sign that the enemy wishes for a truce.

[Tu Mu says: "If the enemy open friendly relations be sending hostages, it is a sign that they are anxious for an armistice, either because their strength is exhausted or for some other reason." But it hardly needs a Sun Tzŭ to draw such an obvious inference.]

39 If the enemy's troops march up angrily and remain facing ours for a long time without either joining battle or taking themselves off again, the situation is one that demands great vigilance and circumspection.

[Ts'ao Kung says a manœuver of this sort may be only a ruse to gain time for an unexpected flank attack or the laying of an ambush.]

40 If our troops are no more in number than the enemy, that is amply sufficient; it only means that no direct attack can be made.

[Literally, "no martial advance." That is to say, *chéng* tactics and frontal attacks must be eschewed, and stratagem resorted to instead.]

What we can do is simply to concentrate all our available strength, keep a close watch on the enemy, and obtain reinforcements.

[This is an obscure sentence, and none of the commentators succeed in squeezing very good sense out of it. I follow Li Ch'üan, who appears to offer the simplest explanation: "Only the side that gets more men will win." Fortunately we have Chang Yü to expound its meaning to us in language which is lucidity itself: "When the numbers are even, and no favourable opening presents itself, although we may not be strong enough to deliver a sustained attack, we can find additional recruits amongst our sutlers and camp-followers, and then, concentrating our forces and keeping a close watch on the enemy, contrive to snatch the victory. But we must avoid borrowing foreign soldiers to help us." He then quotes from Wei Liao Tzŭ, ch. 3: "The nominal strength of mercenary troops may be 100,000, but their real value will be not more than half that figure."]

41 He who exercises no forethought but makes light of his opponents is sure to be captured by them.

[Ch'ên Hao, quoting from the *Tso Chüan*, says: "If bees and scorpions carry poison, how much more will a hostile state! Even a puny opponent, then, should not be treated with contempt."]

42 If soldiers are punished before they have grown attached to you, they will not prove submissive; and, unless submissive, then will be practically useless. If, when the soldiers have become attached to you, punishments are not enforced, they will still be useless.

43 Therefore soldiers must be treated in the first instance with humanity, but kept under control by means of iron discipline.

[Yen Tzŭ [B.C. 493] said of Ssŭ-ma Jang-chü: "His civil virtues endeared him to the people; his martial prowess kept his enemies in awe." Cf. Wu Tzŭ, ch. 4 init.: "The ideal commander unites culture with a warlike temper; the profession of arms requires a combination of hardness and tenderness."]

This is a certain road to victory.

44 If in training soldiers commands are habitually enforced, the army will be well-disciplined; if not, its discipline will be bad.

45 If a general shows confidence in his men but always insists on his orders being obeyed,

[Tu Mu says: "A general ought in time of peace to show kindly confidence in his men and also make his authority respected, so that when they come to face the enemy, orders may be executed and discipline maintained, because they all trust and look up to him." What Sun Tzŭ has said in § 44, however, would lead one rather to expect something like this: "If a general is always confident that his orders will be carried out," etc."]

the gain will be mutual.

[Chang Yü says: "The general has confidence in the men under his command, and the men are docile, having confidence in him. Thus the gain is mutual." He quotes a pregnant sentence from Wei Liao Tzŭ, ch. 4: "The art of giving orders is not to try to rectify minor blunders and not to be swayed by petty doubts." Vacillation and fussiness are the surest means of sapping the confidence of an army.]

[1] "Aids to Scouting," p. 26.

Chapter 10
Terrain

[Only about a third of the chapter, comprising §§ 1-13, deals with "terrain," the subject being more fully treated in ch. XI. The "six calamities" are discussed in §§ 14-20, and the rest of the chapter is again a mere string of desultory remarks, though not less interesting, perhaps, on that account.]

1 Sun Tzŭ said: We may distinguish six kinds of terrain, to wit:

(1) Accessible ground;

[Mei Yao-ch'ên says: "plentifully provided with roads and means of communications."]

(2) entangling ground;

[The same commentator says: "Net-like country, venturing into which you become entangled."]

(3) temporising ground;

[Ground which allows you to "stave off" or "delay."]

(4) narrow passes;

(5) precipitous heights;

(6) positions at a great distance from the enemy.

[It is hardly necessary to point out the faultiness of this classification. A strange lack of logical perception is shown in the Chinaman's unquestioning acceptance of glaring cross-divisions such as the above.]

2 Ground which can be freely traversed by both sides is called *accessible*.

3 With regard to ground of this nature, be before the enemy in occupying the raised and sunny spots, and carefully guard your line of supplies.

[The general meaning of the last phrase is doubtlessly, as Tu Yu says, "not to allow the enemy to cut your communications." In view of Napoleon's dictum, "the secret of war lies in the communications," [1] we could wish that Sun Tzŭ had done more than skirt the edge of this important subject here and in I. § 10, VII. § 11. Col. Henderson says: "The line of supply may be said to be as vital to the existence of an army as the heart to the life of a human being. Just as the duelist who finds his adversary's point menacing him with certain death, and his own guard astray, is compelled to conform to his adversary's movements, and to content himself with warding off his thrusts, so the commander whose communications are suddenly threatened finds himself in a false position, and he will be fortunate if he has not to change all his plans, to split up his force into more or less isolated detachments, and to fight with inferior numbers on ground which he has not had time to prepare, and where defeat will not be an ordinary failure, but will entail the ruin or surrender of his whole army." [2]

Then you will be able to fight with advantage.

4 Ground which can be abandoned but is hard to re-occupy is called *entangling*.

5 From a position of this sort, if the enemy is unprepared, you may sally forth and defeat him. But if the enemy is prepared for your coming, and you fail to defeat him, then, return being impossible, disaster will ensue.

6 When the position is such that neither side will gain by making the first move, it is called *temporising* ground.

[Tu Mu says: "Each side finds it inconvenient to move, and the situation remains at a deadlock."]

7 In a position of this sort, even though the enemy should offer us an attractive bait,

[Tu Yu says, "turning their backs on us and pretending to flee." But this is only one of the lures which might induce us to quit our position.]

it will be advisable not to stir forth, but rather to retreat, thus enticing the enemy in his turn; then, when part of his army has come out, we may deliver our attack with advantage.

8 With regard to *narrow passes*, if you can occupy them first, let them be strongly garrisoned and await the advent of the enemy.

[Because then, as Tu Yu observes, "the initiative will lie with us, and by making sudden and unexpected attacks we shall have the enemy at our mercy."]

9 Should the enemy forestall you in occupying a pass, do not go after him if the pass is fully garrisoned, but only if it is weakly garrisoned.

10 With regard to *precipitous heights*, if you are beforehand with your adversary, you should occupy the raised and sunny spots, and there wait for him to come up.

[Ts'ao Kung says: "The particular advantage of securing heights and defiles is that your actions cannot then be dictated by the enemy." (For the enunciation of the grand principle alluded to, see VI. § 2). Chang Yü tells the following anecdote of P'ei Hsing-chien (A.D. 619-682), who was sent on a punitive expedition against the Turkic tribes. "At night he pitched his camp as usual, and it had already been completely fortified by wall and ditch, when suddenly he gave orders that the army should shift its quarters to a hill near by. This was highly displeasing to his officers, who protested loudly against the extra fatigue which it would entail on the men. P'ei Hsing-chien, however, paid no heed to their remonstrances and had the camp moved as quickly as possible. The same night, a terrific storm came on, which flooded their former place of encampment to the depth of over twelve feet. The recalcitrant officers were amazed at the sight, and owned that they had been in the wrong. 'How did you know what was going to happen?' they asked. P'ei Hsing-chien replied: 'From this time forward be content to obey orders without asking unnecessary questions.' From this it may be seen," Chang Yü continues, "that high and sunny places are advantageous not only for fighting, but also because they are immune from disastrous floods."]

11 If the enemy has occupied them before you, do not follow him, but retreat and try to entice him away.

[The turning point of Li Shih-min's campaign in 621 A.D. against the two rebels, Tou Chien-tê, King of Hsia, and Wang Shih-ch'ung, Prince of Chéng, was his seizure of the heights of Wu-lao, in spite of which Tou Chien-tê persisted in his attempt to relieve his ally in Lo-yang, was defeated and taken prisoner. See *Chiu T'ang Shu*, ch. 2, fol. 5 verso, and also ch. 54.]

12 If you are situated at a great distance from the enemy, and the strength of the two armies is equal, it is not easy to provoke a battle,

[The point is that we must not think of undertaking a long and wearisome march, at the end of which, as Tu Yu says, "we should be exhausted and our adversary fresh and keen."]

and fighting will be to your disadvantage.

13 These six are the principles connected with Earth.

[Or perhaps, "the principles relating to ground." See, however, I. § 8.]

The general who has attained a responsible post must be careful to study them.

14 Now an army is exposed to six several calamities, not arising from natural causes, but from faults for which the general is responsible. These are: (1) Flight; (2) insubordination; (3) collapse; (4) ruin; (5) disorganisation; (6) rout.

15 Other conditions being equal, if one force is hurled against another ten times its size, the result will be the *flight* of the former.

16 When the common soldiers are too strong and their officers too weak, the result is *insubordination*.

[Tu Mu cites the unhappy case of T'ien Pu (*Hsin T'ang Shu*, ch. 148), who was sent to Wei in 821 A.D. with orders to lead an army against Wang T'ing-ts'ou. But the whole time he was in command, his soldiers treated him with the utmost contempt, and openly flouted his authority by riding about the camp on donkeys, several thousands at a time. T'ien Pu was powerless to put a stop to this conduct, and when, after some months had passed, he made an attempt to engage the enemy, his troops turned tail and dispersed in every direction. After that, the unfortunate man committed suicide by cutting his throat.]

When the officers are too strong and the common soldiers too weak, the result is *collapse*.

[Ts'ao Kung says: "The officers are energetic and want to press on, the common soldiers are feeble and suddenly collapse."]

17 When the higher officers are angry and insubordinate, and on meeting the enemy give battle on their own account from a feeling of resentment, before the commander-in-chief can tell whether or no he is in a position to fight, the result is *ruin*.

[Wang Hsi's note is: "This means, the general is angry without cause, and at the same time does not appreciate the ability of his subordinate officers; thus he arouses fierce resentment and brings an avalanche of ruin upon his head."]

18 When the general is weak and without authority; when his orders are not clear and distinct;

[Wei Liao Tzŭ (ch. 4) says: "If the commander gives his orders with decision, the soldiers will not wait to hear them twice; if his moves are made without vacillation, the soldiers will not be in two minds about doing their duty." General Baden-Powell says, italicizing the words: "The secret of getting successful work out of your trained men lies in one nutshell—in the clearness of the instructions they receive." [3] Cf. also Wu Tzŭ ch. 3: "the most fatal defect in a military leader is difference; the worst calamities that befall an army arise from hesitation."]

when there are no fixed duties assigned to officers and men,

[Tu Mu says: "Neither officers nor men have any regular routine."]

and the ranks are formed in a slovenly haphazard manner, the result is utter *disorganization*.

19 When a general, unable to estimate the enemy's strength, allows an inferior force to engage a larger one, or hurls a weak detachment against a powerful one, and neglects to place picked soldiers in the front rank, the result must be a *rout*.

[Chang Yü paraphrases the latter part of the sentence and continues: "Whenever there is fighting to be done, the keenest spirits should be appointed to serve in the front ranks, both in order to strengthen the resolution of our own men and to demoralize the enemy." Cf. the primi ordines of Caesar ("De Bello Gallico," V. 28, 44, et al.).]

20 These are six ways of courting defeat, which must be carefully noted by the general who has attained a responsible post.

[See *supra*, § 13.]

21 The natural formation of the country is the soldier's best ally;

[Ch'ên Hao says: "The advantages of weather and season are not equal to those connected with ground."]

but a power of estimating the adversary, of controlling the forces of victory, and of shrewdly calculating difficulties, dangers and distances, constitutes the test of a great general.

22 He who knows these things, and in fighting puts his knowledge into practice, will win his battles. He who knows them not, nor practises them, will surely be defeated.

23 If fighting is sure to result in victory, then you must fight, even though the ruler forbid it; if fighting will not result in victory, then you must not fight even at the ruler's bidding.

[Cf. VIII. § 3 fin. Huang Shih-kung of the Ch'in dynasty, who is said to have been the patron of Chang Liang and to have written the *San*

Lüeh, has these words attributed to him: "The responsibility of setting an army in motion must devolve on the general alone; if advance and retreat are controlled from the Palace, brilliant results will hardly be achieved. Hence the god-like ruler and the enlightened monarch are content to play a humble part in furthering their country's cause (lit., kneel down to push the chariot wheel)." This means that "in matters lying outside the zenana, the decision of the military commander must be absolute." Chang Yü also quote the saying: "Decrees from the Son of Heaven do not penetrate the walls of a camp."]

24 The general who advances without coveting fame and retreats without fearing disgrace,

[It was Wellington, I think, who said that the hardest thing of all for a soldier is to retreat.]

whose only thought is to protect his country and do good service for his sovereign, is the jewel of the kingdom.

[A noble presentiment, in few words, of the Chinese "happy warrior." Such a man, says Ho Shih, "even if he had to suffer punishment, would not regret his conduct."]

25 Regard your soldiers as your children, and they will follow you into the deepest valleys; look on them as your own beloved sons, and they will stand by you even unto death.

[Cf. I. § 6. In this connection, Tu Mu draws for us an engaging picture of the famous general Wu Ch'i, from whose treatise on war I have frequently had occasion to quote: "He wore the same clothes and ate the same food as the meanest of his soldiers, refused to have either a horse to ride or a mat to sleep on, carried his own surplus rations wrapped in a parcel, and shared every hardship with his men. One of his soldiers was suffering from an abscess, and Wu Ch'i himself sucked out the virus. The soldier's mother, hearing this, began wailing and lamenting. Somebody asked her, saying: 'Why do you cry? Your son is only a common soldier, and yet the commander-in-chief himself has sucked the poison from his sore.' The woman replied, 'Many years ago, Lord Wu performed a similar service for my husband, who never left him afterwards, and finally met his death at the hands of the enemy. And now that he has done the same for my son, he too will fall fighting I know not where.'" Li Ch'üan mentions the Viscount of Ch'u, who invaded the small state of Hsiao during the winter. The Duke of Shen said to him: "Many of the soldiers are suffering severely from the cold." So he made a round of the whole army, comforting and encouraging the men; and straightway they felt as if they were clothed in garments lined with floss silk.]

26 If, however, you are indulgent, but unable to make your authority felt; kind-hearted, but unable to enforce your commands; and incapable, moreover, of quelling disorder: then your soldiers must be likened to spoilt children; they are useless for any practical purpose.

[Li Ching once said that if you could make your soldiers afraid of you, they would not be afraid of the enemy. Tu Mu recalls an instance of stern military discipline which occurred in 219 A.D., when Lü Mêng was occupying the town of Chiang-ling. He had given stringent orders to his army not to molest the inhabitants nor take anything from them by force. Nevertheless, a certain officer serving under his banner, who happened to be a fellow-townsman, ventured to appropriate a bamboo hat belonging to one of the people, in order to wear it over his regulation helmet as a protection against the rain. Lü Mêng considered that the fact of his being also a native of Ju-nan should not be allowed to palliate a clear breach of discipline, and accordingly he ordered his summary execution, the tears rolling down his face, however, as he did so. This act of severity filled the army with wholesome awe, and from that time forth even articles dropped in the highway were not picked up.]

27 If we know that our own men are in a condition to attack, but are unaware that the enemy is not open to attack, we have gone only halfway towards victory.

[That is, Ts'ao Kung says, "the issue in this case is uncertain."]

28 If we know that the enemy is open to attack, but are unaware that our own men are not in a condition to attack, we have gone only halfway towards victory.

[Cf. III. § 13 (1).]

29 If we know that the enemy is open to attack, and also know that our men are in a condition to attack, but are unaware that the nature of the ground makes fighting impracticable, we have still gone only halfway towards victory.

30 Hence the experienced soldier, once in motion, is never bewildered; once he has broken camp, he is never at a loss.

[The reason being, according to Tu Mu, that he has taken his measures so thoroughly as to ensure victory beforehand. "He does not move recklessly," says Chang Yü, "so that when he does move, he makes no mistakes."]

31 Hence the saying: If you know the enemy and know yourself, your victory will not stand in doubt; if you know Heaven and know Earth, you may make your victory complete.

[Li Ch'üan sums up as follows: "Given a knowledge of three things—the affairs of men, the seasons of heaven and the natural advantages of earth—, victory will invariably crown your battles."]

[1] See "Pensees de Napoleon 1er," no. 47.

[2] "The Science of War," chap. 2.

[3] "Aids to Scouting," p. xii.

Chapter 11
The Nine Situations

1 Sun Tzŭ said: The art of war recognises nine varieties of ground:

(1) Dispersive ground;

(2) facile ground;

(3) contentious ground;

(4) open ground;

(5) ground of intersecting highways;

(6) serious ground;

(7) difficult ground;

(8) hemmed-in ground;

(9) desperate ground.

2 When a chieftain is fighting in his own territory, it is dispersive ground.

[So called because the soldiers, being near to their homes and anxious to see their wives and children, are likely to seize the opportunity afforded by a battle and scatter in every direction. "In their advance," observes Tu Mu, "they will lack the valor of desperation, and when they retreat, they will find harbors of refuge."]

3 When he has penetrated into hostile territory, but to no great distance, it is facile ground.

[Li Ch'üan and Ho Shih say "because of the facility for retreating," and the other commentators give similar explanations. Tu Mu remarks: "When your army has crossed the border, you should burn your boats and bridges, in order to make it clear to everybody that you have no hankering after home."]

4 Ground the possession of which imports great advantage to either side, is contentious ground.

[Tu Mu defines the ground as ground "to be contended for." Ts'ao Kung says: "ground on which the few and the weak can defeat the many and the strong," such as "the neck of a pass," instanced by Li Ch'üan. Thus, Thermopylae was of this classification because the possession of it, even for a few days only, meant holding the entire invading army in check and thus gaining invaluable time. Cf. Wu Tzŭ, ch. V. ad init.: "For those who have to fight in the ratio of one to ten, there is nothing better than a narrow pass." When Lü Kuang was returning from his triumphant expedition to Turkestan in 385 A.D., and had got as far as I-ho, laden with spoils, Liang Hsi, administrator of Liang-chou, taking advantage of the death of Fu Chien, King of Ch'in, plotted against him and was for barring his way into the province. Yang Han, governor of Kao-ch'ang, counseled him, saying: "Lü Kuang is fresh from his victories in the west, and his soldiers are vigorous and mettlesome. If we oppose him in the shifting sands of the desert, we shall be no match for him, and we must therefore try a different plan. Let us hasten to occupy the defile at the mouth of the Kao-wu pass, thus cutting him off from supplies of water, and when his troops are prostrated with thirst, we can dictate our own terms without moving. Or if you think that the pass I mention is too far off, we could make a stand against him at the I-wu pass, which is nearer. The cunning and resource of Tzŭ-fang himself would be expended in vain against the enormous strength of these two positions." Liang Hsi, refusing to act on this advice, was overwhelmed and swept away by the invader.]

5 Ground on which each side has liberty of movement is open ground.

[There are various interpretations of the Chinese adjective for this type of ground. Ts'ao Kung says it means "ground covered with a network of roads," like a chessboard. Ho Shih suggested: "ground on which intercommunication is easy."]

6 Ground which forms the key to three contiguous states,

[Ts'au Kung defines this as: "Our country adjoining the enemy's and a third country conterminous with both." Mêng Shih instances the small principality of Chéng, which was bounded on the north-east by Ch'i, on the west by Chin, and on the south by Ch'u.]

so that he who occupies it first has most of the Empire at his command,

[The belligerent who holds this dominating position can constrain most of them to become his allies.]

is ground of intersecting highways.

7 When an army has penetrated into the heart of a hostile country, leaving a number of fortified cities in its rear, it is serious ground.

[Wang Hsi explains the name by saying that "when an army has reached such a point, its situation is serious."]

8 Mountain forests,

[Or simply "forests."]

rugged steeps, marshes and fens—all country that is hard to traverse: this is difficult ground.

9 Ground which is reached through narrow gorges, and from which we can only retire by tortuous paths, so that a small number of the enemy would suffice to crush a large body of our men: this is hemmed in ground.

10 Ground on which we can only be saved from destruction by fighting without delay, is desperate ground.

[The situation, as pictured by Ts'ao Kung, is very similar to the "hemmed-in ground" except that here escape is no longer possible:

"A lofty mountain in front, a large river behind, advance impossible, retreat blocked." Ch'ên Hao says: "to be on 'desperate ground' is like sitting in a leaking boat or crouching in a burning house." Tu Mu quotes from Li Ching a vivid description of the plight of an army thus entrapped: "Suppose an army invading hostile territory without the aid of local guides:—it falls into a fatal snare and is at the enemy's mercy. A ravine on the left, a mountain on the right, a pathway so perilous that the horses have to be roped together and the chariots carried in slings, no passage open in front, retreat cut off behind, no choice but to proceed in single file. Then, before there is time to range our soldiers in order of battle, the enemy is overwhelming strength suddenly appears on the scene. Advancing, we can nowhere take a breathing-space; retreating, we have no haven of refuge. We seek a pitched battle, but in vain; yet standing on the defensive, none of us has a moment's respite. If we simply maintain our ground, whole days and months will crawl by; the moment we make a move, we have to sustain the enemy's attacks on front and rear. The country is wild, destitute of water and plants; the army is lacking in the necessaries of life, the horses are jaded and the men worn-out, all the resources of strength and skill unavailing, the pass so narrow that a single man defending it can check the onset of ten thousand; all means of offense in the hands of the enemy, all points of vantage already forfeited by ourselves:—in this terrible plight, even though we had the most valiant soldiers and the keenest of weapons, how could they be employed with the slightest effect?" Students of Greek history may be reminded of the awful close to the Sicilian expedition, and the agony of the Athenians under Nicias and Demonsthenes. [See Thucydides, VII. 78 sqq.].]

11 On dispersive ground, therefore, fight not. On facile ground, halt not. On contentious ground, attack not.

[But rather let all your energies be bent on occupying the advantageous position first. So Ts'ao Kung. Li Ch'üan and others, however, suppose the meaning to be that the enemy has already forestalled us, sot that it would be sheer madness to attack. In the *Sun Tzŭ Hsü Lu*, when the King of Wu inquires what should be done in this case, Sun Tzŭ replies: "The rule with regard to contentious ground is that those in possession have the advantage over the other side. If a position of this kind is secured first by the enemy, beware of attacking him. Lure him away by pretending to flee—show your banners and sound your drums—make a dash for other places that he cannot afford to lose—trail brushwood and raise a dust—confound his ears and eyes—detach a body of your best troops, and place it secretly in ambuscade. Then your opponent will sally forth to the rescue."]

12 On open ground, do not try to block the enemy's way.

[Because the attempt would be futile, and would expose the blocking force itself to serious risks. There are two interpretations available here. I follow that of Chang Yü The other is indicated in Ts'ao Kung's brief note: "Draw closer together"—i.e., see that a portion of your own army is not cut off.]

On ground of intersecting highways, join hands with your allies.

[Or perhaps, "form alliances with neighbouring states."]

13 On serious ground, gather in plunder.

[On this, Li Ch'üan has the following delicious note: "When an army penetrates far into the enemy's country, care must be taken not to alienate the people by unjust treatment. Follow the example of the Han Emperor Kao Tsu, whose march into Ch'in territory was marked by no violation of women or looting of valuables. [Nota bene: this was in 207 B.C., and may well cause us to blush for the Christian armies that entered Peking in 1900 A.D.] Thus he won the hearts of all. In the present passage, then, I think that the true reading must be, not 'plunder,' but 'do not plunder.'" Alas, I fear that in this instance the worthy commentator's feelings outran his judgment. Tu Mu, at least, has no such illusions. He says: "When encamped on 'serious ground,' there being no inducement as yet to advance further, and no possibility of retreat, one ought to take measures for a protracted resistance by bringing in provisions from all sides, and keep a close watch on the enemy."]

In difficult ground, keep steadily on the march.

[Or, in the words of VIII. § 2, "do not encamp.]

14 On hemmed-in ground, resort to stratagem.

[Ts'au Kung says: "Try the effect of some unusual artifice;" and Tu Yu amplifies this by saying: "In such a position, some scheme must be devised which will suit the circumstances, and if we can succeed in deluding the enemy, the peril may be escaped." This is exactly what happened on the famous occasion when Hannibal was hemmed in among the mountains on the road to Casilinum, and to all appearances entrapped by the dictator Fabius. The stratagem which Hannibal devised to baffle his foes was remarkably like that which T'ien Tan had also employed with success exactly 62 years before. [See IX. § 24, note.] When night came on, bundles of twigs were fastened to the horns of some 2000 oxen and set on fire, the terrified animals being then quickly driven along the mountain side towards the passes which were beset by the enemy. The strange spectacle of these rapidly moving lights so alarmed and discomfited the Romans that they withdrew from their position, and Hannibal's army passed safely through the defile. [See Polybius, III. 93, 94; Livy, XXII. 16 17.]

On desperate ground, fight.

[For, as Chia Lin remarks: "if you fight with all your might, there is a chance of life; where as death is certain if you cling to your corner."]

15 Those who were called skillful leaders of old knew how to drive a wedge between the enemy's front and rear;

[More literally, "cause the front and rear to lose touch with each other."]

to prevent co-operation between his large and small divisions; to hinder the good troops from rescuing the bad, the officers from rallying their men.

16 When the enemy's men were scattered, they prevented them from concentrating; even when their forces were united, they managed to keep them in disorder.

17 When it was to their advantage, they made a forward move; when otherwise, they stopped still.

[Mei Yao-ch'ên connects this with the foregoing: "Having succeeded in thus dislocating the enemy, they would push forward in order to secure any advantage to be gained; if there was no advantage to be gained, they would remain where they were."]

18 If asked how to cope with a great host of the enemy in orderly array and on the point of marching to the attack, I should say: "Begin by seizing something which your opponent holds dear; then he will be amenable to your will."

[Opinions differ as to what Sun Tzŭ had in mind. Ts'ao Kung thinks it is "some strategical advantage on which the enemy is depending." Tu Mu says: "The three things which an enemy is anxious to do, and on the accomplishment of which his success depends, are: (1) to capture our favourable positions; (2) to ravage our cultivated land; (3) to guard his own communications." Our object then must be to thwart his plans in these three directions and thus render him helpless. [Cf. III. § 3.] By boldly seizing the initiative in this way, you at once throw the other side on the defensive.]

19 Rapidity is the essence of war:

[According to Tu Mu, "this is a summary of leading principles in warfare," and he adds: "These are the profoundest truths of military science, and the chief business of the general." The following anecdotes, told by Ho Shih, shows the importance attached to speed by two of China's greatest generals. In 227 A.D., Mêng Ta, governor of Hsin-ch'êng under the Wei Emperor Wên Ti, was meditating defection to the House of Shu, and had entered into correspondence with Chu-ko Liang, Prime Minister of that State. The Wei general Ssŭ-ma I was then military governor of Wan, and getting wind of Mêng Ta's treachery, he at once set off with an army to anticipate his revolt, having previously cajoled him by a specious message of friendly import. Ssŭ-ma's officers came to him and said: "If Mêng Ta has leagued himself with Wu and Shu, the matter should be thoroughly investigated before we make a move." Ssŭ-ma I replied: "Mêng Ta is an unprincipled man, and we ought to go and punish him at once, while he is still wavering and before he has thrown off the mask." Then, by a series of forced marches, be brought his army under the walls of Hsin-ch'êng with in a space of eight days. Now Mêng Ta had previously said in a letter to Chu-ko Liang: "Wan is 1200 *li* from here. When the news of my revolt reaches Ssŭ-ma I, he will at once inform his imperial master, but it will be a whole month before any steps can be taken, and by that time my city will be well fortified. Besides, Ssŭ-ma I is sure not to come himself, and the generals that will be sent against us are not worth troubling about." The next letter, however, was filled with consternation: "Though only eight days have passed since I threw off my allegiance, an army is already at the city-gates. What miraculous rapidity is this!" A fortnight later, Hsin-ch'eng had fallen and Mêng Ta had lost his head. [See *Chin Shu*, ch. 1, f. 3.] In 621 A.D., Li Ching was sent from K'uei-chou in Ssŭ-ch'uan to reduce the successful rebel Hsiao Hsien, who had set up as Emperor at the modern Ching-chou Fu in Hupeh. It was autumn, and the Yangtsze being then in flood, Hsiao Hsien never dreamt that his adversary would venture to come down through the gorges, and consequently made no preparations. But Li Ching embarked his army without loss of time, and was just about to start when the other generals implored him to postpone his departure until the river was in a less dangerous state for navigation. Li Ching replied: "To the soldier, overwhelming speed is of paramount importance, and he must never miss opportunities. Now is the time to strike, before Hsiao Hsien even knows that we have got an army together. If we seize the present moment when the river is in flood, we shall appear before his capital with startling suddenness, like the thunder which is heard before you have time to stop your ears against it. [See VII. § 19, note.] This is the great principle in war. Even if he gets to know of our approach, he will have to levy his soldiers in such a hurry that they will not be fit to oppose us. Thus the full fruits of victory will be ours." All came about as he predicted, and Hsiao Hsien was obliged to surrender, nobly stipulating that his people should be spared and he alone suffer the penalty of death.]

take advantage of the enemy's unreadiness, make your way by unexpected routes, and attack unguarded spots.

20 The following are the principles to be observed by an invading force: The further you penetrate into a country, the greater will be the solidarity of your troops, and thus the defenders will not prevail against you.

21 Make forays in fertile country in order to supply your army with food.

[Cf. *supra*, § 13. Li Ch'üan does not venture on a note here.]

22 Carefully study the well-being of your men,

[For "well-being", Wang Hsi means, "Pet them, humor them, give them plenty of food and drink, and look after them generally."]

and do not overtax them. Concentrate your energy and hoard your strength.

[Ch'en recalls the line of action adopted in 224 B.C. by the famous general Wang Chien, whose military genius largely contributed to the success of the First Emperor. He had invaded the Ch'u State, where a universal levy was made to oppose him. But, being doubtful of the temper of his troops, he declined all invitations to fight and remained strictly on the defensive. In vain did the Ch'u general try to force a battle: day after day Wang Chien kept inside his walls and would not come out, but devoted his whole time and energy to winning the affection and confidence of his men. He took care that they should be well fed, sharing his own meals with them, provided facilities for bathing, and employed every method of judicious indulgence to weld them into a loyal and homogenous body. After some time had elapsed, he told off certain persons to find out how the men were amusing themselves. The answer was, that they were contending with one another in putting the weight and long-jumping. When Wang Chien heard that they were engaged in these athletic pursuits, he knew that their spirits had been strung up to the required pitch and that they were now ready for fighting. By this time the Ch'u army, after repeating their challenge again and again, had marched away eastwards in disgust. The Ch'in general immediately broke up his camp and followed them, and in the battle that ensued they were routed with great slaughter. Shortly afterwards, the whole of Ch'u was conquered by Ch'in, and the king Fu-ch'u led into captivity.]

Keep your army continually on the move,

[In order that the enemy may never know exactly where you are. It has struck me, however, that the true reading might be "link your army together."]

and devise unfathomable plans.

23 Throw your soldiers into positions whence there is no escape, and they will prefer death to flight. If they will face death, there is nothing they may not achieve.

[Chang Yü quotes his favourite Wei Liao Tzŭ (ch. 3): "If one man were to run amok with a sword in the market-place, and everybody else tried to get our of his way, I should not allow that this man alone had courage and that all the rest were contemptible cowards. The truth is, that a desperado and a man who sets some value on his life do not meet on even terms."]

Officers and men alike will put forth their uttermost strength.

[Chang Yü says: "If they are in an awkward place together, they will surely exert their united strength to get out of it."]

24 Soldiers when in desperate straits lose the sense of fear. If there is no place of refuge, they will stand firm. If they are in the heart of a hostile country, they will show a stubborn front. If there is no help for it, they will fight hard.

25 Thus, without waiting to be marshalled, the soldiers will be constantly on the *qui vive;* without waiting to be asked, they will do your will;

[Literally, "without asking, you will get."]

without restrictions, they will be faithful; without giving orders, they can be trusted.

26 Prohibit the taking of omens, and do away with superstitious doubts. Then, until death itself comes, no calamity need be feared.

[The superstitious, "bound in to saucy doubts and fears," degenerate into cowards and "die many times before their deaths." Tu Mu quotes Huang Shih-kung: "'Spells and incantations should be strictly forbidden, and no officer allowed to inquire by divination into the fortunes of an army, for fear the soldiers' minds should be seriously perturbed.' The meaning is," he continues, "that if all doubts and scruples are discarded, your men will never falter in their resolution until they die."]

27 If our soldiers are not overburdened with money, it is not because they have a distaste for riches; if their lives are not unduly long, it is not because they are disinclined to longevity.

[Chang Yü has the best note on this passage: "Wealth and long life are things for which all men have a natural inclination. Hence, if they burn or fling away valuables, and sacrifice their own lives, it is not that they dislike them, but simply that they have no choice." Sun Tzŭ is slyly insinuating that, as soldiers are but human, it is for the general to see that temptations to shirk fighting and grow rich are not thrown in their way.]

28 On the day they are ordered out to battle, your soldiers may weep,

[The word in the Chinese is "snivel.' This is taken to indicate more genuine grief than tears alone.]

those sitting up bedewing their garments, and those lying down letting the tears run down their cheeks.

[Not because they are afraid, but because, as Ts'ao Kung says, "all have embraced the firm resolution to do or die." We may remember that the heroes of the Iliad were equally childlike in showing their emotion. Chang Yü alludes to the mournful parting at the I River between Ching K'o and his friends, when the former was sent to attempt the life of the King of Ch'in (afterwards First Emperor) in 227 B.C. The tears of all flowed down like rain as he bade them farewell and uttered the following lines: "The shrill blast is blowing, Chilly the burn; Your champion is going—Not to return." [1]]

But let them once be brought to bay, and they will display the courage of a Chu or a Kuei.

[Chu was the personal name of Chüan Chu, a native of the Wu State and contemporary with Sun Tzŭ himself, who was employed by Kung-tzu Kuang, better known as Ho Lü Wang, to assassinate his sovereign Wang Liao with a dagger which he secreted in the belly of a fish served up at a banquet. He succeeded in his attempt, but was immediately hacked to pieces by the king's bodyguard. This was in 515 B.C. The other hero referred to, Ts'ao Kuei (or Ts'ao Mo), performed the exploit which has made his name famous 166 years earlier, in 681 B.C. Lu had been thrice defeated by Ch'i, and was just about to conclude a treaty surrendering a large slice of territory, when Ts'ao Kuei suddenly seized Huan Kung, the Duke of Ch'i, as he stood on the altar steps and held a dagger against his chest. None of the duke's retainers dared to move a muscle, and Ts'ao Kuei proceeded to demand full restitution, declaring the Lu was being unjustly treated because she was a smaller and a weaker state. Huan Kung, in peril of his life, was obliged to consent, whereupon Ts'ao Kuei flung away his dagger and quietly resumed his place amid the terrified assemblage without having so much as changed color. As was to be expected, the Duke wanted afterwards to repudiate the bargain, but his wise old counselor Kuan Chung pointed out to him the impolicy of breaking his word, and the upshot was that this bold stroke regained for Lu the whole of what she had lost in three pitched battles.]

29 The skillful tactician may be likened to the *shuai-jan*. Now the *shuai-jan* is a snake that is found in the Ch'ang mountains.

["*Shuai-jan*" means "suddenly" or "rapidly," and the snake in question was doubtless so called owing to the rapidity of its movements. Through this passage, the term in the Chinese has now come to be used in the sense of "military manœuvers."]

Strike at its head, and you will be attacked by its tail; strike at its tail, and you will be attacked by its head; strike at its middle, and you will be attacked by head and tail both.

30 Asked if an army can be made to imitate the *shuai-jan*,

[That is, as Mei Yao-ch'ên says, "Is it possible to make the front and rear of an army each swiftly responsive to attack on the other, just as though they were part of a single living body?"]

I should answer, Yes. For the men of Wu and the men of Yüeh are enemies;

[Cf. VI. § 21.]

yet if they are crossing a river in the same boat and are caught by a storm, they will come to each other's assistance just as the left hand helps the right.

[The meaning is: If two enemies will help each other in a time of common peril, how much more should two parts of the same army, bound together as they are by every tie of interest and fellow-feeling. Yet it is notorious that many a campaign has been ruined through lack of cooperation, especially in the case of allied armies.]

31 Hence it is not enough to put one's trust in the tethering of horses, and the burying of chariot wheels in the ground.

[These quaint devices to prevent one's army from running away recall the Athenian hero Sophanes, who carried the anchor with him at the battle of Plataea, by means of which he fastened himself firmly to one spot. (See Herodotus, IX. 74.) It is not enough, says Sun Tzŭ, to render flight impossible by such mechanical means. You will not succeed unless your men have tenacity and unity of purpose, and, above all, a spirit of sympathetic cooperation. This is the lesson which can be learned from the *shuai-jan*.]

32 The principle on which to manage an army is to set up one standard of courage which all must reach.

[Literally, "level the courage [of all] as though [it were that of] one." If the ideal army is to form a single organic whole, then it follows that the resolution and spirit of its component parts must be of the same quality, or at any rate must not fall below a certain standard. Wellington's seemingly ungrateful description of his army at Waterloo as "the worst he had ever commanded" meant no more than that it was deficient in this important particular—unity of spirit and courage.

Had he not foreseen the Belgian defections and carefully kept those troops in the background, he would almost certainly have lost the day.]

33 How to make the best of both strong and weak—that is a question involving the proper use of ground.

[Mei Yao-ch'ên's paraphrase is: "The way to eliminate the differences of strong and weak and to make both serviceable is to utilize accidental features of the ground." Less reliable troops, if posted in strong positions, will hold out as long as better troops on more exposed terrain. The advantage of position neutralizes the inferiority in stamina and courage. Col. Henderson says: "With all respect to the text books, and to the ordinary tactical teaching, I am inclined to think that the study of ground is often overlooked, and that by no means sufficient importance is attached to the selection of positions… and to the immense advantages that are to be derived, whether you are defending or attacking, from the proper utilization of natural features." [2]]

34 Thus the skillful general conducts his army just as though he were leading a single man, willy-nilly, by the hand.

[Tu Mu says: "The simile has reference to the ease with which he does it."]

35 It is the business of a general to be quiet and thus ensure secrecy; upright and just, and thus maintain order.

36 He must be able to mystify his officers and men by false reports and appearances,

[Literally, "to deceive their eyes and ears."]

and thus keep them in total ignorance.

[Ts'ao Kung gives us one of his excellent apophthegms: "The troops must not be allowed to share your schemes in the beginning; they may only rejoice with you over their happy outcome." "To mystify, mislead, and surprise the enemy," is one of the first principles in war, as had been frequently pointed out. But how about the other process—the mystification of one's own men? Those who may think that Sun Tzŭ is over-emphatic on this point would do well to read Col. Henderson's remarks on Stonewall Jackson's Valley campaign: "The infinite pains," he says, "with which Jackson sought to conceal, even from his most trusted staff officers, his movements, his intentions, and his thoughts, a commander less thorough would have pronounced useless"—etc. etc. [3] In the year 88 A.D., as we read in ch. 47 of the *Hou Han Shu*, "Pan Ch'ao took the field with 25,000 men from Khotan and other Central Asian states with the object of crushing Yarkand. The King of Kutcha replied by dispatching his chief commander to succour the place with an army drawn from the kingdoms of Wen-su, Ku-mo, and Wei-t'ou, totaling 50,000 men. Pan Ch'ao summoned his officers and also the King of Khotan to a council of war, and said: 'Our forces are now outnumbered and unable to make head against the enemy. The best plan, then, is for us to separate and disperse, each in a different direction. The King of Khotan will march away by the easterly route, and I will then return myself towards the west. Let us wait until the evening drum has sounded and then start.' Pan Ch'ao now secretly released the prisoners whom he had taken alive, and the King of Kutcha was thus informed of his plans. Much elated by the news, the latter set off at once at the head of 10,000 horsemen to bar Pan Ch'ao's retreat in the west, while the King of Wen-su rode eastward with 8000 horse in order to intercept the King of Khotan. As soon as Pan Ch'ao knew that the two chieftains had gone, he called his divisions together, got them well in hand, and at cock-crow hurled them against the army of Yarkand, as it lay encamped. The barbarians, panic-stricken, fled in confusion, and were closely pursued by Pan Ch'ao. Over 5000 heads were brought back as trophies, besides immense spoils in the shape of horses and cattle and valuables of every description. Yarkand then capitulating, Kutcha and the other kingdoms drew off their respective forces. From that time forward, Pan Ch'ao's prestige completely overawed the countries of the west." In this case, we see that the Chinese general not only kept his own officers in ignorance of his real plans, but actually took the bold step of dividing his army in order to deceive the enemy.]

37 By altering his arrangements and changing his plans,

[Wang Hsi thinks that this means not using the same stratagem twice.]

he keeps the enemy without definite knowledge.

[Chang Yü, in a quotation from another work, says: "The axiom, that war is based on deception, does not apply only to deception of the enemy. You must deceive even your own soldiers. Make them follow you, but without letting them know why."]

By shifting his camp and taking circuitous routes, he prevents the enemy from anticipating his purpose.

38 At the critical moment, the leader of an army acts like one who has climbed up a height and then kicks away the ladder behind him. He carries his men deep into hostile territory before he shows his hand.

[Literally, "releases the spring" (see V. § 15), that is, takes some decisive step which makes it impossible for the army to return—like Hsiang Yu, who sunk his ships after crossing a river. Ch'ên Hao, followed by Chia Lin, understands the words less well as "puts forth every artifice at his command."]

39 He burns his boats and breaks his cooking-pots; like a shepherd driving a flock of sheep, he drives his men this way and that, and none knows whither he is going.

[Tu Mu says: "The army is only cognizant of orders to advance or retreat; it is ignorant of the ulterior ends of attacking and conquering."]

40 To muster his host and bring it into danger:—this may be termed the business of the general.

[Sun Tzŭ means that after mobilization there should be no delay in aiming a blow at the enemy's heart. Note how he returns again and again to this point. Among the warring states of ancient China, desertion was no doubt a much more present fear and serious evil than it is in the armies of today.]

41 The different measures suited to the nine varieties of ground;

[Chang Yü says: "One must not be hide-bound in interpreting the rules for the nine varieties of ground."]

the expediency of aggressive or defensive tactics; and the fundamental laws of human nature: these are things that must most certainly be studied.

42 When invading hostile territory, the general principle is, that penetrating deeply brings cohesion; penetrating but a short way means dispersion.

[Cf. *supra*, § 20.]

43 When you leave your own country behind, and take your army across neighbourhood territory, you find yourself on critical ground.

[This "ground" is curiously mentioned in VIII. § 2, but it does not figure among the Nine Situations or the Six Calamities in chap. X. One's first impulse would be to translate it "distant ground," but this, if we can trust the commentators, is precisely what is not meant here. Mei Yao-ch'ên says it is "a position not far enough advanced to be called 'facile,' and not near enough to home to be 'dispersive,' but something between the two." Wang Hsi says: "It is ground separated from home by an interjacent state, whose territory we have had to cross in order to reach it. Hence, it is incumbent on us to settle our business there quickly." He adds that this position is of rare occurrence, which is the reason why it is not included among the Nine Situations.]

When there are means of communication on all four sides, the ground is one of intersecting highways.

44 When you penetrate deeply into a country, it is serious ground. When you penetrate but a little way, it is facile ground.

45 When you have the enemy's strongholds on your rear, and narrow passes in front, it is hemmed-in ground. When there is no place of refuge at all, it is desperate ground.

46 Therefore, on dispersive ground, I would inspire my men with unity of purpose.

[This end, according to Tu Mu, is best attained by remaining on the defensive, and avoiding battle. Cf. *supra*, § 11.]

On facile ground, I would see that there is close connection between all parts of my army.

[As Tu Mu says, the object is to guard against two possible contingencies: "(1) the desertion of our own troops; (2) a sudden attack on the part of the enemy." Cf. VII. § 17. Mei Yao-ch'ên says: "On the march, the regiments should be in close touch; in an encampment, there should be continuity between the fortifications."]

47 On contentious ground, I would hurry up my rear.

[This is Ts'ao Kung's interpretation. Chang Yü adopts it, saying: "We must quickly bring up our rear, so that head and tail may both reach the goal." That is, they must not be allowed to straggle up a long way apart. Mei Yao-ch'en offers another equally plausible explanation: "Supposing the enemy has not yet reached the coveted position, and we are behind him, we should advance with all speed in order to dispute its possession." Ch'ên Hao, on the other hand, assuming that the enemy has had time to select his own ground, quotes VI. § 1, where Sun Tzŭ warns us against coming exhausted to the attack. His own idea of the situation is rather vaguely expressed: "If there is a favourable position lying in front of you, detach a picked body of troops to occupy it, then if the enemy, relying on their numbers, come up to make a fight for it, you may fall quickly on their rear with your main body, and victory will be assured." It was thus, he adds, that Chao Shê beat the army of Ch'in. (See p. 57.)]

48 On open ground, I would keep a vigilant eye on my defenses. On ground of intersecting highways, I would consolidate my alliances.

49 On serious ground, I would try to ensure a continuous stream of supplies.

[The commentators take this as referring to forage and plunder, not, as one might expect, to an unbroken communication with a home base.]

On difficult ground, I would keep pushing on along the road.

50 On hemmed-in ground, I would block any way of retreat.

[Mêng Shih says: "To make it seem that I meant to defend the position, whereas my real intention is to burst suddenly through the enemy's lines." Mei Yao-ch'ên says: "in order to make my soldiers fight with desperation." Wang Hsi says, "fearing lest my men be tempted to run away." Tu Mu points out that this is the converse of VII. § 36, where it is the enemy who is surrounded. In 532 A.D., Kao Huan, afterwards Emperor and canonized as Shen-wu, was surrounded by a great army under Erh-chu Chao and others. His own force was comparatively small, consisting only of 2000 horse and something under 30,000 foot. The lines of investment had not been drawn very closely together, gaps being left at certain points. But Kao Huan, instead of trying to escape, actually made a shift to block all the remaining outlets himself by driving into them a number of oxen and donkeys roped together. As soon as his officers and men saw that there was nothing for it but to conquer or die, their spirits rose to an extraordinary pitch of exaltation, and they charged with such desperate ferocity that the opposing ranks broke and crumbled under their onslaught.]

On desperate ground, I would proclaim to my soldiers the hopelessness of saving their lives.

Tu Yu says: "Burn your baggage and impedimenta, throw away your stores and provisions, choke up the wells, destroy your cooking-stoves, and make it plain to your men that they cannot survive, but must fight to the death." Mei Yao-ch'ên says: "The only chance of life lies in giving up all hope of it." This concludes what Sun Tzŭ has to say about "grounds" and the "variations" corresponding to them. Reviewing the passages which bear on this important subject, we cannot fail to be struck by the desultory and unmethodical fashion in which it is treated. Sun Tzŭ begins abruptly in VIII. § 2 to enumerate "variations" before touching on "grounds" at all, but only mentions five, namely nos. 7, 5, 8 and 9 of the subsequent list, and one that is not included in it. A few varieties of ground are dealt with in the earlier portion of chap. IX, and then chap. X sets forth six new grounds, with six variations of plan to match. None of these is mentioned again, though the first is hardly to be distinguished from ground no. 4 in the next chapter. At last, in chap. XI, we come to the Nine Grounds par excellence, immediately followed by the variations. This takes us down to § 14. In §§ 43-45, fresh definitions are provided for nos. 5, 6, 2, 8 and 9 (in the order given), as well as for the tenth ground noticed in chap. VIII; and finally, the nine variations are enumerated once more from beginning to end, all, with the exception of 5, 6 and 7, being different from those previously given. Though it is impossible to account for the present state of Sun Tzŭ's text, a few suggestive facts maybe brought into prominence: (1) Chap. VIII, according to the title, should deal with nine variations, whereas only five appear. (2) It is an abnormally short chapter. (3) Chap. XI is entitled The Nine Grounds. Several of these are defined twice over, besides which there are two distinct lists of the corresponding variations. (4) The length of the chapter is disproportionate, being double that of any other except IX. I do not propose to draw any inferences from these facts, beyond the general conclusion that Sun Tzŭ's work cannot have come down to us in the shape in which it left his hands: chap. VIII is obviously defective and probably out of place, while XI seems to contain matter that has either been added by a later hand or ought to appear elsewhere.]

51 For it is the soldier's disposition to offer an obstinate resistance when surrounded, to fight hard when he cannot help himself, and to obey promptly when he has fallen into danger.

[Chang Yü alludes to the conduct of Pan Ch'ao's devoted followers in 73 A.D. The story runs thus in the *Hou Han Shu*, ch. 47: "When Pan Ch'ao arrived at Shan-shan, Kuang, the King of the country, received him at first with great politeness and respect; but shortly afterwards his behavior underwent a sudden change, and he became remiss and negligent. Pan Ch'ao spoke about this to the officers of his suite: 'Have you noticed,' he said, 'that Kuang's polite intentions are on the wane? This must signify that envoys have come from the Northern barbarians, and that consequently he is in a state of indecision, not knowing with which side to throw in his lot. That surely is the reason. The truly wise man, we are told, can perceive things before they have come to pass; how much more, then, those that are already manifest!' Thereupon he called one of the natives who had been assigned to his service, and set a trap for him, saying: 'Where are those envoys from the Hsiung-nu who arrived some day ago?' The man was so taken aback that between surprise and fear he presently blurted out the whole truth. Pan Ch'ao, keeping his informant carefully under lock and key, then summoned a general gathering of his officers, thirty-six in all, and began drinking with them. When the wine had mounted into their heads a little, he tried to rouse their spirit still further by addressing them thus: 'Gentlemen, here we are in the heart of an isolated region, anxious to achieve riches and honour by some great exploit. Now it happens that an ambassador from the Hsiung-no arrived in this kingdom only a few days ago, and the result is that the respectful courtesy extended towards us by our royal host has disappeared. Should this envoy prevail upon him to seize our party and hand us over to the Hsiung-no, our bones will become food for the wolves of the desert. What are we to do?' With one accord, the officers replied: 'Standing as we do in peril of our lives, we will follow our commander through life and death.' For the sequel of this adventure, see chap. XII. § 1, note.]

52 We cannot enter into alliance with neighbouring princes until we are acquainted with their designs. We are not fit to lead an army on the march unless we are familiar with the face of the country—its mountains and forests, its pitfalls and precipices, its marshes and swamps. We shall be unable to turn natural advantages to account unless we make use of local guides.

[These three sentences are repeated from VII. §§ 12-14—in order to emphasize their importance, the commentators seem to think. I prefer to regard them as interpolated here in order to form an antecedent to the following words. With regard to local guides, Sun Tzŭ might have added that there is always the risk of going wrong, either through their treachery or some misunderstanding such as Livy records (XXII. 13): Hannibal, we are told, ordered a guide to lead him into the neighbourhood of Casinum, where there was an important pass to be occupied; but his Carthaginian accent, unsuited to the pronunciation of Latin names, caused the guide to understand Casilinum instead of Casinum, and turning from his proper route, he took the army in that direction, the mistake not being discovered until they had almost arrived.]

53 To be ignorant of any one of the following four or five principles does not befit a warlike prince.

54 When a warlike prince attacks a powerful state, his generalship shows itself in preventing the concentration of the enemy's forces. He overawes his opponents, and their allies are prevented from joining against him.

[Mei Tao-ch'ên constructs one of the chains of reasoning that are so much affected by the Chinese: "In attacking a powerful state, if you can divide her forces, you will have a superiority in strength; if you have a superiority in strength, you will overawe the enemy; if you overawe the enemy, the neighbouring states will be frightened; and if the neighbouring states are frightened, the enemy's allies will be prevented from joining her." The following gives a stronger meaning: "If the great state has once been defeated (before she has had time to summon her allies), then the lesser states will hold aloof and refrain from massing their forces." Ch'ên Hao and Chang Yü take the sentence in quite another way. The former says: "Powerful though a prince may be, if he attacks a large state, he will be unable to raise enough troops, and must rely to some extent on external aid; if he dispenses with this, and with overweening confidence in his own strength, simply tries to intimidate the enemy, he will surely be defeated." Chang Yü puts his view thus: "If we recklessly attack a large state, our own people will be discontented and hang back. But if (as will then be the case) our display of military force is inferior by half to that of the enemy, the other chieftains will take fright and refuse to join us."]

55 Hence he does not strive to ally himself with all and sundry, nor does he foster the power of other states. He carries out his own secret designs, keeping his antagonists in awe.

[The train of thought, as said by Li Ch'üan, appears to be this: Secure against a combination of his enemies, "he can afford to reject entangling alliances and simply pursue his own secret designs, his prestige enable him to dispense with external friendships."]

Thus he is able to capture their cities and overthrow their kingdoms.

[This paragraph, though written many years before the Ch'in State became a serious menace, is not a bad summary of the policy by which the famous Six Chancellors gradually paved the way for her final triumph under Shih Huang Ti. Chang Yü, following up his previous note, thinks that Sun Tzŭ is condemning this attitude of cold-blooded selfishness and haughty isolation.]

56 Bestow rewards without regard to rule,

[Wu Tzŭ (ch. 3) less wisely says: "Let advance be richly rewarded and retreat be heavily punished."]

issue orders

[Literally, "hang" or post up."]

without regard to previous arrangements;

["In order to prevent treachery," says Wang Hsi. The general meaning is made clear by Ts'ao Kung's quotation from the *Ssŭ-ma Fa*: "Give instructions only on sighting the enemy; give rewards when you see deserving deeds." Ts'ao Kung's paraphrase: "The final instructions you give to your army should not correspond with those that have been previously posted up." Chang Yü simplifies this into "your arrangements should not be divulged beforehand." And Chia Lin says: "there should be no fixity in your rules and arrangements." Not only is there danger in letting your plans be known, but war often necessitates the entire reversal of them at the last moment.]

and you will be able to handle a whole army as though you had to do with but a single man.

[Cf. *supra*, § 34.]

57 Confront your soldiers with the deed itself; never let them know your design.

[Literally, "do not tell them words;" i.e. do not give your reasons for any order. Lord Mansfield once told a junior colleague to "give no reasons" for his decisions, and the maxim is even more applicable to a general than to a judge.]

When the outlook is bright, bring it before their eyes; but tell them nothing when the situation is gloomy.

58 Place your army in deadly peril, and it will survive; plunge it into desperate straits, and it will come off in safety.

[These words of Sun Tzŭ were once quoted by Han Hsin in explanation of the tactics he employed in one of his most brilliant battles, already alluded to on p. 28. In 204 B.C., he was sent against the army of Chao, and halted ten miles from the mouth of the Ching-hsing pass, where the enemy had mustered in full force. Here, at midnight, he detached a body of 2000 light cavalry, every man of which was furnished with a red flag. Their instructions were to make their way through narrow defiles and keep a secret watch on the enemy. "When the men of Chao see me in full flight," Han Hsin said, "they will abandon their fortifications and give chase. This must be the sign for you to rush in, pluck down the Chao standards and set up the red banners of Han in their stead." Turning then to his other officers, he remarked: "Our adversary holds a strong position, and is not likely to come out and attack us until he sees the standard and drums of the commander-in-chief, for fear I should turn back and escape through the mountains." So saying, he first of all sent out a division consisting of 10,000 men, and ordered them to form in line of battle with their backs to the River Ti. Seeing this manœuver, the whole army of Chao broke into loud laughter. By this time it was broad daylight, and Han Hsin, displaying the generalissimo's flag, marched out of the pass with drums beating, and was immediately engaged by the enemy. A great battle followed, lasting for some time; until at length Han Hsin and his colleague Chang Ni, leaving drums and banner on the field, fled to the division on the river bank, where another fierce battle was raging. The enemy rushed out to pursue them and to secure the trophies, thus denuding their ramparts of men; but the two generals succeeded in joining the other army, which was fighting with the utmost desperation. The time had now come for the 2000 horsemen to play their part. As soon as they saw the men of Chao following up their advantage, they galloped behind the deserted walls, tore up the enemy's flags and replaced them by those of Han. When the Chao army looked back from the pursuit, the sight of these red flags struck them with terror. Convinced that the Hans had got in and overpowered their king, they broke up in wild disorder, every effort of their leader to stay the panic being in vain. Then the Han army fell on them from both sides and completed the rout, killing a number and capturing the rest, amongst whom was King Ya himself... After the battle, some of Han Hsin's officers came to him and said: "In the *Art of War* we are told to have a hill or tumulus on the right rear, and a river or marsh on the left front. (This appears to be a blend of Sun Tzŭ and T'ai Kung. See IX § 9, and note.) You, on the contrary, ordered us to draw up our troops with the river at our back. Under these conditions, how did you manage to gain the victory?" The general replied: "I fear you gentlemen have not studied the Art of War with sufficient care. Is it not written there: 'Plunge your army into desperate straits and it will come off in safety; place it in deadly peril and it will survive'? Had I taken the usual course, I should never have been able to bring my colleague round. What says the Military Classic—'Swoop down on the market-place and drive the men off to fight.' [This passage does not occur in the present text of Sun Tzŭ.] If I had not placed my troops in a position where they were obliged to fight for their lives, but had allowed each man to follow his own discretion, there would have been a general *débandade*, and it would have been impossible to do anything with them." The officers admitted the force of his argument, and said: "These are higher tactics than we should have been capable of." [See *Ch'ien Han Shu*, ch. 34, ff. 4, 5.]]

59 For it is precisely when a force has fallen into harm's way that is capable of striking a blow for victory.

[Danger has a bracing effect.]

60 Success in warfare is gained by carefully accommodating ourselves to the enemy's purpose.

[Ts'ao Kung says: "Feign stupidity"—by an appearance of yielding and falling in with the enemy's wishes. Chang Yü's note makes the meaning clear: "If the enemy shows an inclination to advance, lure him on to do so; if he is anxious to retreat, delay on purpose that he may carry out his intention." The object is to make him remiss and contemptuous before we deliver our attack.]

61 By persistently hanging on the enemy's flank,

[I understand the first four words to mean "accompanying the enemy in one direction." Ts'ao Kung says: "unite the soldiers and make for the enemy." But such a violent displacement of characters is quite indefensible.]

we shall succeed in the long run

[Literally, "after a thousand *li*."]

in killing the commander-in-chief.

[Always a great point with the Chinese.]

62 This is called ability to accomplish a thing by sheer cunning.

63 On the day that you take up your command, block the frontier passes, destroy the official tallies,

[These were tablets of bamboo or wood, one half of which was issued as a permit or passport by the official in charge of a gate. Cf. the "border-warden" of *Lun Yü* III. 24, who may have had similar duties. When this half was returned to him, within a fixed period, he was authorized to open the gate and let the traveler through.]

and stop the passage of all emissaries.

[Either to or from the enemy's country.]

64 Be stern in the council-chamber,

[Show no weakness, and insist on your plans being ratified by the sovereign.]

so that you may control the situation.

[Mei Yao-ch'ên understands the whole sentence to mean: Take the strictest precautions to ensure secrecy in your deliberations.]

65 If the enemy leaves a door open, you must rush in.

66 Forestall your opponent by seizing what he holds dear,

[Cf. *supra*, § 18.]

and subtly contrive to time his arrival on the ground.

[Ch'ên Hao's explanation: "If I manage to seize a favourable position, but the enemy does not appear on the scene, the advantage thus obtained cannot be turned to any practical account. He who intends therefore, to occupy a position of importance to the enemy, must begin by making an artful appointment, so to speak, with his antagonist, and cajole him into going there as well." Mei Yao-ch'ên explains that this "artful appointment" is to be made through the medium of the enemy's own spies, who will carry back just the amount of information that we choose to give them. Then, having cunningly disclosed our intentions, "we must manage, though starting after the enemy, to arrive before him (VII. § 4). We must start after him in order to ensure his marching thither; we must arrive before him in order to capture the place without trouble. Taken thus, the present passage lends some support to Mei Yao-ch'ên's interpretation of § 47.]

67 Walk in the path defined by rule,

[Chia Lin says: "Victory is the only thing that matters, and this cannot be achieved by adhering to conventional canons." It is unfortunate that this variant rests on very slight authority, for the sense yielded is certainly much more satisfactory. Napoleon, as we know, according to the veterans of the old school whom he defeated, won his battles by violating every accepted canon of warfare.]

and accommodate yourself to the enemy until you can fight a decisive battle.

[Tu Mu says: "Conform to the enemy's tactics until a favourable opportunity offers; then come forth and engage in a battle that shall prove decisive."]

68 At first, then, exhibit the coyness of a maiden, until the enemy gives you an opening; afterwards emulate the rapidity of a running hare, and it will be too late for the enemy to oppose you.

[As the hare is noted for its extreme timidity, the comparison hardly appears felicitous. But of course Sun Tzŭ was thinking only of its speed. The words have been taken to mean: You must flee from the enemy as quickly as an escaping hare; but this is rightly rejected by Tu Mu.]

[1] Giles' Biographical Dictionary, no. 399.
[2] "The Science of War," p. 333.
[3] "Stonewall Jackson," vol. I, p. 421.

Chapter 12
The Attack by Fire

[Rather more than half the chapter (§§ 1-13) is devoted to the subject of fire, after which the author branches off into other topics.]

1 Sun Tzŭ said: There are five ways of attacking with fire. The first is to burn soldiers in their camp;

[So Tu Mu. Li Ch'üan says: "Set fire to the camp, and kill the soldiers" (when they try to escape from the flames). Pan Ch'ao, sent on a diplomatic mission to the King of Shan-shan (see XI. § 51, note), found himself placed in extreme peril by the unexpected arrival of an envoy from the Hsiung-nu (the mortal enemies of the Chinese). In consultation with his officers, he exclaimed: "Never venture, never win! [1] The only course open to us now is to make an assault by fire on the barbarians under cover of night, when they will not be able to discern our numbers. Profiting by their panic, we shall exterminate them completely; this will cool the King's courage and cover us with glory, besides ensuring the success of our mission.' The officers all replied that it would be necessary to discuss the matter first with the Intendant. Pan Ch'ao then fell into a passion: 'It is today,' he cried, 'that our fortunes must be decided! The Intendant is only a humdrum civilian, who on hearing of our project will certainly be afraid, and everything will be brought to light. An inglorious death is no worthy fate for valiant warriors.' All then agreed to do as he wished. Accordingly, as soon as night came on, he and his little band quickly made their way to the barbarian camp. A strong gale was blowing at the time. Pan Ch'ao ordered ten of the party to take drums and hide behind the enemy's barracks, it being arranged that when they saw flames shoot up, they should begin drumming and yelling with all their might. The rest of his men, armed with bows and crossbows, he posted in ambuscade at the gate of the camp. He then set fire to the place from the windward side, whereupon a deafening noise of drums and shouting arose on the front and rear of the Hsiung-nu, who rushed out pell-mell in frantic disorder. Pan Ch'ao slew three of them with his own hand, while his companions cut off the heads of the envoy and thirty of his suite. The remainder, more than a hundred in all, perished in the flames. On the following day, Pan Ch'ao, divining his thoughts, said with uplifted hand: 'Although you did not go with us last night, I should not think, Sir, of taking sole credit for our exploit.' This satisfied Kuo Hsun, and Pan Ch'ao, having sent for Kuang, King of Shan-shan, showed him the head of the barbarian envoy. The whole kingdom was seized with fear and trembling, which Pan Ch'ao took steps to allay by issuing a public proclamation. Then, taking the king's sons as hostage, he returned to make his report to Tou Ku." *Hou Han Shu*, ch. 47, ff. 1, 2.]]

the second is to burn stores;

[Tu Mu says: "Provisions, fuel and fodder." In order to subdue the rebellious population of Kiangnan, Kao Keng recommended Wên Ti of the Sui dynasty to make periodical raids and burn their stores of grain, a policy which in the long run proved entirely successful.]

the third is to burn baggage-trains;

[An example given is the destruction of Yüan Shao's wagons and impedimenta by Ts'ao Ts'ao in 200 A.D.]

the fourth is to burn arsenals and magazines;

[Tu Mu says that the things contained in "arsenals" and "magazines" are the same. He specifies weapons and other implements, bullion and clothing. Cf. VII. § 11.]

the fifth is to hurl dropping fire amongst the enemy.

[Tu Yu says in the *T'ung Tien:* "To drop fire into the enemy's camp. The method by which this may be done is to set the tips of arrows alight by dipping them into a brazier, and then shoot them from powerful crossbows into the enemy's lines."]

2 In order to carry out an attack, we must have means available.

[T'sao Kung thinks that "traitors in the enemy's camp" are referred to. But Ch'ên Hao is more likely to be right in saying: "We must have favourable circumstances in general, not merely traitors to help us." Chia Lin says: "We must avail ourselves of wind and dry weather."]

the material for raising fire should always be kept in readiness.

[Tu Mu suggests as material for making fire: "dry vegetable matter, reeds, brushwood, straw, grease, oil, etc." Here we have the material cause. Chang Yü says: "vessels for hoarding fire, stuff for lighting fires."]

3 There is a proper season for making attacks with fire, and special days for starting a conflagration.

4 The proper season is when the weather is very dry; the special days are those when the moon is in the constellations of the Sieve, the Wall, the Wing or the Cross-bar;

[These are, respectively, the 7th, 14th, 27th, and 28th of the Twenty-eight Stellar Mansions, corresponding roughly to Sagittarius, Pegasus, Crater and Corvus.]

for these four are all days of rising wind.

5 In attacking with fire, one should be prepared to meet five possible developments:

6 (1) When fire breaks out inside the enemy's camp, respond at once with an attack from without.

7 (2) If there is an outbreak of fire, but the enemy's soldiers remain quiet, bide your time and do not attack.

[The prime object of attacking with fire is to throw the enemy into confusion. If this effect is not produced, it means that the enemy is ready to receive us. Hence the necessity for caution.]

8 (3) When the force of the flames has reached its height, follow it up with an attack, if that is practicable; if not, stay where you are.

[Ts'ao Kung says: "If you see a possible way, advance; but if you find the difficulties too great, retire."]

9 (4) If it is possible to make an assault with fire from without, do not wait for it to break out within, but deliver your attack at a favourable moment.

[Tu Mu says that the previous paragraphs had reference to the fire breaking out (either accidentally, we may suppose, or by the agency of incendiaries) inside the enemy's camp. "But," he continues, "if the enemy is settled in a waste place littered with quantities of grass, or if he has pitched his camp in a position which can be burnt out, we must carry our fire against him at any seasonable opportunity, and not await on in hopes of an outbreak occurring within, for fear our opponents should themselves burn up the surrounding vegetation, and thus render our own attempts fruitless." The famous Li Ling once baffled the leader of the Hsiung-nu in this way. The latter, taking advantage of a favourable wind, tried to set fire to the Chinese general's camp, but found that every scrap of combustible vegetation in the neighbourhood had already been burnt down. On the other hand, Po-ts'ai, a general of the Yellow Turban rebels, was badly defeated in 184 A.D. through his neglect of this simple precaution. "At the head of a large army he was besieging Ch'ang-she, which was held by Huang-fu Sung. The garrison was very small, and a general feeling of nervousness pervaded the ranks; so Huang-fu Sung called his officers together and said: "In war, there are various indirect methods of attack, and numbers do not count for everything. (The commentator here quotes Sun Tzŭ, V. §§ 5, 6 and 10.) Now the rebels have pitched their camp in the midst of thick grass which will easily burn when the wind blows. If we set fire to it at night, they will be thrown into a panic, and we can make a sortie and attack them on all sides at once, thus emulating the achievement of T'ien Tan.' [See p. 90.] That same evening, a strong breeze sprang up; so Huang-fu Sung instructed his soldiers to bind reeds together into torches and mount guard on the city walls, after which he sent out a band of daring men, who stealthily made their way through the lines and started the fire with loud shouts and yells. Simultaneously, a glare of light shot up from the city walls, and Huang-fu Sung, sounding his drums, led a rapid charge, which threw the rebels into confusion and put them to headlong flight." [*Hou Han Shu*, ch. 71.]]

10 (5) When you start a fire, be to windward of it. Do not attack from the leeward.

[Chang Yü, following Tu Yu, says: "When you make a fire, the enemy will retreat away from it; if you oppose his retreat and attack him then, he will fight desperately, which will not conduce to your success." A rather more obvious explanation is given by Tu Mu: "If the wind is in the east, begin burning to the east of the enemy, and follow up the attack yourself from that side. If you start the fire on the east side, and then attack from the west, you will suffer in the same way as your enemy."]

11 A wind that rises in the daytime lasts long, but a night breeze soon falls.

[Cf. Lao Tzŭ's saying: "A violent wind does not last the space of a morning." (*Tao Te Ching*, chap. 23.) Mei Yao-ch'ên and Wang Hsi say: "A day breeze dies down at nightfall, and a night breeze at daybreak. This is what happens as a general rule." The phenomenon observed may be correct enough, but how this sense is to be obtained is not apparent.]

12 In every army, the five developments connected with fire must be known, the movements of the stars calculated, and a watch kept for the proper days.

[Tu Mu says: "We must make calculations as to the paths of the stars, and watch for the days on which wind will rise, before making our attack with fire." Chang Yü seems to interpret the text differently: "We must not only know how to assail our opponents with fire, but also be on our guard against similar attacks from them."]

13 Hence those who use fire as an aid to the attack show intelligence; those who use water as an aid to the attack gain an accession of strength.

14 By means of water, an enemy may be intercepted, but not robbed of all his belongings.

[Ts'ao Kung's note is: "We can merely obstruct the enemy's road or divide his army, but not sweep away all his accumulated stores." Water can do useful service, but it lacks the terrible destructive power of fire. This is the reason, Chang Yü concludes, why the former is dismissed in a couple of sentences, whereas the attack by fire is discussed in detail. Wu Tzŭ speaks thus of the two elements: "If an army is encamped on low-lying marshy ground, from which the water cannot run off, and where the rainfall is heavy, it may be submerged by a flood. If an army is encamped in wild marsh lands thickly overgrown with weeds and brambles, and visited by frequent gales, it may be exterminated by fire."]

15 Unhappy is the fate of one who tries to win his battles and succeed in his attacks without cultivating the spirit of enterprise; for the result is waste of time and general stagnation.

[This is one of the most perplexing passages in Sun Tzŭ. Ts'ao Kung says: "Rewards for good service should not be deferred a single day." And Tu Mu: "If you do not take opportunity to advance and reward the deserving, your subordinates will not carry out your commands, and disaster will ensue." For several reasons, however, and in spite of the formidable array of scholars on the other side, I prefer the interpretation suggested by Mei Yao-ch'ên alone, whose words I will quote: "Those who want to make sure of succeeding in their battles and assaults must seize the favourable moments when they come and not shrink on occasion from heroic measures: that is to say, they must resort to such means of attack of fire, water and the like. What they must not do, and what will prove fatal, is to sit still and simply hold to the advantages they have got."]

16 Hence the saying: The enlightened ruler lays his plans well ahead; the good general cultivates his resources.

[Tu Mu quotes the following from the *San Lüeh*, ch. 2: "The warlike prince controls his soldiers by his authority, kits them together by good faith, and by rewards makes them serviceable. If faith decays, there will be disruption; if rewards are deficient, commands will not be respected."]

17 Move not unless you see an advantage; use not your troops unless there is something to be gained; fight not unless the position is critical.

[Sun Tzŭ may at times appear to be over-cautious, but he never goes so far in that direction as the remarkable passage in the *Tao Te Ching*, ch. 69. "I dare not take the initiative, but prefer to act on the defensive; I dare not advance an inch, but prefer to retreat a foot."]

18 No ruler should put troops into the field merely to gratify his own spleen; no general should fight a battle simply out of pique.

19 If it is to your advantage, make a forward move; if not, stay where you are.

[This is repeated from XI. § 17. Here I feel convinced that it is an interpolation, for it is evident that § 20 ought to follow immediately on § 18.]

20 Anger may in time change to gladness; vexation may be succeeded by content.

21 But a kingdom that has once been destroyed can never come again into being;

[The Wu State was destined to be a melancholy example of this saying.]

nor can the dead ever be brought back to life.

22 Hence the enlightened ruler is heedful, and the good general full of caution. This is the way to keep a country at peace and an army intact.

[1] "Unless you enter the tiger's lair, you cannot get hold of the tiger's cubs."

Chapter 13
The Use of Spies

1 Sun Tzŭ said: Raising a host of a hundred thousand men and marching them great distances entails heavy loss on the people and a drain on the resources of the State. The daily expenditure will amount to a thousand ounces of silver.

[Cf. II. §§ 1, 13, 14.]

There will be commotion at home and abroad, and men will drop down exhausted on the highways.

[Cf. *Tao Te Ching*, ch. 30: "Where troops have been quartered, brambles and thorns spring up. Chang Yü has the note: "We may be reminded of the saying: 'On serious ground, gather in plunder.' Why then should carriage and transportation cause exhaustion on the highways?—The answer is, that not victuals alone, but all sorts of munitions of war have to be conveyed to the army. Besides, the injunction to 'forage on the enemy' only means that when an army is deeply engaged in hostile territory, scarcity of food must be provided against. Hence, without being solely dependent on the enemy for corn, we must forage in order that there may be an uninterrupted flow of supplies. Then, again, there are places like salt deserts where provisions being unobtainable, supplies from home cannot be dispensed with."]

As many as seven hundred thousand families will be impeded in their labor.

[Mei Yao-ch'ên says: "Men will be lacking at the plough-tail." The allusion is to the system of dividing land into nine parts, each consisting of about 15 acres, the plot in the center being cultivated on behalf of the State by the tenants of the other eight. It was here also, so Tu Mu tells us, that their cottages were built and a well sunk, to be used by all in common. (See II. § 12, note.) In time of war, one of the families had to serve in the army, while the other seven contributed to its support. Thus, by a levy of 100,000 men (reckoning one able-bodied soldier to each family) the husbandry of 700,000 families would be affected.]

2 Hostile armies may face each other for years, striving for the victory which is decided in a single day. This being so, to remain in ignorance of the enemy's condition simply because one grudges the outlay of a hundred ounces of silver in honours and emoluments,

["For spies" is of course the meaning, though it would spoil the effect of this curiously elaborate exordium if spies were actually mentioned at this point.]

is the height of inhumanity.

[Sun Tzŭ's agreement is certainly ingenious. He begins by adverting to the frightful misery and vast expenditure of blood and treasure which war always brings in its train. Now, unless you are kept informed of the enemy's condition, and are ready to strike at the right moment, a war may drag on for years. The only way to get this information is to employ spies, and it is impossible to obtain trustworthy spies unless they are properly paid for their services. But it is surely false economy to grudge a comparatively trifling amount for this purpose, when every day that the war lasts eats up an incalculably greater sum. This grievous burden falls on the shoulders of the poor, and hence Sun Tzŭ concludes that to neglect the use of spies is nothing less than a crime against humanity.]

3 One who acts thus is no leader of men, no present help to his sovereign, no master of victory.

[This idea, that the true object of war is peace, has its root in the national temperament of the Chinese. Even so far back as 597 B.C., these memorable words were uttered by Prince Chüang of the Ch'u State: "The (Chinese) character for 'prowess' is made up of (the characters for) 'to stay' and 'a spear' (cessation of hostilities). Military prowess is seen in the repression of cruelty, the calling in of weapons, the preservation of the appointment of Heaven, the firm establishment of merit, the bestowal of happiness on the people, putting harmony between the princes, the diffusion of wealth."]

4 Thus, what enables the wise sovereign and the good general to strike and conquer, and achieve things beyond the reach of ordinary men, is *foreknowledge*.

[That is, knowledge of the enemy's dispositions, and what he means to do.]

5 Now this foreknowledge cannot be elicited from spirits; it cannot be obtained inductively from experience,

[Tu Mu's note is: "[knowledge of the enemy] cannot be gained by reasoning from other analogous cases."]

nor by any deductive calculation.

[Li Ch'üan says: "Quantities like length, breadth, distance and magnitude, are susceptible of exact mathematical determination; human actions cannot be so calculated."]

6 Knowledge of the enemy's dispositions can only be obtained from other men.

[Mei Yao-ch'ên has rather an interesting note: "Knowledge of the spirit-world is to be obtained by divination; information in natural science may be sought by inductive reasoning; the laws of the universe can be verified by mathematical calculation: but the dispositions of an enemy are ascertainable through spies and spies alone."]

7 Hence the use of spies, of whom there are five classes: (1) Local spies; (2) inward spies; (3) converted spies; (4) doomed spies; (5) surviving spies.

8 When these five kinds of spy are all at work, none can discover the secret system. This is called "divine manipulation of the threads." It is the sovereign's most precious faculty.

[Cromwell, one of the greatest and most practical of all cavalry leaders, had officers styled 'scout masters,' whose business it was to collect all possible information regarding the enemy, through scouts and spies, etc., and much of his success in war was traceable to the previous knowledge of the enemy's moves thus gained." [1]]

9 Having *local spies* means employing the services of the inhabitants of a district.

[Tu Mu says: "In the enemy's country, win people over by kind treatment, and use them as spies."]

10 Having *inward spies*, making use of officials of the enemy.

[Tu Mu enumerates the following classes as likely to do good service in this respect: "Worthy men who have been degraded from office, criminals who have undergone punishment; also, favourite concubines who are greedy for gold, men who are aggrieved at being in subordinate positions, or who have been passed over in the distribution of posts, others who are anxious that their side should be defeated in order that they may have a chance of displaying their ability and talents, fickle turncoats who always want to have a foot in each boat. Officials of these several kinds," he continues, "should be secretly approached and bound to one's interests by means of rich presents. In this way you will be able to find out the state of affairs in the enemy's country, ascertain the plans that are being formed against you, and moreover disturb the harmony and create a breach between the sovereign and his ministers." The necessity for extreme caution, however, in dealing with "inward spies," appears from an historical incident related by Ho Shih: "Lo Shang, Governor of I-Chou, sent his general Wei Po to attack the rebel Li Hsiung of Shu in his stronghold at P'i. After each side had experienced a number of victories and defeats, Li Hsiung had recourse to the services of a certain P'o-t'ai, a native of Wu-tu. He began to have him whipped until the blood came, and then sent him off to Lo Shang, whom he was to delude by offering to cooperate with him from inside the city, and to give a fire signal at the right moment for making a general assault. Lo Shang, confiding in these promises, march out all his best troops, and placed Wei Po and others at their head with orders to attack at P'o-t'ai's bidding. Meanwhile, Li Hsiung's general, Li Hsiang, had prepared an ambuscade on their line of march; and P'o-t'ai, having reared long scaling-ladders against the city walls, now lighted the beacon-fire. Wei Po's men raced up on seeing the signal and began climbing the ladders as fast as they could, while others were drawn up by ropes lowered from above. More than a hundred of Lo Shang's soldiers entered the city in this way, every one of whom was forthwith beheaded. Li Hsiung then charged with all his forces, both inside and outside the city, and routed the enemy completely." (This happened in 303 A.D. I do not know where Ho Shih got the story from. It is not given in the biography of Li Hsiung or that of his father Li T'e, *Chin Shu*, ch. 120, 121.)

11 Having *converted spies*, getting hold of the enemy's spies and using them for our own purposes.

[By means of heavy bribes and liberal promises detaching them from the enemy's service, and inducing them to carry back false information as well as to spy in turn on their own countrymen. On the other hand, Hsiao Shih-hsien says that we pretend not to have detected him, but contrive to let him carry away a false impression of what is going on. Several of the commentators accept this as an alternative definition; but that it is not what Sun Tzŭ meant is conclusively proved by his subsequent remarks about treating the converted spy generously (§ 21 sqq.). Ho Shih notes three occasions on which converted spies were used with conspicuous success: (1) by T'ien Tan in his defense of Chi-mo (see *supra*, p. 90); (2) by Chao Shê on his march to O-yü (see p. 57); and by the wily Fan Chu in 260 B.C., when Lien P'o was conducting a defensive campaign against Ch'in. The King of Chao strongly disapproved of Lien P'o's cautious and dilatory methods, which had been unable to avert a series of minor disasters, and therefore lent a ready ear to the reports of his spies, who had secretly gone over to the enemy and were already in Fan Chu's pay. They said: "The only thing which causes Ch'in anxiety is lest Chao Kua should be made general. Lien P'o they consider an easy opponent, who is sure to be vanquished in the long run." Now this Chao Kua was a son of the famous Chao Shê. From his boyhood, he had been wholly engrossed in the study of war and military matters, until at last he came to believe that there was no commander in the whole Empire who could stand against him. His father was much disquieted by this overweening conceit, and the flippancy with which he spoke of such a serious thing as war, and solemnly declared that if ever Kua was appointed general, he would bring ruin on the armies of Chao. This was the man who, in spite of earnest protests from his own mother and the veteran statesman Lin Hsiang-ju, was now sent to succeed Lien P'o. Needless to say, he proved no match for the redoubtable Po Ch'i and the great military power of Ch'in. He fell into a trap by which his army was divided into two and his communications cut; and after a desperate resistance lasting 46 days, during which the famished soldiers devoured one another, he was himself killed by an arrow, and his whole force, amounting, it is said, to 400,000 men, ruthlessly put to the sword.]

12 Having *doomed spies*, doing certain things openly for purposes of deception, and allowing our own spies to know of them and report them to the enemy.

[Tu Yu gives the best exposition of the meaning: "We ostentatiously do things calculated to deceive our own spies, who must be led to believe that they have been unwittingly disclosed. Then, when these spies are captured in the enemy's lines, they will make an entirely false report, and the enemy will take measures accordingly, only to find that we do something quite different. The spies will thereupon be put to death." As an example of doomed spies, Ho Shih mentions the prisoners released by Pan Ch'ao in his campaign against Yarkand. (See p. 132.) He also refers to T'ang Chien, who in 630 A.D. was sent by T'ai Tsung to lull the Turkish Kahn Chieh-li into fancied security, until Li Ching was able to deliver a crushing blow against him. Chang Yü says that the Turks revenged themselves by killing T'ang Chien, but this is a mistake, for we read in both the old and the New T'ang History (ch. 58, fol. 2 and ch. 89, fol. 8 respectively) that he escaped and lived on until 656. Li I-chi played a somewhat similar part in 203 B.C., when sent by the King of Han to open peaceful negotiations with Ch'i. He has certainly more claim to be described a "doomed spy", for the king of Ch'i, being subsequently attacked without warning by Han Hsin, and infuriated by what he considered the treachery of Li I-chi, ordered the unfortunate envoy to be boiled alive.]

13 *Surviving spies*, finally, are those who bring back news from the enemy's camp.

[This is the ordinary class of spies, properly so called, forming a regular part of the army. Tu Mu says: "Your surviving spy must be a man of keen intellect, though in outward appearance a fool; of shabby exterior, but with a will of iron. He must be active, robust, endowed with physical strength and courage; thoroughly accustomed to all sorts of dirty work, able to endure hunger and cold, and to put up with shame and ignominy." Ho Shih tells the following story of Ta'hsi Wu of the Sui dynasty: "When he was governor of Eastern Ch'in, Shen-wu of Ch'i made a hostile movement upon Sha-Yüan. The Emperor T'ai Tsu sent Ta-hsi Wu to spy upon the enemy. He was accompanied by two other men. All three were on horseback and wore the enemy's uniform. When it was dark, they dismounted a few hundred feet away from the enemy's camp and stealthily crept up to listen, until they succeeded in catching the passwords used in the army. Then they got on their horses again and boldly passed through the camp under the guise of night-watchmen; and more than once, happening to come across a soldier who was committing some breach of discipline, they actually stopped to give the culprit a sound cudgeling! Thus they managed to return with the fullest possible information about the enemy's dispositions, and received warm commendation from the Emperor, who in consequence of their report was able to inflict a severe defeat on his adversary."]

14 Hence it is that with none in the whole army are more intimate relations to be maintained than with spies.

[Tu Mu and Mei Yao-ch'ên point out that the spy is privileged to enter even the general's private sleeping-tent.]

None should be more liberally rewarded. In no other business should greater secrecy be preserved.

[Tu Mu gives a graphic touch: all communication with spies should be carried "mouth-to-ear." The following remarks on spies may be quoted from Turenne, who made perhaps larger use of them than any previous commander: "Spies are attached to those who give them most, he who pays them ill is never served. They should never be known to anybody; nor should they know one another. When they propose anything very material, secure their persons, or have in your possession their wives and children as hostages for their fidelity. Never communicate anything to them but what is absolutely necessary that they should know. [2]]

15 Spies cannot be usefully employed without a certain intuitive sagacity.

[Mei Yao-ch'ên says: "In order to use them, one must know fact from falsehood, and be able to discriminate between honesty and double-dealing." Wang Hsi in a different interpretation thinks more along the lines of "intuitive perception" and "practical intelligence." Tu Mu strangely refers these attributes to the spies themselves: "Before using spies we must assure ourselves as to their integrity of character and the extent of their experience and skill." But he continues: "A brazen face and a crafty disposition are more dangerous than mountains or rivers; it takes a man of genius to penetrate such." So that we are left in some doubt as to his real opinion on the passage."]

16 They cannot be properly managed without benevolence and straightforwardness.

[Chang Yü says: "When you have attracted them by substantial offers, you must treat them with absolute sincerity; then they will work for you with all their might."]

17 Without subtle ingenuity of mind, one cannot make certain of the truth of their reports.

[Mei Yao-ch'ên says: "Be on your guard against the possibility of spies going over to the service of the enemy."]

18 Be subtle! be subtle! and use your spies for every kind of business.

[Cf. VI. § 9.]

19 If a secret piece of news is divulged by a spy before the time is ripe, he must be put to death together with the man to whom the secret was told.

[Word for word, the translation here is: "If spy matters are heard before [our plans] are carried out," etc. Sun Tzŭ's main point in this passage is: Whereas you kill the spy himself "as a punishment for letting out the secret," the object of killing the other man is only, as Ch'ên Hao puts it, "to stop his mouth' and prevent news leaking any further. If it had already been repeated to others, this object would not be gained. Either way, Sun Tzŭ lays himself open to the charge of inhumanity, though Tu Mu tries to defend him by saying that the man deserves to be put to death, for the spy would certainly not have told the secret unless the other had been at pains to worm it out of him."]

20 Whether the object be to crush an army, to storm a city, or to assassinate an individual, it is always necessary to begin by finding out the names of the attendants, the aides-de- camp,

[Literally "visitors", is equivalent, as Tu Yu says, to "those whose duty it is to keep the general supplied with information," which naturally necessitates frequent interviews with him.]

the door-keepers and sentries of the general in command. Our spies must be commissioned to ascertain these.

[As the first step, no doubt towards finding out if any of these important functionaries can be won over by bribery.]

21 The enemy's spies who have come to spy on us must be sought out, tempted with bribes, led away and comfortably housed. Thus they will become converted spies and available for our service.

22 It is through the information brought by the converted spy that we are able to acquire and employ local and inward spies.

[Tu Yu says: "through conversion of the enemy's spies we learn the enemy's condition." And Chang Yü says: "We must tempt the converted spy into our service, because it is he that knows which of the local inhabitants are greedy of gain, and which of the officials are open to corruption."]

23 It is owing to his information, again, that we can cause the doomed spy to carry false tidings to the enemy.

[Chang Yü says, "because the converted spy knows how the enemy can best be deceived."]

24 Lastly, it is by his information that the surviving spy can be used on appointed occasions.

25 The end and aim of spying in all its five varieties is knowledge of the enemy; and this knowledge can only be derived, in the first instance, from the converted spy.

[As explained in §§ 22-24. He not only brings information himself, but makes it possible to use the other kinds of spy to advantage.]

Hence it is essential that the converted spy be treated with the utmost liberality.

26 Of old, the rise of the Yin dynasty

[Sun Tzŭ means the Shang dynasty, founded in 1766 B.C. Its name was changed to Yin by P'an Kêng in 1401.

was due to Î Chih

[Better known as Î Yin, the famous general and statesman who took part in Ch'êng T'ang's campaign against Chieh Kuei.]

who had served under the Hsia. Likewise, the rise of the Chou dynasty was due to Lü Ya

[Lü Shang rose to high office under the tyrant Chou Hsin, whom he afterwards helped to overthrow. Popularly known as T'ai Kung, a title bestowed on him by Wen Wang, he is said to have composed a treatise on war, erroneously identified with the *Liu T'ao*.]

who had served under the Yin.

[There is less precision in the Chinese than I have thought it well to introduce into my translation, and the commentaries on the passage are by no means explicit. But, having regard to the context, we can hardly doubt that Sun Tzŭ is holding up Î Chih and Lü Ya as illustrious examples of the converted spy, or something closely analogous. His suggestion is, that the Hsia and Yin dynasties were upset owing to the intimate knowledge of their weaknesses and shortcoming which these former ministers were able to impart to the other side. Mei Yao-ch'ên appears to resent any such aspersion on these historic names: "Î Yin and Lü Ya," he says, "were not rebels against the Government. Hsia could not employ the former, hence Yin employed him. Yin could not employ the latter, hence Hou employed him. Their great achievements were all for the good of the people." Ho Shih is also indignant: "How should two divinely inspired men such as I and Lu have acted as common spies? Sun Tzŭ's mention of them simply means that the proper use of the five classes of spies is a matter which requires men of the highest mental caliber like I and Lu, whose wisdom and capacity qualified them for the task. The above words only emphasize this point." Ho Shih believes then that the two heroes are mentioned on account of their supposed skill in the use of spies. But this is very weak.]

27 Hence it is only the enlightened ruler and the wise general who will use the highest intelligence of the army for purposes of spying and thereby they achieve great results.

[Tu Mu closes with a note of warning: "Just as water, which carries a boat from bank to bank, may also be the means of sinking it, so reliance on spies, while production of great results, is oft-times the cause of utter destruction."]

Spies are a most important element in war, because on them depends an army's ability to move.

[Chia Lin says that an army without spies is like a man with ears or eyes.]

[1] "Aids to Scouting," p. 2.
[2] "Marshal Turenne," p. 311.

THE ART OF WAR
SUN TZŬ

Translated from the Chinese

LIONEL GILES, M.A.

Contents

Chapter 1
Laying Plans

1 Sun Tzŭ said: The art of war is of vital importance to the State.

2 It is a matter of life and death, a road either to safety or to ruin. Hence it is a subject of inquiry which can on no account be neglected.

3 The art of war, then, is governed by five constant factors, to be taken into account in one's deliberations, when seeking to determine the conditions obtaining in the field.

4 These are:

(1) The Moral Law;

(2) Heaven;

(3) Earth;

(4) The Commander;

(5) Method and discipline.

5 The Moral Law causes the people to be in complete accord with their ruler, so that they will follow him regardless of their lives, undismayed by any danger.

6 Heaven signifies night and day, cold and heat, times and seasons.

7 Earth comprises distances, great and small; danger and security; open ground and narrow passes; the chances of life and death.

8 The Commander stands for the virtues of wisdom, sincerity, benevolence, courage and strictness.

9 By Method and Discipline are to be understood the marshalling of the army in its proper subdivisions, the gradations of rank among the officers, the maintenance of roads by which supplies may reach the army, and the control of military expenditure.

10 These five heads should be familiar to every general: he who knows them will be victorious; he who knows them not will fail.

11 Therefore, in your deliberations, when seeking to determine the military conditions, let them be made the basis of a comparison, in this wise:—

12

(1) Which of the two sovereigns is imbued with the Moral law?

(2) Which of the two generals has most ability?

(3) With whom lie the advantages derived from Heaven and Earth?

(4) On which side is Discipline most rigorously enforced?

(5) Which army is the stronger?

(6) On which side are officers and men more highly trained?

(7) In which army is there the greater constancy both in reward and punishment?

13 By means of these seven considerations I can forecast victory or defeat.

14 The general that hearkens to my counsel and acts upon it, will conquer: let such a one be retained in command! The general that hearkens not to my counsel nor acts upon it, will suffer defeat:—let such a one be dismissed!

15 While heeding the profit of my counsel, avail yourself also of any helpful circumstances over and beyond the ordinary rules.

16 According as circumstances are favorable, one should modify one's plans.

17 All warfare is based on deception.

18 Hence, when able to attack, we must seem unable; when using our forces, we must seem inactive; when we are near, we must make the enemy believe we are far away; when far away, we must make him believe we are near.

19 Hold out baits to entice the enemy. Feign disorder, and crush him.

20 If he is secure at all points, be prepared for him. If he is in superior strength, evade him.

21 If your opponent is of choleric temper, seek to irritate him. Pretend to be weak, that he may grow arrogant.

22 If he is taking his ease, give him no rest. If his forces are united, separate them.

23 Attack him where he is unprepared, appear where you are not expected.

24 These military devices, leading to victory, must not be divulged beforehand.

25 Now the general who wins a battle makes many calculations in his temple ere the battle is fought. The general who loses a battle makes but few calculations beforehand. Thus do many calculations lead to victory, and few calculations to defeat: how much more no calculation at all! It is by attention to this point that I can foresee who is likely to win or lose.

Chapter 2
Waging War

1 Sun Tzŭ said: In the operations of war, where there are in the field a thousand swift chariots, as many heavy chariots, and a hundred thousand mail-clad soldiers, with provisions enough to carry them a thousand *li*, the expenditure at home and at the front, including entertainment of guests, small items such as glue and paint, and sums spent on chariots and armor, will reach the total of a thousand ounces of silver per day. Such is the cost of raising an army of 100,000 men.

2 When you engage in actual fighting, if victory is long in coming, the men's weapons will grow dull and their ardor will be damped. If you lay siege to a town, you will exhaust your strength.

3 Again, if the campaign is protracted, the resources of the State will not be equal to the strain.

4 Now, when your weapons are dulled, your ardor damped, your strength exhausted and your treasure spent, other chieftains will spring up to take advantage of your extremity. Then no man, however wise, will be able to avert the consequences that must ensue.

5 Thus, though we have heard of stupid haste in war, cleverness has never been seen associated with long delays.

6 There is no instance of a country having benefited from prolonged warfare.

7 It is only one who is thoroughly acquainted with the evils of war that can thoroughly understand the profitable way of carrying it on.

8 The skillful soldier does not raise a second levy, neither are his supply-wagons loaded more than twice.

9 Bring war material with you from home, but forage on the enemy. Thus the army will have food enough for its needs.

10 Poverty of the State exchequer causes an army to be maintained by contributions from a distance. Contributing to maintain an army at a distance causes the people to be impoverished.

11 On the other hand, the proximity of an army causes prices to go up; and high prices cause the people's substance to be drained away.

12 When their substance is drained away, the peasantry will be afflicted by heavy exactions.

13, 14 With this loss of substance and exhaustion of strength, the homes of the people will be stripped bare, and three-tenths of their incomes will be dissipated; while Government expenses for broken chariots, worn-out horses, breast-plates and helmets, bows and arrows, spears and shields, protective mantlets, draught-oxen and heavy wagons, will amount to four-tenths of its total revenue.

15 Hence a wise general makes a point of foraging on the enemy. One cartload of the enemy's provisions is equivalent to twenty of one's own, and likewise a single *picul*[1] of his provender is equivalent to twenty from one's own store.

1 Approximately 133 pounds

16 Now in order to kill the enemy, our men must be roused to anger; that there may be advantage from defeating the enemy, they must have their rewards.

17 Therefore in chariot fighting, when ten or more chariots have been taken, those should be rewarded who took the first. Our own flags should be substituted for those of the enemy, and the chariots mingled and used in conjunction with ours. The captured soldiers should be kindly treated and kept.

18 This is called using the conquered foe to augment one's own strength.

19 In war, then, let your great object be victory, not lengthy campaigns.

20 Thus it may be known that the leader of armies is the arbiter of the people's fate, the man on whom it depends whether the nation shall be in peace or in peril.

Chapter 3
Attack Stratagems

1 Sun Tzŭ said: In the practical art of war, the best thing of all is to take the enemy's country whole and intact; to shatter and destroy it is not so good. So, too, it is better to capture an army entire than to destroy it, to capture a regiment, a detachment or a company entire than to destroy them.

2 Hence to fight and conquer in all your battles is not supreme excellence; supreme excellence consists in breaking the enemy's resistance without fighting.

3 Thus the highest form of generalship is to baulk the enemy's plans; the next best is to prevent the junction of the enemy's forces; the next in order is to attack the enemy's army in the field; and the worst policy of all is to besiege walled cities.

4 The rule is, not to besiege walled cities if it can possibly be avoided. The preparation of mantlets, movable shelters, and various implements of war, will take up three whole months; and the piling up of mounds over against the walls will take three months more.

5 The general, unable to control his irritation, will launch his men to the assault like swarming ants, with the result that one-third of his men are slain, while the town still remains untaken. Such are the disastrous effects of a siege.

6 Therefore the skillful leader subdues the enemy's troops without any fighting; he captures their cities without laying siege to them; he overthrows their kingdom without lengthy operations in the field.

7 With his forces intact he will dispute the mastery of the Empire, and thus, without losing a man, his triumph will be complete. This is the method of attacking by stratagem.

8 It is the rule in war, if our forces are ten to the enemy's one, to surround him; if five to one, to attack him; if twice as numerous, to divide our army into two.

9 If equally matched, we can offer battle; if slightly inferior in numbers, we can avoid the enemy; if quite unequal in every way, we can flee from him.

10 Hence, though an obstinate fight may be made by a small force, in the end it must be captured by the larger force.

11 Now the general is the bulwark of the State: if the bulwark is complete at all points; the State will be strong; if the bulwark is defective, the State will be weak.

12 There are three ways in which a ruler can bring misfortune upon his army:—

13 (1) By commanding the army to advance or to retreat, being ignorant of the fact that it cannot obey. This is called hobbling the army.

14 (2) By attempting to govern an army in the same way as he administers a kingdom, being ignorant of the conditions which obtain in an army. This causes restlessness in the soldier's minds.

15 (3) By employing the officers of his army without discrimination, through ignorance of the military principle of adaptation to circumstances. This shakes the confidence of the soldiers.

16 But when the army is restless and distrustful, trouble is sure to come from the other feudal princes. This is simply bringing anarchy into the army, and flinging victory away.

17 Thus we may know that there are five essentials for victory:

(1) He will win who knows when to fight and when not to fight.

(2) He will win who knows how to handle both superior and inferior forces.

(3) He will win whose army is animated by the same spirit throughout all its ranks.

(4) He will win who, prepared himself, waits to take the enemy unprepared.

(5) He will win who has military capacity and is not interfered with by the sovereign.

18 Hence the saying: If you know the enemy and know yourself, you need not fear the result of a hundred battles. If you know yourself but not the enemy, for every victory gained you will also suffer a defeat. If you know neither the enemy nor yourself, you will succumb in every battle.

Chapter 4
Tactical Dispositions

1 Sun Tzŭ said: The good fighters of old first put themselves beyond the possibility of defeat, and then waited for an opportunity of defeating the enemy.

2 To secure ourselves against defeat lies in our own hands, but the opportunity of defeating the enemy is provided by the enemy himself.

3 Thus the good fighter is able to secure himself against defeat, but cannot make certain of defeating the enemy.

4 Hence the saying: One may *know* how to conquer without being able to *do* it.

5 Security against defeat implies defensive tactics; ability to defeat the enemy means taking the offensive.

6 Standing on the defensive indicates insufficient strength; attacking, a superabundance of strength.

7 The general who is skilled in defense hides in the most secret recesses of the earth; he who is skilled in attack flashes forth from the topmost heights of heaven. Thus on the one hand we have ability to protect ourselves; on the other, a victory that is complete.

8 To see victory only when it is within the ken of the common herd is not the acme of excellence.

9 Neither is it the acme of excellence if you fight and conquer and the whole Empire says, "Well done!"

10 To lift an autumn hair is no sign of great strength; to see sun and moon is no sign of sharp sight; to hear the noise of thunder is no sign of a quick ear.

11 What the ancients called a clever fighter is one who not only wins, but excels in winning with ease.

12 Hence his victories bring him neither reputation for wisdom nor credit for courage.

13 He wins his battles by making no mistakes. Making no mistakes is what establishes the certainty of victory, for it means conquering an enemy that is already defeated.

14 Hence the skillful fighter puts himself into a position which makes defeat impossible, and does not miss the moment for defeating the enemy.

15 Thus it is that in war the victorious strategist only seeks battle after the victory has been won, whereas he who is destined to defeat first fights and afterwards looks for victory.

16 The consummate leader cultivates the moral law, and strictly adheres to method and discipline; thus it is in his power to control success.

17 In respect of military method, we have, firstly, Measurement; secondly, Estimation of quantity; thirdly, Calculation; fourthly, Balancing of chances; fifthly, Victory.

18 Measurement owes its existence to Earth; Estimation of quantity to Measurement; Calculation to Estimation of quantity; Balancing of chances to Calculation; and Victory to Balancing of chances.

19 A victorious army opposed to a routed one, is as a pound's weight placed in the scale against a single grain.

20 The onrush of a conquering force is like the bursting of pent-up waters into a chasm a thousand fathoms deep. So much for tactical dispositions.

Chapter 5
Energy

1 Sun Tzŭ said: The control of a large force is the same principle as the control of a few men: it is merely a question of dividing up their numbers.

2 Fighting with a large army under your command is nowise different from fighting with a small one: it is merely a question of instituting signs and signals.

3 To ensure that your whole host may withstand the brunt of the enemy's attack and remain unshaken—this is effected by maneuvers direct and indirect.

4 That the impact of your army may be like a grindstone dashed against an egg—this is effected by the science of weak points and strong.

5 In all fighting, the direct method may be used for joining battle, but indirect methods will be needed in order to secure victory.

6 Indirect tactics, efficiently applied, are inexhaustible as Heaven and Earth, unending as the flow of rivers and streams; like the sun and moon, they end but to begin anew; like the four seasons, they pass away but to return once more.

7 There are not more than five musical notes, yet the combinations of these five give rise to more melodies than can ever be heard.

8 There are not more than five primary colours (blue, yellow, red, white, and black), yet in combination they produce more hues than can ever be seen.

9 There are not more than five cardinal tastes (sour, acrid, salt, sweet, bitter), yet combinations of them yield more flavours than can ever be tasted.

10 In battle, there are not more than two methods of attack—the direct and the indirect; yet these two in combination give rise to an endless series of maneuvers.

11 The direct and the indirect lead on to each other in turn. It is like moving in a circle—you never come to an end. Who can exhaust the possibilities of their combination?

12 The onset of troops is like the rush of a torrent which will even roll stones along in its course.

13 The quality of decision is like the well-timed swoop of a falcon which enables it to strike and destroy its victim.

14 Therefore the good fighter will be terrible in his onset, and prompt in his decision.

15 Energy may be likened to the bending of a crossbow; decision, to the releasing of the trigger.

16 Amid the turmoil and tumult of battle, there may be seeming disorder and yet no real disorder at all; amid confusion and chaos, your array may be without head or tail, yet it will be proof against defeat.

17 Simulated disorder postulates perfect discipline; simulated fear postulates courage; simulated weakness postulates strength.

18 Hiding order beneath the cloak of disorder is simply a question of subdivision; concealing courage under a show of timidity presupposes a fund of latent energy; masking strength with weakness is to be effected by tactical dispositions.

19 Thus one who is skillful at keeping the enemy on the move maintains deceitful appearances, according to which the enemy will act. He sacrifices something, that the enemy may snatch at it.

20 By holding out baits, he keeps him on the march; then with a body of picked men he lies in wait for him.

21 The clever combatant looks to the effect of combined energy, and does not require too much from individuals. Hence his ability to pick out the right men and utilize combined energy.

22 When he utilizes combined energy, his fighting men become as it were like unto rolling logs or stones. For it is the nature of a log or stone to remain motionless on level ground, and to move when on a slope; if four-cornered, to come to a standstill, but if round-shaped, to go rolling down.

23 Thus the energy developed by good fighting men is as the momentum of a round stone rolled down a mountain thousands of feet in height. So much on the subject of energy.

Chapter 6

Weak Points and Strong

1 Sun Tzŭ said: Whoever is first in the field and awaits the coming of the enemy, will be fresh for the fight; whoever is second in the field and has to hasten to battle, will arrive exhausted.

2 Therefore the clever combatant imposes his will on the enemy, but does not allow the enemy's will to be imposed on him.

3 By holding out advantages to him, he can cause the enemy to approach of his own accord; or, by inflicting damage, he can make it impossible for the enemy to draw near.

4 If the enemy is taking his ease, he can harass him; if well supplied with food, he can starve him out; if quietly encamped, he can force him to move.

5 Appear at points which the enemy must hasten to defend; march swiftly to places where you are not expected.

6 An army may march great distances without distress, if it marches through country where the enemy is not.

7 You can be sure of succeeding in your attacks if you only attack places which are undefended. You can ensure the safety of your defense if you only hold positions that cannot be attacked.

8 Hence that general is skillful in attack whose opponent does not know what to defend; and he is skillful in defense whose opponent does not know what to attack.

9 O divine art of subtlety and secrecy! Through you we learn to be invisible, through you inaudible; and hence we can hold the enemy's fate in our hands.

10 You may advance and be absolutely irresistible, if you make for the enemy's weak points; you may retire and be safe from pursuit if your movements are more rapid than those of the enemy.

11 If we wish to fight, the enemy can be forced to an engagement even though he be sheltered behind a high rampart and a deep ditch. All we need do is attack some other place that he will be obliged to relieve.

12 If we do not wish to fight, we can prevent the enemy from engaging us even though the lines of our encampment be merely traced out on the ground. All we need do is to throw something odd and unaccountable in his way.

13 By discovering the enemy's dispositions and remaining invisible ourselves, we can keep our forces concentrated, while the enemy's must be divided.

14 We can form a single united body, while the enemy must split up into fractions. Hence there will be a whole pitted against separate parts of a whole, which means that we shall be many to the enemy's few.

15 And if we are able thus to attack an inferior force with a superior one, our opponents will be in dire straits.

16 The spot where we intend to fight must not be made known; for then the enemy will have to prepare against a possible attack at several different points; and his forces being thus distributed in many directions, the numbers we shall have to face at any given point will be proportionately few.

17 For should the enemy strengthen his van, he will weaken his rear; should he strengthen his rear, he will weaken his van; should he strengthen his left, he will weaken his right; should he strengthen his right, he will weaken his left. If he sends reinforcements everywhere, he will everywhere be weak.

18 Numerical weakness comes from having to prepare against possible attacks; numerical strength, from compelling our adversary to make these preparations against us.

19 Knowing the place and the time of the coming battle, we may concentrate from the greatest distances in order to fight.

20 But if neither time nor place be known, then the left wing will be impotent to succor the right, the right equally impotent to succor the left, the van unable to relieve the rear, or the rear to support the van. How much more so if the furthest portions of the army are anything under a hundred *li* apart, and even the nearest are separated by several *li!*

21 Though according to my estimate the soldiers of Yüeh exceed our own in number, that shall advantage them nothing in the matter of victory. I say then that victory can be achieved.

22 Though the enemy be stronger in numbers, we may prevent him from fighting. Scheme so as to discover his plans and the likelihood of their success.

23 Rouse him, and learn the principle of his activity or inactivity. Force him to reveal himself, so as to find out his vulnerable spots.

24 Carefully compare the opposing army with your own, so that you may know where strength is superabundant and where it is deficient.

25 In making tactical dispositions, the highest pitch you can attain is to conceal them; conceal your dispositions, and you will be safe from the prying of the subtlest spies, from the machinations of the wisest brains.

26 How victory may be produced for them out of the enemy's own tactics—that is what the multitude cannot comprehend.

27 All men can see the tactics whereby I conquer, but what none can see is the strategy out of which victory is evolved.

28 Do not repeat the tactics which have gained you one victory, but let your methods be regulated by the infinite variety of circumstances.

29 Military tactics are like unto water; for water in its natural course runs away from high places and hastens downwards.

30 So in war, the way is to avoid what is strong and to strike at what is weak.

31 Water shapes its course according to the nature of the ground over which it flows; the soldier works out his victory in relation to the foe whom he is facing.

32 Therefore, just as water retains no constant shape, so in warfare there are no constant conditions.

33 He who can modify his tactics in relation to his opponent and thereby succeed in winning, may be called a heaven-born captain.

34 The five elements (water, fire, wood, metal, earth) are not always equally predominant; the four seasons make way for each other in turn. There are short days and long; the moon has its periods of waning and waxing.

Chapter 7
Maneuvering

1 Sun Tzŭ said: In war, the general receives his commands from the sovereign.

2 Having collected an army and concentrated his forces, he must blend and harmonize the different elements thereof before pitching his camp.

3 After that, comes tactical maneuvering, than which there is nothing more difficult. The difficulty of tactical maneuvering consists in turning the devious into the direct, and misfortune into gain.

4 Thus, to take a long and circuitous route, after enticing the enemy out of the way, and though starting after him, to contrive to reach the goal before him, shows knowledge of the artifice of deviation.

5 Maneuvering with an army is advantageous, with an undisciplined multitude, most dangerous.

6 If you set a fully equipped army in march in order to snatch an advantage, the chances are that you will be too late. On the other hand, to detach a flying column for the purpose involves the sacrifice of its baggage and stores.

7 Thus, if you order your men to roll up their buff-coats, and make forced marches without halting day or night, covering

double the usual distance at a stretch, doing a hundred *li* in order to wrest an advantage, the leaders of all your three divisions will fall into the hands of the enemy.

8 The stronger men will be in front, the jaded ones will fall behind, and on this plan only one-tenth of your army will reach its destination.

9 If you march fifty *li* in order to outmaneuver the enemy, you will lose the leader of your first division, and only half your force will reach the goal.

10 If you march thirty *li* with the same object, two-thirds of your army will arrive.

11 We may take it then that an army without its baggage-train is lost; without provisions it is lost; without bases of supply it is lost.

12 We cannot enter into alliances until we are acquainted with the designs of our neighbours.

13 We are not fit to lead an army on the march unless we are familiar with the face of the country—its mountains and forests, its pitfalls and precipices, its marshes and swamps.

14 We shall be unable to turn natural advantages to account unless we make use of local guides.

15 In war, practice dissimulation, and you will succeed. Move only if there is a real advantage to be gained.

16 Whether to concentrate or to divide your troops, must be decided by circumstances.

17 Let your rapidity be that of the wind, your compactness that of the forest.

18 In raiding and plundering be like fire, in immovability like a mountain.

19 Let your plans be dark and impenetrable as night, and when you move, fall like a thunderbolt.

20 When you plunder a countryside, let the spoil be divided amongst your men; when you capture new territory, cut it up into allotments for the benefit of the soldiery.

21 Ponder and deliberate before you make a move.

22 He will conquer who has learnt the artifice of deviation. Such is the art of maneuvering.

23 The Book of Army Management says: On the field of battle, the spoken word does not carry far enough: hence the institution of gongs and drums. Nor can ordinary objects be seen clearly enough: hence the institution of banners and flags.

24 Gongs and drums, banners and flags, are means whereby the ears and eyes of the host may be focused on one particular point.

25 The host thus forming a single united body, is it impossible either for the brave to advance alone, or for the cowardly to retreat alone. This is the art of handling large masses of men.

26 In night-fighting, then, make much use of signal-fires and drums, and in fighting by day, of flags and banners, as a means of influencing the ears and eyes of your army.

27 A whole army may be robbed of its spirit; a commander-in-chief may be robbed of his presence of mind.

28 Now a soldier's spirit is keenest in the morning; by noonday it has begun to flag; and in the evening, his mind is bent only on returning to camp.

29 A clever general, therefore, avoids an army when its spirit is keen, but attacks it when it is sluggish and inclined to return. This is the art of studying moods.

30 Disciplined and calm, to await the appearance of disorder and hubbub amongst the enemy:—this is the art of retaining self-possession.

31 To be near the goal while the enemy is still far from it, to wait at ease while the enemy is toiling and struggling, to be well-fed while the enemy is famished:—this is the art of husbanding one's strength.

32 To refrain from intercepting an enemy whose banners are in perfect order, to refrain from attacking an army drawn up in calm and confident array:—this is the art of studying circumstances.

33 It is a military axiom not to advance uphill against the enemy, nor to oppose him when he comes downhill.

34 Do not pursue an enemy who simulates flight; do not attack soldiers whose temper is keen.

35 Do not swallow a bait offered by the enemy. Do not interfere with an army that is returning home.

36 When you surround an army, leave an outlet free. Do not press a desperate foe too hard.

37 Such is the art of warfare.

Chapter 8
Variation of Tactics

1 Sun Tzŭ said: In war, the general receives his commands from the sovereign, collects his army and concentrates his forces.

2 When in difficult country, do not encamp. In country where high roads intersect, join hands with your allies. Do not linger in dangerously isolated positions. In hemmed-in situations, you must resort to stratagem. In a desperate position, you must fight.

3 There are roads which must not be followed, armies which must be not attacked, towns which must not be besieged, positions which must not be contested, commands of the sovereign which must not be obeyed.

4 The general who thoroughly understands the advantages that accompany variation of tactics knows how to handle his troops.

5 The general who does not understand these, may be well acquainted with the configuration of the country, yet he will not be able to turn his knowledge to practical account.

6 So, the student of war who is unversed in the art of war of varying his plans, even though he be acquainted with the Five Advantages, will fail to make the best use of his men.

7 Hence in the wise leader's plans, considerations of advantage and of disadvantage will be blended together.

8 If our expectation of advantage be tempered in this way, we may succeed in accomplishing the essential part of our schemes.

9 If, on the other hand, in the midst of difficulties we are always ready to seize an advantage, we may extricate ourselves from misfortune.

10 Reduce the hostile chiefs by inflicting damage on them; and make trouble for them, and keep them constantly engaged; hold out specious allurements, and make them rush to any given point.

11 The art of war teaches us to rely not on the likelihood of the enemy's not coming, but on our own readiness to receive him; not on the chance of his not attacking, but rather on the fact that we have made our position unassailable.

12 There are five dangerous faults which may affect a general:

(1) recklessness, which leads to destruction;

(2) cowardice, which leads to capture;

(3) hasty temper, which can be provoked by insults;

(4) a delicacy of honour which is sensitive to shame;

(5) over-solicitude for his men, which exposes him to worry and trouble.

13 These are the five besetting sins of a general, ruinous to the conduct of war.

14 When an army is overthrown and its leader slain, the cause will surely be found among these five dangerous faults. Let them be a subject of meditation.

Chapter 9

The Army on the March

1 Sun Tzŭ said: We come now to the question of encamping the army, and observing signs of the enemy. Pass quickly over mountains, and keep in the neighborhood of valleys.

2 Camp in high places, facing the sun. Do not climb heights in order to fight. So much for mountain warfare.

3 After crossing a river, you should get far away from it.

4 When an invading force crosses a river in its onward march, do not advance to meet it in mid-stream. It will be best to let half the army get across, and then deliver your attack.

5 If you are anxious to fight, you should not go to meet the invader near a river which he has to cross.

6 Moor your craft higher up than the enemy, and facing the sun. Do not move up-stream to meet the enemy. So much for river warfare.

7 In crossing salt-marshes, your sole concern should be to get over them quickly, without any delay.

8 If forced to fight in a salt-marsh, you should have water and grass near you, and get your back to a clump of trees. So much for operations in salt-marshes.

9 In dry, level country, take up an easily accessible position with rising ground to your right and on your rear, so that the danger may be in front, and safety lie behind. So much for campaigning in flat country.

10 These are the four useful branches of military knowledge which enabled the Yellow Emperor to vanquish four several sovereigns.

11 All armies prefer high ground to low, and sunny places to dark.

12 If you are careful of your men, and camp on hard ground, the army will be free from disease of every kind, and this will spell victory.

13 When you come to a hill or a bank, occupy the sunny side, with the slope on your right rear. Thus you will at once act for the benefit of your soldiers and utilize the natural advantages of the ground.

14 When, in consequence of heavy rains up-country, a river which you wish to ford is swollen and flecked with foam, you must wait until it subsides.

15 Country in which there are precipitous cliffs with torrents running between, deep natural hollows, confined places, tangled thickets, quagmires and crevasses, should be left with all possible speed and not approached.

16 While we keep away from such places, we should get the enemy to approach them; while we face them, we should let the enemy have them on his rear.

17 If in the neighborhood of your camp there should be any hilly country, ponds surrounded by aquatic grass, hollow basins filled with reeds, or woods with thick undergrowth, they must be carefully routed out and searched; for these are places where men in ambush or insidious spies are likely to be lurking.

18 When the enemy is close at hand and remains quiet, he is relying on the natural strength of his position.

19 When he keeps aloof and tries to provoke a battle, he is anxious for the other side to advance

20 If his place of encampment is easy of access, he is tendering a bait.

21 Movement amongst the trees of a forest shows that the **enemy is advancing**. The appearance of a number of screens in the midst of thick grass means that the enemy wants to make us suspicious.

22 The rising of birds in their flight is the sign of an ambuscade. Startled beasts indicate that a sudden attack is coming.

23 When there is dust rising in a high column, it is the sign of chariots advancing; when the dust is low, but spread over a wide area, it betokens the approach of infantry. When it branches out in different directions, it shows that parties have been sent to collect firewood. A few clouds of dust moving to and fro signify that the army is encamping.

24 Humble words and increased preparations are signs that the enemy is about to advance. Violent language and driving forward as if to the attack are signs that he will retreat.

25 When the light chariots come out first and take up a position on the wings, it is a sign that the enemy is forming for battle.

26 Peace proposals unaccompanied by a sworn covenant indicate a plot.

27 When there is much running about and the soldiers fall into rank, it means that the critical moment has come.

28 When some are seen advancing and some retreating, it is a lure.

29 When the soldiers stand leaning on their spears, they are faint from want of food.

30 If those who are sent to draw water begin by drinking themselves, the army is suffering from thirst.

31 If the enemy sees an advantage to be gained and makes no effort to secure it, the soldiers are exhausted.

32 If birds gather on any spot, it is unoccupied. Clamor by night betokens nervousness.

33 If there is disturbance in the camp, the general's authority is weak. If the banners and flags are shifted about, sedition is afoot. If the officers are angry, it means that the men are weary.

34 When an army feeds its horses with grain and kills its cattle for food, and when the men do not hang their cooking-pots over the camp-fires, showing that they will not return to their tents, you may know that they are determined to fight to the death.

35 The sight of men whispering together in small knots or speaking in subdued tones points to disaffection amongst the rank and file.

36 Too frequent rewards signify that the enemy is at the end of his resources; too many punishments betray a condition of dire distress.

37 To begin by bluster, but afterwards to take fright at the enemy's numbers, shows a supreme lack of intelligence.

38 When envoys are sent with compliments in their mouths, it is a sign that the enemy wishes for a truce.

39 If the enemy's troops march up angrily and remain facing ours for a long time without either joining battle or taking themselves off again, the situation is one that demands great vigilance and circumspection.

40 If our troops are no more in number than the enemy, that is amply sufficient; it only means that no direct attack can be made. What we can do is simply to concentrate all our available strength, keep a close watch on the enemy, and obtain reinforcements.

41 He who exercises no forethought but makes light of his opponents is sure to be captured by them.

42 If soldiers are punished before they have grown attached to you, they will not prove submissive; and, unless submissive, then will be practically useless. If, when the soldiers have become attached to you, punishments are not enforced, they will still be useless.

43 Therefore soldiers must be treated in the first instance with humanity, but kept under control by means of iron discipline. This is a certain road to victory.

44 If in training soldiers commands are habitually enforced, the army will be well-disciplined; if not, its discipline will be bad.

45 If a general shows confidence in his men but always insists on his orders being obeyed, the gain will be mutual.

Chapter 10
Terrain

1 Sun Tzŭ said: We may distinguish six kinds of terrain, to wit:

(1) Accessible ground;

(2) entangling ground;

(3) temporising ground;

(4) narrow passes;

(5) precipitous heights;

(6) positions at a great distance from the enemy.

2 Ground which can be freely traversed by both sides is called accessible.

3 With regard to ground of this nature, be before the enemy in occupying the raised and sunny spots, and carefully guard your line of supplies. Then you will be able to fight with advantage.

4 Ground which can be abandoned but is hard to re-occupy is called entangling.

5 From a position of this sort, if the enemy is unprepared, you may sally forth and defeat him. But if the enemy is prepared for your coming, and you fail to defeat him, then, return being impossible, disaster will ensue.

6 When the position is such that neither side will gain by making the first move, it is called temporizing ground.

7 In a position of this sort, even though the enemy should offer us an attractive bait, it will be advisable not to stir forth, but rather to retreat, thus enticing the enemy in his turn; then, when part of his army has come out, we may deliver our attack with advantage.

8 With regard to narrow passes, if you can occupy them first, let them be strongly garrisoned and await the advent of the enemy.

9 Should the enemy forestall you in occupying a pass, do not go after him if the pass is fully garrisoned, but only if it is weakly garrisoned.

10 With regard to precipitous heights, if you are beforehand with your adversary, you should occupy the raised and sunny spots, and there wait for him to come up.

11 If the enemy has occupied them before you, do not follow him, but retreat and try to entice him away.

12 If you are situated at a great distance from the enemy, and the strength of the two armies is equal, it is not easy to provoke a battle, and fighting will be to your disadvantage.

13 These six are the principles connected with Earth. The general who has attained a responsible post must be careful to study them.

14 Now an army is exposed to six several calamities, not arising from natural causes, but from faults for which the general is responsible. These are:

(1) Flight;

(2) insubordination;

(3) collapse;

(4) ruin;

(5) disorganisation;

(6) rout.

15 Other conditions being equal, if one force is hurled against another ten times its size, the result will be the *flight* of the former.

16 When the common soldiers are too strong and their officers too weak, the result is *insubordination*. When the officers are too strong and the common soldiers too weak, the result is *collapse*.

17 When the higher officers are angry and insubordinate, and on meeting the enemy give battle on their own account from a feeling of resentment, before the commander-in-chief can tell whether or no he is in a position to fight, the result is *ruin*.

18 When the general is weak and without authority; when his orders are not clear and distinct; when there are no fixed duties assigned to officers and men, and the ranks are formed in a slovenly haphazard manner, the result is utter *disorganization*.

19 When a general, unable to estimate the enemy's strength, allows an inferior force to engage a larger one, or hurls a weak detachment against a powerful one, and neglects to place picked soldiers in the front rank, the result must be a *rout*.

20 These are six ways of courting defeat, which must be carefully noted by the general who has attained a responsible post.

21 The natural formation of the country is the soldier's best ally; but a power of estimating the adversary, of controlling the forces of victory, and of shrewdly calculating difficulties, dangers and distances, constitutes the test of a great general.

22 He who knows these things, and in fighting puts his knowledge into practice, will win his battles. He who knows them not, nor practices them, will surely be defeated.

23 If fighting is sure to result in victory, then you must fight, even though the ruler forbid it; if fighting will not result in victory, then you must not fight even at the ruler's bidding.

24 The general who advances without coveting fame and retreats without fearing disgrace, whose only thought is to protect his country and do good service for his sovereign, is the jewel of the kingdom.

25 Regard your soldiers as your children, and they will follow you into the deepest valleys; look on them as your own beloved sons, and they will stand by you even unto death.

26 If, however, you are indulgent, but unable to make your authority felt; kind-hearted, but unable to enforce your commands; and incapable, moreover, of quelling disorder: then your soldiers must be likened to spoilt children; they are useless for any practical purpose.

27 If we know that our own men are in a condition to attack, but are unaware that the enemy is not open to attack, we have gone only halfway towards victory.

28 If we know that the enemy is open to attack, but are unaware that our own men are not in a condition to attack, we have gone only halfway towards victory.

29 If we know that the enemy is open to attack, and also know that our men are in a condition to attack, but are unaware that the nature of the ground makes fighting impracticable, we have still gone only halfway towards victory.

30 Hence the experienced soldier, once in motion, is never bewildered; once he has broken camp, he is never at a loss.

31 Hence the saying: If you know the enemy and know yourself, your victory will not stand in doubt; if you know Heaven and know Earth, you may make your victory complete.

Chapter 11

The Nine Situations

1 Sun Tzŭ said: The art of war recognizes nine varieties of ground:

(1) Dispersive ground;

(2) facile ground;

(3) contentious ground;

(4) open ground;

(5) ground of intersecting highways;

(6) serious ground;

(7) difficult ground;

(8) hemmed-in ground;

(9) desperate ground.

2 When a chieftain is fighting in his own territory, it is dispersive ground.

3 When he has penetrated into hostile territory, but to no great distance, it is facile ground.

4 Ground the possession of which imports great advantage to either side, is contentious ground.

5 Ground on which each side has liberty of movement is open ground.

6 Ground which forms the key to three contiguous states, so that he who occupies it first has most of the Empire at his command, is ground of intersecting highways.

7 When an army has penetrated into the heart of a hostile country, leaving a number of fortified cities in its rear, it is serious ground.

8 Mountain forests, rugged steeps, marshes and fens—all country that is hard to traverse: this is difficult ground.

9 Ground which is reached through narrow gorges, and from which we can only retire by tortuous paths, so that a small number of the enemy would suffice to crush a large body of our men: this is hemmed in ground.

10 Ground on which we can only be saved from destruction by fighting without delay, is desperate ground.

11 On dispersive ground, therefore, fight not. On facile ground, halt not. On contentious ground, attack not.

12 On open ground, do not try to block the enemy's way. On ground of intersecting highways, join hands with your allies.

13 On serious ground, gather in plunder. In difficult ground, keep steadily on the march.

14 On hemmed-in ground, resort to stratagem. On desperate ground, fight.

15 Those who were called skillful leaders of old knew how to drive a wedge between the enemy's front and rear; to prevent co-operation between his large and small divisions; to hinder the good troops from rescuing the bad, the officers from rallying their men.

16 When the enemy's men were scattered, they prevented them from concentrating; even when their forces were united, they managed to keep them in disorder.

17 When it was to their advantage, they made a forward move; when otherwise, they stopped still.

18 If asked how to cope with a great host of the enemy in orderly array and on the point of marching to the attack, I should say: "Begin by seizing something which your opponent holds dear; then he will be amenable to your will."

19 Rapidity is the essence of war: take advantage of the enemy's unreadiness, make your way by unexpected routes, and attack unguarded spots.

20 The following are the principles to be observed by an invading force: The further you penetrate into a country, the greater will be the solidarity of your troops, and thus the defenders will not prevail against you.

21 Make forays in fertile country in order to supply your army with food.

22 Carefully study the well-being of your men, and do not overtax them. Concentrate your energy and hoard your strength. Keep your army continually on the move, and devise unfathomable plans.

23 Throw your soldiers into positions whence there is no escape, and they will prefer death to flight. If they will face death, there is nothing they may not achieve. Officers and men alike will put forth their uttermost strength.

24 Soldiers when in desperate straits lose the sense of fear. If there is no place of refuge, they will stand firm. If they are in the heart of a hostile country, they will show a stubborn front. If there is no help for it, they will fight hard.

25 Thus, without waiting to be marshalled, the soldiers will be constantly on the *qui vive;* without waiting to be asked, they will do your will; without restrictions, they will be faithful; without giving orders, they can be trusted.

26 Prohibit the taking of omens, and do away with superstitious doubts. Then, until death itself comes, no calamity need be feared.

27 If our soldiers are not overburdened with money, it is not because they have a distaste for riches; if their lives are not unduly long, it is not because they are disinclined to longevity.

28 On the day they are ordered out to battle, your soldiers may weep, those sitting up bedewing their garments, and those lying down letting the tears run down their cheeks. But let them once be brought to bay, and they will display the courage of a Chu or a Kuei.

29 The skillful tactician may be likened to the *shuai-jan*. Now the *shuai-jan* is a snake that is found in the Ch'ang mountains. Strike at its head, and you will be attacked by its tail; strike at its tail, and you will be attacked by its head; strike at its middle, and you will be attacked by head and tail both.

30 Asked if an army can be made to imitate the *shuai-jan*, I should answer, Yes. For the men of Wu and the men of Yüeh are enemies; yet if they are crossing a river in the same boat and are caught by a storm, they will come to each other's assistance just as the left hand helps the right.

31 Hence it is not enough to put one's trust in the tethering of horses, and the burying of chariot wheels in the ground.

32 The principle on which to manage an army is to set up one standard of courage which all must reach.

33 How to make the best of both strong and weak—that is a question involving the proper use of ground.

34 Thus the skilful general conducts his army just as though he were leading a single man, willy-nilly, by the hand.

35 It is the business of a general to be quiet and thus ensure secrecy; upright and just, and thus maintain order.

36 He must be able to mystify his officers and men by false reports and appearances, and thus keep them in total ignorance.

37 By altering his arrangements and changing his plans, he keeps the enemy without definite knowledge. By shifting his camp and taking circuitous routes, he prevents the enemy from anticipating his purpose.

38 At the critical moment, the leader of an army acts like one who has climbed up a height and then kicks away the ladder behind him. He carries his men deep into hostile territory before he shows his hand.

39 He burns his boats and breaks his cooking-pots; like a shepherd driving a flock of sheep, he drives his men this way and that, and none knows whither he is going.

40 To muster his host and bring it into danger:—this may be termed the business of the general.

41 The different measures suited to the nine varieties of ground; the expediency of aggressive or defensive tactics; and the fundamental laws of human nature: these are things that must most certainly be studied.

42 When invading hostile territory, the general principle is, that penetrating deeply brings cohesion; penetrating but a short way means dispersion.

43 When you leave your own country behind, and take your army across neighborhood territory, you find yourself on critical ground. When there are means of communication on all four sides, the ground is one of intersecting highways.

44 When you penetrate deeply into a country, it is serious ground. When you penetrate but a little way, it is facile ground.

45 When you have the enemy's strongholds on your rear, and narrow passes in front, it is hemmed-in ground. When there is no place of refuge at all, it is desperate ground.

46 Therefore, on dispersive ground, I would inspire my men with unity of purpose. On facile ground, I would see that there is close connection between all parts of my army.

47 On contentious ground, I would hurry up my rear.

48 On open ground, I would keep a vigilant eye on my defenses. On ground of intersecting highways, I would consolidate my alliances.

49 On serious ground, I would try to ensure a continuous stream of supplies. On difficult ground, I would keep pushing on along the road.

50 On hemmed-in ground, I would block any way of retreat. On desperate ground, I would proclaim to my soldiers the hopelessness of saving their lives.

51 For it is the soldier's disposition to offer an obstinate resistance when surrounded, to fight hard when he cannot help himself, and to obey promptly when he has fallen into danger.

52 We cannot enter into alliance with neighbouring princes until we are acquainted with their designs. We are not fit to lead an army on the march unless we are familiar with the face of the country—its mountains and forests, its pitfalls and precipices, its marshes and swamps. We shall be unable to turn natural advantages to account unless we make use of local guides.

53 To be ignorant of any one of the following four or five principles does not befit a warlike prince.

54 When a warlike prince attacks a powerful state, his generalship shows itself in preventing the concentration of the enemy's

forces. He overawes his opponents, and their allies are prevented from joining against him.

55 Hence he does not strive to ally himself with all and sundry, nor does he foster the power of other states. He carries out his own secret designs, keeping his antagonists in awe. Thus he is able to capture their cities and overthrow their kingdoms.

56 Bestow rewards without regard to rule, issue orders without regard to previous arrangements; and you will be able to handle a whole army as though you had to do with but a single man.

57 Confront your soldiers with the deed itself; never let them know your design. When the outlook is bright, bring it before their eyes; but tell them nothing when the situation is gloomy.

58 Place your army in deadly peril, and it will survive; plunge it into desperate straits, and it will come off in safety.

59 For it is precisely when a force has fallen into harm's way that is capable of striking a blow for victory.

60 Success in warfare is gained by carefully accommodating ourselves to the enemy's purpose.

61 By persistently hanging on the enemy's flank, we shall succeed in the long run in killing the commander-in-chief.

62 This is called ability to accomplish a thing by sheer cunning.

63 On the day that you take up your command, block the frontier passes, destroy the official tallies, and stop the passage of all emissaries.

64 Be stern in the council-chamber, so that you may control the situation.

65 If the enemy leaves a door open, you must rush in.

66 Forestall your opponent by seizing what he holds dear, and subtly contrive to time his arrival on the ground.

67 Walk in the path defined by rule, and accommodate yourself to the enemy until you can fight a decisive battle.

68 At first, then, exhibit the coyness of a maiden, until the enemy gives you an opening; afterwards emulate the rapidity of a running hare, and it will be too late for the enemy to oppose you.

Chapter 12

The Attack by Fire

1 Sun Tzŭ said: There are five ways of attacking with fire. The first is to burn soldiers in their camp; the second is to burn stores; the third is to burn baggage-trains; the fourth is to burn arsenals and magazines; the fifth is to hurl dropping fire amongst the enemy.

2 In order to carry out an attack, we must have means available. The material for raising fire should always be kept in readiness.

3 There is a proper season for making attacks with fire, and special days for starting a conflagration.

4 The proper season is when the weather is very dry; the special days are those when the moon is in the constellations of the Sieve, the Wall, the Wing or the Cross-bar; for these four are all days of rising wind.

5 In attacking with fire, one should be prepared to meet five possible developments:

6 (1) When fire breaks out inside the enemy's camp, respond at once with an attack from without.

7 (2) If there is an outbreak of fire, but the enemy's soldiers remain quiet, bide your time and do not attack.

8 (3) When the force of the flames has reached its height, follow it up with an attack, if that is practicable; if not, stay where you are.

9 (4) If it is possible to make an assault with fire from without, do not wait for it to break out within, but deliver your attack at a favorable moment.

10 (5) When you start a fire, be to windward of it. Do not attack from the leeward.

11 A wind that rises in the daytime lasts long, but a night breeze soon falls.

12 In every army, the five developments connected with fire must be known, the movements of the stars calculated, and a watch kept for the proper days.

13 Hence those who use fire as an aid to the attack show intelligence; those who use water as an aid to the attack gain an accession of strength.

14 By means of water, an enemy may be intercepted, but not robbed of all his belongings.

15 Unhappy is the fate of one who tries to win his battles and succeed in his attacks without cultivating the spirit of enterprise; for the result is waste of time and general stagnation.

16 Hence the saying: The enlightened ruler lays his plans well ahead; the good general cultivates his resources.

17 Move not unless you see an advantage; use not your troops unless there is something to be gained; fight not unless the position is critical.

18 No ruler should put troops into the field merely to gratify his own spleen; no general should fight a battle simply out of pique.

19 If it is to your advantage, make a forward move; if not, stay where you are.

20 Anger may in time change to gladness; vexation may be succeeded by content.

21 But a kingdom that has once been destroyed can never come again into being; nor can the dead ever be brought back to life.

22 Hence the enlightened ruler is heedful, and the good general full of caution. This is the way to keep a country at peace and an army intact.

Chapter 13
The Use of Spies

1 Sun Tzŭ said: Raising a host of a hundred thousand men and marching them great distances entails heavy loss on the people and a drain on the resources of the State. The daily expenditure will amount to a thousand ounces of silver. There will be commotion at home and abroad, and men will drop down exhausted on the highways. As many as seven hundred thousand families will be impeded in their labor.

2 Hostile armies may face each other for years, striving for the victory which is decided in a single day. This being so, to remain in ignorance of the enemy's condition simply because one grudges the outlay of a hundred ounces of silver in honours and emoluments, is the height of inhumanity.

3 One who acts thus is no leader of men, no present help to his sovereign, no master of victory.

4 Thus, what enables the wise sovereign and the good general to strike and conquer, and achieve things beyond the reach of ordinary men, is *foreknowledge*.

5 Now this foreknowledge cannot be elicited from spirits; it cannot be obtained inductively from experience, nor by any deductive calculation.

6 Knowledge of the enemy's dispositions can only be obtained from other men.

7 Hence the use of spies, of whom there are five classes:

(1) Local spies;

(2) inward spies;

(3) converted spies;

(4) doomed spies;

(5) surviving spies.

8 When these five kinds of spy are all at work, none can discover the secret system. This is called "divine manipulation of the threads." It is the sovereign's most precious faculty.

9 Having *local spies* means employing the services of the inhabitants of a district.

10 Having *inward spies*, making use of officials of the enemy.

11 Having *converted spies*, getting hold of the enemy's spies and using them for our own purposes.

12 Having *doomed spies*, doing certain things openly for purposes of deception, and allowing our own spies to know of them and report them to the enemy.

13 *Surviving spies*, finally, are those who bring back news from the enemy's camp.

14 Hence it is that with none in the whole army are more intimate relations to be maintained than with spies. None should be more liberally rewarded. In no other business should greater secrecy be preserved.

15 Spies cannot be usefully employed without a certain intuitive sagacity.

16 They cannot be properly managed without benevolence and straightforwardness.

17 Without subtle ingenuity of mind, one cannot make certain of the truth of their reports.

18 Be subtle! be subtle! and use your spies for every kind of business.

19 If a secret piece of news is divulged by a spy before the time is ripe, he must be put to death together with the man to whom the secret was told.

20 Whether the object be to crush an army, to storm a city, or to assassinate an individual, it is always necessary to begin by finding out the names of the attendants, the aides-de-camp, the door-keepers and sentries of the general in command. Our spies must be commissioned to ascertain these.

21 The enemy's spies who have come to spy on us must be sought out, tempted with bribes, led away and comfortably housed. Thus they will become converted spies and available for our service.

22 It is through the information brought by the converted spy that we are able to acquire and employ local and inward spies.

23 It is owing to his information, again, that we can cause the doomed spy to carry false tidings to the enemy.

24 Lastly, it is by his information that the surviving spy can be used on appointed occasions.

25 The end and aim of spying in all its five varieties is knowledge of the enemy; and this knowledge can only be derived, in the first instance, from the converted spy. Hence it is essential that the converted spy be treated with the utmost liberality.

26 Of old, the rise of the Yin dynasty was due to Î Chih who had served under the Hsia. Likewise, the rise of the Chou dynasty was due to Lü Ya who had served under the Yin.

27 Hence it is only the enlightened ruler and the wise general who will use the highest intelligence of the army for purposes of spying and thereby they achieve great results. Spies are a most important element in war, because on them depends an army's ability to move.

THE TAO TE CHING,

OR

THE TAO AND ITS CHARACTERISTICS

by Lao Tzŭ

Translated by James Legge

Contents

PART I.

I

1 The Tao that can be trodden is not the enduring and unchanging Tao. The name that can be named is not the enduring and unchanging name.

2 (Conceived of as) having no name, it is the Originator of heaven and earth; (conceived of as) having a name, it is the Mother of all things.

3

Always without desire we must be found,
If its deep mystery we would sound;
But if desire always within us be,
Its outer fringe is all that we shall see.

4 Under these two aspects, it is really the same; but as development takes place, it receives the different names. Together we call them the Mystery. Where the Mystery is the deepest is the gate of all that is subtle and wonderful.

II

1 All in the world know the beauty of the beautiful, and in doing this they have (the idea of) what ugliness is; they all know the skill of the skilful, and in doing this they have (the idea of) what the want of skill is.

2 So it is that existence and non-existence give birth the one to (the idea of) the other; that difficulty and ease produce the one (the idea of) the other; that length and shortness fashion out the one the figure of the other; that (the ideas of) height and lowness arise from the contrast of the one with the other; that the musical notes and tones become harmonious through the relation of one with another; and that being before and behind give the idea of one following another.

3 Therefore the sage manages affairs without doing anything, and conveys his instructions without the use of speech.

4 All things spring up, and there is not one which declines to show itself; they grow, and there is no claim made for their ownership; they go through their processes, and there is no expectation (of a reward for the results). The work is accomplished, and there is no resting in it (as an achievement).

The work is done, but how no one can see;
'Tis this that makes the power not cease to be.

III

1 Not to value and employ men of superior ability is the way to keep the people from rivalry among themselves; not to prize articles which are difficult to procure is the way to keep them from becoming thieves; not to show them what is likely to excite their desires is the way to keep their minds from disorder.

2 Therefore the sage, in the exercise of his government, empties their minds, fills their bellies, weakens their wills, and strengthens their bones.

3 He constantly (tries to) keep them without knowledge and without desire, and where there are those who have knowledge, to keep them from presuming to act (on it). When there is this abstinence from action, good order is universal.

IV

1 The Tao is (like) the emptiness of a vessel; and in our employment of it we must be on our guard against all fulness. How deep and unfathomable it is, as if it were the Honoured Ancestor of all things!

2 We should blunt our sharp points, and unravel the complications of things; we should attemper our brightness, and bring

ourselves into agreement with the obscurity of others. How pure and still the Tao is, as if it would ever so continue!

3 I do not know whose son it is. It might appear to have been before God.

V

1 Heaven and earth do not act from (the impulse of) any wish to be benevolent; they deal with all things as the dogs of grass are dealt with. The sages do not act from (any wish to be) benevolent; they deal with the people as the dogs of grass are dealt with.

2 May not the space between heaven and earth be compared to a bellows?

'Tis emptied, yet it loses not its power;
'Tis moved again, and sends forth air the more.
Much speech to swift exhaustion lead we see;
Your inner being guard, and keep it free.

VI

The valley spirit dies not, aye the same;
The female mystery thus do we name.
Its gate, from which at first they issued forth,
Is called the root from which grew heaven and earth.
Long and unbroken does its power remain,
Used gently, and without the touch of pain.

VII

1 Heaven is long-enduring and earth continues long. The reason why heaven and earth are able to endure and continue thus long is because they do not live of, or for, themselves. This is how they are able to continue and endure.

2 Therefore the sage puts his own person last, and yet it is found in the foremost place; he treats his person as if it were foreign to him, and yet that person is preserved. Is it not because he has no personal and private ends, that therefore such ends are realised?

VIII

1 The highest excellence is like (that of) water. The excellence of water appears in its benefiting all things, and in its occupying, without striving (to the contrary), the low place which all men dislike. Hence (its way) is near to (that of) the Tao.

2 The excellence of a residence is in (the suitability of) the place; that of the mind is in abysmal stillness; that of associations is in their being with the virtuous; that of government is in its securing good order; that of (the conduct of) affairs is in its ability; and that of (the initiation of) any movement is in its timeliness.

3 And when (one with the highest excellence) does not wrangle (about his low position), no one finds fault with him.

IX

1 It is better to leave a vessel unfilled, than to attempt to carry it when it is full. If you keep feeling a point that has been sharpened, the point cannot long preserve its sharpness.

2 When gold and jade fill the hall, their possessor cannot keep them safe. When wealth and honours lead to arrogancy, this brings its evil on itself. When the work is done, and one's name is becoming distinguished, to withdraw into obscurity is the way of Heaven.

X

1 When the intelligent and animal souls are held together in one embrace, they can be kept from separating. When one gives undivided attention to the (vital) breath, and brings it to the utmost degree of pliancy, he can become as a (tender) babe. When he has cleansed away the most mysterious sights (of his imagination), he can become without a flaw.

2 In loving the people and ruling the state, cannot he proceed without any (purpose of) action? In the opening and shutting of his gates of heaven, cannot he do so as a female bird? While his intelligence reaches in every direction, cannot he (appear to) be without knowledge?

3 The Tao) produces (all things) and nourishes them; it produces them and does not claim them as its own; it does all, and yet does not boast of it; it presides over all, and yet does not control them. This is what is called 'The mysterious Quality' (of the Tao).

XI

The thirty spokes unite in the one nave; but it is on the empty space (for the axle), that the use of the wheel depends. Clay is fashioned into vessels; but it is on their empty hollowness, that their use depends. The door and windows are cut out (from the walls) to form an apartment; but it is on the empty space (within), that its use depends. Therefore, what has a (positive) existence serves for profitable adaptation, and what has not that for (actual) usefulness.

XII

1

Colour's five hues from th' eyes their sight will take;
Music's five notes the ears as deaf can make;

The flavours five deprive the mouth of taste;
The chariot course, and the wild hunting waste
Make mad the mind; and objects rare and strange,
Sought for, men's conduct will to evil change.

2 Therefore the sage seeks to satisfy (the craving of) the belly, and not the (insatiable longing of the) eyes. He puts from him the latter, and prefers to seek the former.

XIII

1 Favour and disgrace would seem equally to be feared; honour and great calamity, to be regarded as personal conditions (of the same kind).

2 What is meant by speaking thus of favour and disgrace? Disgrace is being in a low position (after the enjoyment of favour). The getting that (favour) leads to the apprehension (of losing it), and the losing it leads to the fear of (still greater calamity):—this is what is meant by saying that favour and disgrace would seem equally to be feared.

And what is meant by saying that honour and great calamity are to be (similarly) regarded as personal conditions? What makes me liable to great calamity is my having the body (which I call myself); if I had not the body, what great calamity could come to me?

3 Therefore he who would administer the kingdom, honouring it as he honours his own person, may be employed to govern it, and he who would administer it with the love which he bears to his own person may be entrusted with it.

XIV

1 We look at it, and we do not see it, and we name it 'the Equable.' We listen to it, and we do not hear it, and we name it 'the Inaudible.' We try to grasp it, and do not get hold of it, and we name it 'the Subtle.' With these three qualities, it cannot be made the subject of description; and hence we blend them together and obtain The One.

2 Its upper part is not bright, and its lower part is not obscure. Ceaseless in its action, it yet cannot be named, and then it again returns and becomes nothing. This is called the Form of the Formless, and the Semblance of the Invisible; this is called the Fleeting and Indeterminable.

3 We meet it and do not see its Front; we follow it, and do not see its Back. When we can lay hold of the Tao of old to direct the things of the present day, and are able to know it as it was of old in the beginning, this is called (unwinding) the clue of Tao.

XV

1 The skilful masters (of the Tao) in old times, with a subtle and exquisite penetration, comprehended its mysteries, and were deep (also) so as to elude men's knowledge. As they were thus beyond men's knowledge, I will make an effort to describe of what sort they appeared to be.

2 Shrinking looked they like those who wade through a stream in winter; irresolute like those who are afraid of all around them; grave like a guest (in awe of his host); evanescent like ice that is melting away; unpretentious like wood that has not been fashioned into anything; vacant like a valley, and dull like muddy water.

3 Who can (make) the muddy water (clear)? Let it be still, and it will gradually become clear. Who can secure the condition of rest? Let movement go on, and the condition of rest will gradually arise.

4 They who preserve this method of the Tao do not wish to be full (of themselves). It is through their not being full of themselves that they can afford to seem worn and not appear new and complete.

XVI

1 The (state of) vacancy should be brought to the utmost degree, and that of stillness guarded with unwearying vigour. All things alike go through their processes of activity, and (then) we see them return (to their original state). When things (in the vegetable world) have displayed their luxuriant growth, we see each of them return to its root. This returning to their root is what we call the state of stillness; and that stillness may be called a reporting that they have fulfilled their appointed end.

2 The report of that fulfilment is the regular, unchanging rule. To know that unchanging rule is to be intelligent; not to know it leads to wild movements and evil issues. The knowledge of that unchanging rule produces a (grand) capacity and forbearance, and that capacity and forbearance lead to a community (of feeling with all things). From this community of feeling comes a kingliness of character; and he who is king-like goes on to be heaven-like. In that likeness to heaven he possesses the Tao. Possessed of the Tao, he endures long; and to the end of his bodily life, is exempt from all danger of decay.

XVII

1 In the highest antiquity, (the people) did not know that there were (their rulers). In the next age they loved them and praised

them. In the next they feared them; in the next they despised them. Thus it was that when faith (in the Tao) was deficient (in the rulers) a want of faith in them ensued (in the people).

2 How irresolute did those (earliest rulers) appear, showing (by their reticence) the importance which they set upon their words! Their work was done and their undertakings were successful, while the people all said, 'We are as we are, of ourselves!'

XVIII

1 When the Great Tao (Way or Method) ceased to be observed, benevolence and righteousness came into vogue. (Then) appeared wisdom and shrewdness, and there ensued great hypocrisy.

2 When harmony no longer prevailed throughout the six kinships, filial sons found their manifestation; when the states and clans fell into disorder, loyal ministers appeared.

XIX

1 If we could renounce our sageness and discard our wisdom, it would be better for the people a hundredfold. If we could renounce our benevolence and discard our righteousness, the people would again become filial and kindly. If we could renounce our artful contrivances and discard our (scheming for) gain, there would be no thieves nor robbers.

2

Those three methods (of government)
Thought olden ways in elegance did fail
And made these names their want of worth to veil;
But simple views, and courses plain and true
Would selfish ends and many lusts eschew.

XX

1

When we renounce learning we have no troubles.
The (ready) 'yes,' and (flattering) 'yea;'—
Small is the difference they display.
But mark their issues, good and ill;—
What space the gulf between shall fill?

What all men fear is indeed to be feared; but how wide and without end is the range of questions (asking to be discussed)!

2 The multitude of men look satisfied and pleased; as if enjoying a full banquet, as if mounted on a tower in spring. I alone seem listless and still, my desires having as yet given no indication of their presence. I am like an infant which has not yet smiled. I look dejected and forlorn, as if I had no home to go to. The multitude of men all have enough and to spare. I alone seem to have lost everything. My mind is that of a stupid man; I am in a state of chaos.

Ordinary men look bright and intelligent, while I alone seem to be benighted. They look full of discrimination, while I alone am dull and confused. I seem to be carried about as on the sea, drifting as if I had nowhere to rest. All men have their spheres of action, while I alone seem dull and incapable, like a rude borderer. (Thus) I alone am different from other men, but I value the nursing-mother (the Tao).

XXI

The grandest forms of active force
From Tao come, their only source.
Who can of Tao the nature tell?
Our sight it flies, our touch as well.

Eluding sight, eluding touch,
The forms of things all in it crouch;
Eluding touch, eluding sight,
There are their semblances, all right.
Profound it is, dark and obscure;
Things' essences all there endure.
Those essences the truth enfold
Of what, when seen, shall then be told.
Now it is so; 'twas so of old.
Its name—what passes not away;
So, in their beautiful array,
Things form and never know decay.

How know I that it is so with all the beauties of existing things? By this (nature of the Tao).

XXII

1 The partial becomes complete; the crooked, straight; the empty, full; the worn out, new. He whose (desires) are few gets them; he whose (desires) are many goes astray.

2 Therefore the sage holds in his embrace the one thing (of humility), and manifests it to all the world. He is free from self-display, and therefore he shines; from self-assertion, and therefore he is distinguished; from self-boasting, and therefore his merit is acknowledged; from self-complacency, and therefore he acquires superiority. It is because he is thus free from striving that therefore no one in the world is able to strive with him.

3 That saying of the ancients that 'the partial becomes complete' was not vainly spoken:—all real completion is comprehended under it.

XXIII

4 Abstaining from speech marks him who is obeying the spontaneity of his nature. A violent wind does not last for a whole morning; a sudden rain does not last for the whole day. To whom is it that these (two) things are owing? To Heaven and Earth. If Heaven and Earth cannot make such (spasmodic) actings last long, how much less can man!

5 Therefore when one is making the Tao his business, those who are also pursuing it, agree with him in it, and those who are making the manifestation of its course their object agree with him in that; while even those who are failing in both these things agree with him where they fail.

6 Hence, those with whom he agrees as to the Tao have the happiness of attaining to it; those with whom he agrees as to its manifestation have the happiness of attaining to it; and those with whom he agrees in their failure have also the happiness of attaining (to the Tao). (But) when there is not faith sufficient (on his part), a want of faith (in him) ensues (on the part of the others).

XXIV

He who stands on his tiptoes does not stand firm; he who stretches his legs does not walk (easily). (So), he who displays himself does not shine; he who asserts his own views is not distinguished; he who vaunts himself does not find his merit acknowledged; he who is self-conceited has no superiority allowed to him. Such conditions, viewed from the standpoint of the Tao, are like remnants of food, or a tumour on the body, which all dislike. Hence those who pursue (the course) of the Tao do not adopt and allow them.

XXV

1 There was something undefined and complete, coming into existence before Heaven and Earth. How still it was and

formless, standing alone, and undergoing no change, reaching everywhere and in no danger (of being exhausted)! It may be regarded as the Mother of all things.

2 I do not know its name, and I give it the designation of the Tao (the Way or Course). Making an effort (further) to give it a name I call it The Great.

3 Great, it passes on (in constant flow). Passing on, it becomes remote. Having become remote, it returns. Therefore the Tao is great; Heaven is great; Earth is great; and the (sage) king is also great. In the universe there are four that are great, and the (sage) king is one of them.

4 Man takes his law from the Earth; the Earth takes its law from Heaven; Heaven takes its law from the Tao. The law of the Tao is its being what it is.

XXVI

1 Gravity is the root of lightness; stillness, the ruler of movement.

2 Therefore a wise prince, marching the whole day, does not go far from his baggage waggons. Although he may have brilliant prospects to look at, he quietly remains (in his proper place), indifferent to them. How should the lord of a myriad chariots carry himself lightly before the kingdom? If he do act lightly, he has lost his root (of gravity); if he proceed to active movement, he will lose his throne.

XXVII

1 The skilful traveller leaves no traces of his wheels or footsteps; the skilful speaker says nothing that can be found fault with or blamed; the skilful reckoner uses no tallies; the skilful closer needs no bolts or bars, while to open what he has shut will be impossible; the skilful binder uses no strings or knots, while

to unloose what he has bound will be impossible. In the same way the sage is always skilful at saving men, and so he does not cast away any man; he is always skilful at saving things, and so he does not cast away anything. This is called 'Hiding the light of his procedure.'

2 Therefore the man of skill is a master (to be looked up to) by him who has not the skill; and he who has not the skill is the helper of (the reputation of) him who has the skill. If the one did not honour his master, and the other did not rejoice in his helper, an (observer), though intelligent, might greatly err about them. This is called 'The utmost degree of mystery.'

XXVIII

1

Who knows his manhood's strength,
Yet still his female feebleness maintains;
As to one channel flow the many drains,
All come to him, yea, all beneath the sky.
Thus he the constant excellence retains;
The simple child again, free from all stains.
Who knows how white attracts,
Yet always keeps himself within black's shade,
The pattern of humility displayed,
Displayed in view of all beneath the sky;
He in the unchanging excellence arrayed,
Endless return to man's first state has made.
Who knows how glory shines,
Yet loves disgrace, nor e'er for it is pale;
Behold his presence in a spacious vale,
To which men come from all beneath the sky.
The unchanging excellence completes its tale;
The simple infant man in him we hail.

2 The unwrought material, when divided and distributed, forms vessels. The sage, when employed, becomes the Head of all the Officers (of government); and in his greatest regulations he employs no violent measures.

XXIX

1 If any one should wish to get the kingdom for himself, and to effect this by what he does, I see that he will not succeed. The kingdom is a spirit-like thing, and cannot be got by active doing. He who would so win it destroys it; he who would hold it in his grasp loses it.

2

The course and nature of things is such that
What was in front is now behind;
What warmed anon we freezing find.
Strength is of weakness oft the spoil;
The store in ruins mocks our toil.

Hence the sage puts away excessive effort, extravagance, and easy indulgence.

XXX

1 He who would assist a lord of men in harmony with the Tao will not assert his mastery in the kingdom by force of arms. Such a course is sure to meet with its proper return.

2 Wherever a host is stationed, briars and thorns spring up. In the sequence of great armies there are sure to be bad years.

3 A skilful (commander) strikes a decisive blow, and stops. He does not dare (by continuing his operations) to assert and complete his mastery. He will strike the blow, but will be on his guard against being vain or boastful or arrogant in consequence

of it. He strikes it as a matter of necessity; he strikes it, but not from a wish for mastery.

4 When things have attained their strong maturity they become old. This may be said to be not in accordance with the Tao: and what is not in accordance with it soon comes to an end.

XXXI

1 Now arms, however beautiful, are instruments of evil omen, hateful, it may be said, to all creatures. Therefore they who have the Tao do not like to employ them.

2 The superior man ordinarily considers the left hand the most honourable place, but in time of war the right hand. Those sharp weapons are instruments of evil omen, and not the instruments of the superior man;—he uses them only on the compulsion of necessity. Calm and repose are what he prizes; victory (by force of arms) is to him undesirable. To consider this desirable would be to delight in the slaughter of men; and he who delights in the slaughter of men cannot get his will in the kingdom.

3 On occasions of festivity to be on the left hand is the prized position; on occasions of mourning, the right hand. The second in command of the army has his place on the left; the general commanding in chief has his on the right;—his place, that is, is assigned to him as in the rites of mourning. He who has killed multitudes of men should weep for them with the bitterest grief; and the victor in battle has his place (rightly) according to those rites.

XXXII

1 The Tao, considered as unchanging, has no name.

2 Though in its primordial simplicity it may be small, the whole world dares not deal with (one embodying) it as a minister. If

a feudal prince or the king could guard and hold it, all would spontaneously submit themselves to him.

3 Heaven and Earth (under its guidance) unite together and send down the sweet dew, which, without the directions of men, reaches equally everywhere as of its own accord.

4 As soon as it proceeds to action, it has a name. When it once has that name, (men) can know to rest in it. When they know to rest in it, they can be free from all risk of failure and error.

5 The relation of the Tao to all the world is like that of the great rivers and seas to the streams from the valleys.

XXXIII

1 He who knows other men is discerning; he who knows himself is intelligent. He who overcomes others is strong; he who overcomes himself is mighty. He who is satisfied with his lot is rich; he who goes on acting with energy has a (firm) will.

2 He who does not fail in the requirements of his position, continues long; he who dies and yet does not perish, has longevity.

XXXIV

1 All-pervading is the Great Tao! It may be found on the left hand and on the right.

2 All things depend on it for their production, which it gives to them, not one refusing obedience to it. When its work is accomplished, it does not claim the name of having done it. It clothes all things as with a garment, and makes no assumption of being their lord;—it may be named in the smallest things. All things return (to their root and disappear), and do not know that it is it which presides over their doing so;—it may be named in the greatest things.

3 Hence the sage is able (in the same way) to accomplish his great achievements. It is through his not making himself great that he can accomplish them.

XXXV

1 To him who holds in his hands the Great Image (of the invisible Tao), the whole world repairs. Men resort to him, and receive no hurt, but (find) rest, peace, and the feeling of ease.

2 Music and dainties will make the passing guest stop (for a time). But though the Tao as it comes from the mouth, seems insipid and has no flavour, though it seems not worth being looked at or listened to, the use of it is inexhaustible.

XXXVI

1 When one is about to take an inspiration, he is sure to make a (previous) expiration; when he is going to weaken another, he will first strengthen him; when he is going to overthrow another, he will first have raised him up; when he is going to despoil another, he will first have made gifts to him:—this is called 'Hiding the light (of his procedure).'

2 The soft overcomes the hard; and the weak the strong.

3 Fishes should not be taken from the deep; instruments for the profit of a state should not be shown to the people.

XXXVII

1 The Tao in its regular course does nothing (for the sake of doing it), and so there is nothing which it does not do.

2 If princes and kings were able to maintain it, all things would of themselves be transformed by them.

3 If this transformation became to me an object of desire, I would express the desire by the nameless simplicity.

Simplicity without a name
Is free from all external aim.
With no desire, at rest and still,
All things go right as of their will.

PART II.

XXXVIII

1 (Those who) possessed in highest degree the attributes (of the Tao) did not (seek) to show them, and therefore they possessed them (in fullest measure). (Those who) possessed in a lower degree those attributes (sought how) not to lose them, and therefore they did not possess them (in fullest measure).

2 Those who) possessed in the highest degree those attributes did nothing (with a purpose), and had no need to do anything. (Those who) possessed them in a lower degree were (always) doing, and had need to be so doing.

3 Those who) possessed the highest benevolence were (always seeking) to carry it out, and had no need to be doing so. (Those who) possessed the highest righteousness were (always seeking) to carry it out, and had need to be so doing.

4 Those who) possessed the highest (sense of) propriety were (always seeking) to show it, and when men did not respond to it, they bared the arm and marched up to them.

5 Thus it was that when the Tao was lost, its attributes appeared; when its attributes were lost, benevolence appeared; when benevolence was lost, righteousness appeared; and when righteousness was lost, the proprieties appeared.

6 Now propriety is the attenuated form of leal-heartedness and good faith, and is also the commencement of disorder; swift apprehension is (only) a flower of the Tao, and is the beginning of stupidity.

7 Thus it is that the Great man abides by what is solid, and eschews what is flimsy; dwells with the fruit and not with the flower. It is thus that he puts away the one and makes choice of the other.

XXXIX

1 The things which from of old have got the One (the Tao) are—

Heaven which by it is bright and pure;
Earth rendered thereby firm and sure;
Spirits with powers by it supplied;
Valleys kept full throughout their void
All creatures which through it do live
Princes and kings who from it get
The model which to all they give.

All these are the results of the One (Tao).

2

If heaven were not thus pure, it soon would rend;
If earth were not thus sure, 'twould break and bend;
Without these powers, the spirits soon would fail;
If not so filled, the drought would parch each vale;
Without that life, creatures would pass away;
Princes and kings, without that moral sway,
However grand and high, would all decay.

3 Thus it is that dignity finds its (firm) root in its (previous) meanness, and what is lofty finds its stability in the lowness (from which it rises). Hence princes and kings call themselves 'Orphans,' 'Men of small virtue,' and as 'Carriages without a nave.' Is not this an acknowledgment that in their considering themselves mean they see the foundation of their dignity? So it is that in the enumeration of the different parts of a carriage we do not come on what makes it answer the ends of a carriage. They do not wish to show themselves elegant-looking as jade, but (prefer) to be coarse-looking as an (ordinary) stone.

XL

1

The movement of the Tao
By contraries proceeds;
And weakness marks the course
Of Tao's mighty deeds.

2 All things under heaven sprang from It as existing (and named); that existence sprang from It as non-existent (and not named).

XLI

1 Scholars of the highest class, when they hear about the Tao, earnestly carry it into practice. Scholars of the middle class, when they have heard about it, seem now to keep it and now to lose it. Scholars of the lowest class, when they have heard about it, laugh greatly at it. If it were not (thus) laughed at, it would not be fit to be the Tao.

2 Therefore the sentence-makers have thus expressed themselves:—

'The Tao, when brightest seen, seems light to lack;
Who progress in it makes, seems drawing back;
Its even way is like a rugged track.
Its highest virtue from the vale doth rise;
Its greatest beauty seems to offend the eyes;
And he has most whose lot the least supplies.
Its firmest virtue seems but poor and low;
Its solid truth seems change to undergo;
Its largest square doth yet no corner show
A vessel great, it is the slowest made;
Loud is its sound, but never word it said;
A semblance great, the shadow of a shade.'

3 The Tao is hidden, and has no name; but it is the Tao which is skilful at imparting (to all things what they need) and making them complete.

XLII

1 The Tao produced One; One produced Two; Two produced Three; Three produced All things. All things leave behind them the Obscurity (out of which they have come), and go forward to embrace the Brightness (into which they have emerged), while they are harmonised by the Breath of Vacancy.

2 What men dislike is to be orphans, to have little virtue, to be as carriages without naves; and yet these are the designations which kings and princes use for themselves. So it is that some things are increased by being diminished, and others are diminished by being increased.

3 What other men (thus) teach, I also teach. The violent and strong do not die their natural death. I will make this the basis of my teaching.

XLIII

1 The softest thing in the world dashes against and overcomes the hardest; that which has no (substantial) existence enters where there is no crevice. I know hereby what advantage belongs to doing nothing (with a purpose).

2 There are few in the world who attain to the teaching without words, and the advantage arising from non-action.

XLIV

1

Or fame or life,
Which do you hold more dear?
Or life or wealth,
To which would you adhere?
Keep life and lose those other things;
Keep them and lose your life:—which brings
Sorrow and pain more near?

2

Thus we may see,
Who cleaves to fame
Rejects what is more great;
Who loves large stores
Gives up the richer state.

3

Who is content
Needs fear no shame.
Who knows to stop
Incurs no blame.
From danger free
Long live shall he.

XLV

1

Who thinks his great achievements poor
Shall find his vigour long endure.
Of greatest fulness, deemed a void,
Exhaustion ne'er shall stem the tide.
Do thou what's straight still crooked deem;

Thy greatest art still stupid seem,
And eloquence a stammering scream.

2 Constant action overcomes cold, being still overcomes heat. Purity and stillness give the correct law to all under heaven.

XLVI

1 When the Tao prevails in the world, they send back their swift horses to (draw) the dung-carts. When the Tao is disregarded in the world, the war-horses breed in the border lands.

2 There is no guilt greater than to sanction ambition; no calamity greater than to be discontented with one's lot; no fault greater than the wish to be getting. Therefore the sufficiency of contentment is an enduring and unchanging sufficiency.

XLVII

1 Without going outside his door, one understands (all that takes place) under the sky; without looking out from his window, one sees the Tao of Heaven. The farther that one goes out (from himself), the less he knows.

2 Therefore the sages got their knowledge without travelling; gave their (right) names to things without seeing them; and accomplished their ends without any purpose of doing so.

XLVIII

1 He who devotes himself to learning (seeks) from day to day to increase (his knowledge); he who devotes himself to the Tao (seeks) from day to day to diminish (his doing).

2 He diminishes it and again diminishes it, till he arrives at doing nothing (on purpose). Having arrived at this point of non-action, there is nothing which he does not do.

3 He who gets as his own all under heaven does so by giving himself no trouble (with that end). If one take trouble (with that end), he is not equal to getting as his own all under heaven.

XLIX

1 The sage has no invariable mind of his own; he makes the mind of the people his mind.

2 To those who are good (to me), I am good; and to those who are not good (to me), I am also good;—and thus (all) get to be good. To those who are sincere (with me), I am sincere; and to those who are not sincere (with me), I am also sincere;—and thus (all) get to be sincere.

3 The sage has in the world an appearance of indecision, and keeps his mind in a state of indifference to all. The people all keep their eyes and ears directed to him, and he deals with them all as his children.

L

1 Men come forth and live; they enter (again) and die.

2 Of every ten three are ministers of life (to themselves); and three are ministers of death.

3 There are also three in every ten whose aim is to live, but whose movements tend to the land (or place) of death. And for what reason? Because of their excessive endeavours to perpetuate life.

4 But I have heard that he who is skilful in managing the life entrusted to him for a time travels on the land without having to shun rhinoceros or tiger, and enters a host without having to avoid buff coat or sharp weapon. The rhinoceros finds no place in him into which to thrust its horn, nor the tiger a place

in which to fix its claws, nor the weapon a place to admit its point. And for what reason? Because there is in him no place of death.

LI

1 All things are produced by the Tao, and nourished by its outflowing operation. They receive their forms according to the nature of each, and are completed according to the circumstances of their condition. Therefore all things without exception honour the Tao, and exalt its outflowing operation.

2 This honouring of the Tao and exalting of its operation is not the result of any ordination, but always a spontaneous tribute.

3 Thus it is that the Tao produces (all things), nourishes them, brings them to their full growth, nurses them, completes them, matures them, maintains them, and overspreads them.

4 It produces them and makes no claim to the possession of them; it carries them through their processes and does not vaunt its ability in doing so; it brings them to maturity and exercises no control over them;—this is called its mysterious operation.

LII

1 (The Tao) which originated all under the sky is to be considered as the mother of them all.

2 When the mother is found, we know what her children should be. When one knows that he is his mother's child, and proceeds to guard (the qualities of) the mother that belong to him, to the end of his life he will be free from all peril.

3 Let him keep his mouth closed, and shut up the portals (of his nostrils), and all his life he will be exempt from laborious

exertion. Let him keep his mouth open, and (spend his breath) in the promotion of his affairs, and all his life there will be no safety for him.

4 The perception of what is small is (the secret of) clear-sightedness; the guarding of what is soft and tender is (the secret of) strength.

5

Who uses well his light,
Reverting to its (source so) bright,
Will from his body ward all blight,
And hides the unchanging from men's sight.

LIII

1 If I were suddenly to become known, and (put into a position to) conduct (a government) according to the Great Tao, what I should be most afraid of would be a boastful display.

2 The great Tao (or way) is very level and easy; but people love the by-ways.

3 Their court(-yards and buildings) shall be well kept, but their fields shall be ill-cultivated, and their granaries very empty. They shall wear elegant and ornamented robes, carry a sharp sword at their girdle, pamper themselves in eating and drinking, and have a superabundance of property and wealth;—such (princes) may be called robbers and boasters. This is contrary to the Tao surely!

LIV

1

What (Tao's) skilful planter plants
Can never be uptorn;

What his skilful arms enfold,
From him can ne'er be borne.
Sons shall bring in lengthening line,
Sacrifices to his shrine.

2

Tao when nursed within one's self,
His vigour will make true;
And where the family it rules
What riches will accrue!
The neighbourhood where it prevails
In thriving will abound;
And when 'tis seen throughout the state,
Good fortune will be found.
Employ it the kingdom o'er,
And men thrive all around.

3 In this way the effect will be seen in the person, by the observation of different cases; in the family; in the neighbourhood; in the state; and in the kingdom.

4 How do I know that this effect is sure to hold thus all under the sky? By this (method of observation).

LV

1 He who has in himself abundantly the attributes (of the Tao) is like an infant. Poisonous insects will not sting him; fierce beasts will not seize him, birds of prey will not strike him.

2 The infant's) bones are weak and its sinews soft, but yet its grasp is firm. It knows not yet the union of male and female, and yet its virile member may be excited;—showing the perfection of its physical essence. All day long it will cry without its throat becoming hoarse;—showing the harmony (in its constitution).

3

To him by whom this harmony is known,
(The secret of) the unchanging (Tao) is shown,
And in the knowledge wisdom finds its throne.
All life-increasing arts to evil turn;
Where the mind makes the vital breath to burn,
(False) is the strength, (and o'er it we should mourn.)

4 When things have become strong, they (then) become old, which may be said to be contrary to the Tao. Whatever is contrary to the Tao soon ends.

LVI

1 He who knows (the Tao) does not (care to) speak (about it); he who is (ever ready to) speak about it does not know it.

2 He (who knows it) will keep his mouth shut and close the portals (of his nostrils). He will blunt his sharp points and unravel the complications of things; he will attemper his brightness, and bring himself into agreement with the obscurity (of others). This is called 'the Mysterious Agreement.'

3 Such an one) cannot be treated familiarly or distantly; he is beyond all consideration of profit or injury; of nobility or meanness:—he is the noblest man under heaven.

LVII

1 A state may be ruled by (measures of) correction; weapons of war may be used with crafty dexterity; (but) the kingdom is made one's own (only) by freedom from action and purpose.

2 How do I know that it is so? By these facts:—In the kingdom the multiplication of prohibitive enactments increases the poverty of the people; the more implements to add to their profit

that the people have, the greater disorder is there in the state and clan; the more acts of crafty dexterity that men possess, the more do strange contrivances appear; the more display there is of legislation, the more thieves and robbers there are.

3 Therefore a sage has said, 'I will do nothing (of purpose), and the people will be transformed of themselves; I will be fond of keeping still, and the people will of themselves become correct. I will take no trouble about it, and the people will of themselves become rich; I will manifest no ambition, and the people will of themselves attain to the primitive simplicity.'

LVIII

1

The government that seems the most unwise,
Oft goodness to the people best supplies;
That which is meddling, touching everything,
Will work but ill, and disappointment bring.

Misery!—happiness is to be found by its side! Happiness!—misery lurks beneath it! Who knows what either will come to in the end?

2 Shall we then dispense with correction? The (method of) correction shall by a turn become distortion, and the good in it shall by a turn become evil. The delusion of the people (on this point) has indeed subsisted for a long time.

3 Therefore the sage is (like) a square which cuts no one (with its angles); (like) a corner which injures no one (with its sharpness). He is straightforward, but allows himself no license; he is bright, but does not dazzle.

LIX

1 For regulating the human (in our constitution) and rendering the (proper) service to the heavenly, there is nothing like moderation.

2 It is only by this moderation that there is effected an early return (to man's normal state). That early return is what I call the repeated accumulation of the attributes (of the Tao). With that repeated accumulation of those attributes, there comes the subjugation (of every obstacle to such return). Of this subjugation we know not what shall be the limit; and when one knows not what the limit shall be, he may be the ruler of a state.

3 He who possesses the mother of the state may continue long. His case is like that (of the plant) of which we say that its roots are deep and its flower stalks firm:—this is the way to secure that its enduring life shall long be seen.

LX

1 Governing a great state is like cooking small fish

2 Let the kingdom be governed according to the Tao, and the manes of the departed will not manifest their spiritual energy. It is not that those manes have not that spiritual energy, but it will not be employed to hurt men. It is not that it could not hurt men, but neither does the ruling sage hurt them.

3 When these two do not injuriously affect each other, their good influences converge in the virtue (of the Tao).

LXI

1 What makes a great state is its being (like) a low-lying, down-flowing (stream);—it becomes the centre to which tend (all the small states) under heaven.

2 To illustrate from) the case of all females:—the female always overcomes the male by her stillness. Stillness may be considered (a sort of) abasement.

3 Thus it is that a great state, by condescending to small states, gains them for itself; and that small states, by abasing themselves to a great state, win it over to them. In the one case the abasement leads to gaining adherents, in the other case to procuring favour.

4 The great state only wishes to unite men together and nourish them; a small state only wishes to be received by, and to serve, the other. Each gets what it desires, but the great state must learn to abase itself.

62

1

Tao has of all things the most honoured place.
No treasures give good men so rich a grace;
Bad men it guards, and doth their ill efface.

2 Its) admirable words can purchase honour; (its) admirable deeds can raise their performer above others. Even men who are not good are not abandoned by it.

3 Therefore when the sovereign occupies his place as the Son of Heaven, and he has appointed his three ducal ministers, though (a prince) were to send in a round symbol-of-rank large enough to fill both the hands, and that as the precursor of the team of horses (in the court-yard), such an offering would not be equal to (a lesson of) this Tao, which one might present on his knees.

4 Why was it that the ancients prized this Tao so much? Was it not because it could be got by seeking for it, and the guilty could escape (from the stain of their guilt) by it? This is the

reason why all under heaven consider it the most valuable thing.

LXIII

1 It is the way of the Tao) to act without (thinking of) acting; to conduct affairs without (feeling the) trouble of them; to taste without discerning any flavour; to consider what is small as great, and a few as many; and to recompense injury with kindness.

2 The master of it) anticipates things that are difficult while they are easy, and does things that would become great while they are small. All difficult things in the world are sure to arise from a previous state in which they were easy, and all great things from one in which they were small. Therefore the sage, while he never does what is great, is able on that account to accomplish the greatest things.

3 He who lightly promises is sure to keep but little faith; he who is continually thinking things easy is sure to find them difficult. Therefore the sage sees difficulty even in what seems easy, and so never has any difficulties.

LXIV

1 That which is at rest is easily kept hold of; before a thing has given indications of its presence, it is easy to take measures against it; that which is brittle is easily broken; that which is very small is easily dispersed. Action should be taken before a thing has made its appearance; order should be secured before disorder has begun.

2 The tree which fills the arms grew from the tiniest sprout; the tower of nine storeys rose from a (small) heap of earth; the journey of a thousand li commenced with a single step.

3 He who acts (with an ulterior purpose) does harm; he who takes hold of a thing (in the same way) loses his hold. The sage does not act (so), and therefore does no harm; he does not lay hold (so), and therefore does not lose his hold. (But) people in their conduct of affairs are constantly ruining them when they are on the eve of success. If they were careful at the end, as (they should be) at the beginning, they would not so ruin them.

4 Therefore the sage desires what (other men) do not desire, and does not prize things difficult to get; he learns what (other men) do not learn, and turns back to what the multitude of men have passed by. Thus he helps the natural development of all things, and does not dare to act (with an ulterior purpose of his own).

LXV

1 The ancients who showed their skill in practising the Tao did so, not to enlighten the people, but rather to make them simple and ignorant.

2 The difficulty in governing the people arises from their having much knowledge. He who (tries to) govern a state by his wisdom is a scourge to it; while he who does not (try to) do so is a blessing.

3 He who knows these two things finds in them also his model and rule. Ability to know this model and rule constitutes what we call the mysterious excellence (of a governor). Deep and far-reaching is such mysterious excellence, showing indeed its possessor as opposite to others, but leading them to a great conformity to him.

LXVI

1 That whereby the rivers and seas are able to receive the homage and tribute of all the valley streams, is their skill in being lower

than they;—it is thus that they are the kings of them all. So it is that the sage (ruler), wishing to be above men, puts himself by his words below them, and, wishing to be before them, places his person behind them.

2 In this way though he has his place above them, men do not feel his weight, nor though he has his place before them, do they feel it an injury to them.

3 Therefore all in the world delight to exalt him and do not weary of him. Because he does not strive, no one finds it possible to strive with him.

LXVII

1 All the world says that, while my Tao is great, it yet appears to be inferior (to other systems of teaching). Now it is just its greatness that makes it seem to be inferior. If it were like any other (system), for long would its smallness have been known!

2 But I have three precious things which I prize and hold fast. The first is gentleness; the second is economy; and the third is shrinking from taking precedence of others.

3 With that gentleness I can be bold; with that economy I can be liberal; shrinking from taking precedence of others, I can become a vessel of the highest honour. Now-a-days they give up gentleness and are all for being bold; economy, and are all for being liberal; the hindmost place, and seek only to be foremost;—(of all which the end is) death.

4 Gentleness is sure to be victorious even in battle, and firmly to maintain its ground. Heaven will save its possessor, by his (very) gentleness protecting him.

68

He who in (Tao's) wars has skill

Assumes no martial port;
He who fights with most good will
To rage makes no resort.
He who vanquishes yet still
Keeps from his foes apart;
He whose hests men most fulfil
Yet humbly plies his art.

Thus we say, 'He ne'er contends,
And therein is his might.
Thus we say, 'Men's wills he bends,
That they with him unite.'
Thus we say, 'Like Heaven's his ends,
No sage of old more bright.'

LXIX

1 A master of the art of war has said, 'I do not dare to be the host (to commence the war); I prefer to be the guest (to act on the defensive). I do not dare to advance an inch; I prefer to retire a foot.' This is called marshalling the ranks where there are no ranks; baring the arms (to fight) where there are no arms to bare; grasping the weapon where there is no weapon to grasp; advancing against the enemy where there is no enemy.

2 There is no calamity greater than lightly engaging in war. To do that is near losing (the gentleness) which is so precious. Thus it is that when opposing weapons are (actually) crossed, he who deplores (the situation) conquers.

LXX

1 My words are very easy to know, and very easy to practise; but there is no one in the world who is able to know and able to practise them.

2 There is an originating and all-comprehending (principle) in my words, and an authoritative law for the things (which I enforce). It is because they do not know these, that men do not know me.

3 They who know me are few, and I am on that account (the more) to be prized. It is thus that the sage wears (a poor garb of) hair cloth, while he carries his (signet of) jade in his bosom.

LXXI

1 To know and yet (think) we do not know is the highest (attainment); not to know (and yet think) we do know is a disease.

2 It is simply by being pained at (the thought of) having this disease that we are preserved from it. The sage has not the disease. He knows the pain that would be inseparable from it, and therefore he does not have it.

LXXII

1 When the people do not fear what they ought to fear, that which is their great dread will come on them.

2 Let them not thoughtlessly indulge themselves in their ordinary life; let them not act as if weary of what that life depends on.

3 It is by avoiding such indulgence that such weariness does not arise.

4 Therefore the sage knows (these things) of himself, but does not parade (his knowledge); loves, but does not (appear to set a) value on, himself. And thus he puts the latter alternative away and makes choice of the former.

LXXIII

1 He whose boldness appears in his daring (to do wrong, in defiance of the laws) is put to death; he whose boldness appears in his not daring (to do so) lives on. Of these two cases the one appears to be advantageous, and the other to be injurious. But

When Heaven's anger smites a man,
Who the cause shall truly scan?

On this account the sage feels a difficulty (as to what to do in the former case).

2 It is the way of Heaven not to strive, and yet it skilfully overcomes; not to speak, and yet it is skilful in obtaining a reply; does not call, and yet men come to it of themselves. Its demonstrations are quiet, and yet its plans are skilful and effective. The meshes of the net of Heaven are large; far apart, but letting nothing escape.

LXXIV

1 The people do not fear death; to what purpose is it to (try to) frighten them with death? If the people were always in awe of death, and I could always seize those who do wrong, and put them to death, who would dare to do wrong?

2 There is always One who presides over the infliction of death. He who would inflict death in the room of him who so presides over it may be described as hewing wood instead of a great carpenter. Seldom is it that he who undertakes the hewing, instead of the great carpenter, does not cut his own hands!

LXXV

1 The people suffer from famine because of the multitude of taxes consumed by their superiors. It is through this that they suffer famine.

2 The people are difficult to govern because of the (excessive) agency of their superiors (in governing them). It is through this that they are difficult to govern.

3 The people make light of dying because of the greatness of their labours in seeking for the means of living. It is this which makes them think light of dying. Thus it is that to leave the subject of living altogether out of view is better than to set a high value on it.

LXXVI

1 Man at his birth is supple and weak; at his death, firm and strong. (So it is with) all things. Trees and plants, in their early growth, are soft and brittle; at their death, dry and withered.

2 Thus it is that firmness and strength are the concomitants of death; softness and weakness, the concomitants of life.

3 Hence he who (relies on) the strength of his forces does not conquer; and a tree which is strong will fill the out-stretched arms, (and thereby invites the feller.)

4 Therefore the place of what is firm and strong is below, and that of what is soft and weak is above.

LXXVII

1 May not the Way (or Tao) of Heaven be compared to the (method of) bending a bow? The (part of the bow) which was high is brought low, and what was low is raised up. (So Heaven) diminishes where there is superabundance, and supplements where there is deficiency.

2 It is the Way of Heaven to diminish superabundance, and to supplement deficiency. It is not so with the way of man. He takes away from those who have not enough to add to his own superabundance.

3 Who can take his own superabundance and therewith serve all under heaven? Only he who is in possession of the Tao!

4 Therefore the (ruling) sage acts without claiming the results as his; he achieves his merit and does not rest (arrogantly) in it:—he does not wish to display his superiority.

LXXVIII

1 There is nothing in the world more soft and weak than water, and yet for attacking things that are firm and strong there is nothing that can take precedence of it;—for there is nothing (so effectual) for which it can be changed.

2 Every one in the world knows that the soft overcomes the hard, and the weak the strong, but no one is able to carry it out in practice.

3

Therefore a sage has said,
'He who accepts his state's reproach,
Is hailed therefore its altars' lord;
To him who bears men's direful woes
They all the name of King accord.'

4 Words that are strictly true seem to be paradoxical.

LXXIX

1 When a reconciliation is effected (between two parties) after a great animosity, there is sure to be a grudge remaining (in the mind of the one who was wrong). And how can this be beneficial (to the other)?

2 Therefore (to guard against this), the sage keeps the left-hand portion of the record of the engagement, and does not insist on the (speedy) fulfilment of it by the other party. (So), he who has the attributes (of the Tao) regards (only) the conditions of the engagement, while he who has not those attributes regards only the conditions favourable to himself.

3 In the Way of Heaven, there is no partiality of love; it is always on the side of the good man.

LXXX

1 In a little state with a small population, I would so order it, that, though there were individuals with the abilities of ten or a hundred men, there should be no employment of them; I would make the people, while looking on death as a grievous thing, yet not remove elsewhere (to avoid it).

2 Though they had boats and carriages, they should have no occasion to ride in them; though they had buff coats and sharp weapons, they should have no occasion to don or use them.

3 Iwould make the people return to the use of knotted cords (instead of the written characters).

4 They should think their (coarse) food sweet; their (plain) clothes beautiful; their (poor) dwellings places of rest; and their common (simple) ways sources of enjoyment.

5 There should be a neighbouring state within sight, and the voices of the fowls and dogs should be heard all the way from it to us, but I would make the people to old age, even to death, not have any intercourse with it.

LXXXI

1 Sincere words are not fine; fine words are not sincere. Those who are skilled (in the Tao) do not dispute (about it); the disputatious are not skilled in it. Those who know (the Tao) are not extensively learned; the extensively learned do not know it.

2 The sage does not accumulate (for himself). The more that he expends for others, the more does he possess of his own; the more that he gives to others, the more does he have himself.

3 With all the sharpness of the Way of Heaven, it injures not; with all the doing in the way of the sage he does not strive.

CONFUCIAN ANALECTS

Translated by James Legge

Contents

BOOK I.
HSIO R.

CHAPTER I.

1 The Master said, 'Is it not pleasant to learn with a constant perseverance and application?

2 'Is it not delightful to have friends coming from distant quarters?

3 'Is he not a man of complete virtue, who feels no discomposure though men may take no note of him?'

CHAPTER II.

1 The philosopher Yû said, 'They are few who, being filial and fraternal, are fond of offending against their superiors. There have been none, who, not liking to offend against their superiors, have been fond of stirring up confusion.

2 'The superior man bends his attention to what is radical. That being established, all practical courses naturally grow up. Filial piety and fraternal submission!– are they not the root of all benevolent actions?'

CHAPTER III.

The Master said, 'Fine words and an insinuating appearance are seldom associated with true virtue.'

CHAPTER IV.

The philosopher Tsăng said, 'I daily examine myself on three points:-- whether, in transacting business for others, I may have been not faithful;-- whether, in intercourse with friends, I may have been not sincere;-- whether I may have not mastered and practised the instructions of my teacher.'

CHAPTER V.

The Master said, 'To rule a country of a thousand chariots, there must be reverent attention to business, and sincerity; economy in expenditure, and love for men; and the employment of the people at the proper seasons.'

CHAPTER VI.

The Master said, 'A youth, when at home, should be filial, and, abroad, respectful to his elders. He should be earnest and truthful. He should overflow in love to all, and cultivate the friendship of the good. When he has time and opportunity, after the performance of these things, he should employ them in polite studies.'

CHAPTER VII.

Tsze-hsiâ said, 'If a man withdraws his mind from the love of beauty, and applies it as sincerely to the love of the virtuous; if, in serving his parents, he can exert his utmost strength; if, in serving his prince, he can devote his life; if, in his intercourse with his friends, his words are sincere:-- although men say that he has not learned, I will certainly say that he has.'

CHAPTER VIII.

1 The Master said, 'If the scholar be not grave, he will not call forth any veneration, and his learning will not be solid.

2 'Hold faithfulness and sincerity as first principles.

3 'Have no friends not equal to yourself

4 'When you have faults, do not fear to abandon them.'

CHAPTER IX.

The philosopher Tsăng said, 'Let there be a careful attention *to perform the funeral rites to parents*, and let them be followed when long *gone with the ceremonies of sacrifice*;-- then the virtue of the people will resume its proper excellence.'

CHAPTER X.

1 Tsze-ch'in asked Tsze-kung, saying, 'When our master comes to any country, he does not fail to learn all about its government. Does he ask his information? or is it given to him?'

2 Tsze-kung said, 'Our master is benign, upright, courteous, temperate, and complaisant, and thus he gets his information. The master's mode of asking information!-- is it not different from that of other men?'

CHAPTER XI.

The Master said, 'While a man's father is alive, look at the bent of his will; when his father is dead, look at his conduct. If for three years he does not alter from the way of his father, he may be called filial.'

CHAPTER XII.

1 The philosopher Yû said, 'In practising the rules of propriety, a natural ease is to be prized. In the ways prescribed by the ancient kings, this is the excellent quality, and in things small and great we follow them.

2 'Yet it is not to be observed in all cases. If one, knowing how such ease should be prized, manifests it, without regulating it by the rules of propriety, this likewise is not to be done.'

CHAPTER XIII.

The philosopher Yû said, 'When agreements are made according to what is right, what is spoken can be made good. When respect is shown according to what is proper, one keeps far from shame and disgrace. When the parties upon whom a man leans are proper persons to be intimate with, he can make them his guides and masters.'

CHAPTER XIV.

The Master said, 'He who aims to be a man of complete virtue in his food does not seek to gratify his appetite, nor in his dwelling place does he seek the appliances of ease; he is earnest in what he is doing, and careful in his speech; he frequents the company of men of principle that he may be rectified:-- such a person may be said indeed to love to learn.'

CHAPTER XV.

1 Tsze-kung said, 'What do you pronounce concerning the poor man who yet does not flatter, and the rich man who is not proud?' The Master replied, 'They will do; but they are not equal to him, who, though poor, is yet cheerful, and to him, who, though rich, loves the rules of propriety.'

2 Tsze-kung replied, 'It is said in the Book of Poetry, "As you cut and then file, as you carve and then polish."-- The meaning is the same, I apprehend, as that which you have just expressed.'

3 The Master said, 'With one like Ts'ze, I can begin to talk about the odes. I told him one point, and he knew its proper sequence.'

CHAPTER XVI.

The Master said, 'I will not be afflicted at men's not knowing me; I will be afflicted that I do not know men.'

BOOK II.
WEI CHĂNG.

CHAPTER I.

The Master said, 'He who exercises government by means of his virtue may be compared to the north polar star, which keeps its place and all the stars turn towards it.'

CHAPTER II.

The Master said, 'In the Book of Poetry are three hundred pieces, but the design of them all may be embraced in one sentence--"Having no depraved thoughts."'

CHAPTER III.

1 The Master said, 'If the people be led by laws, and uniformity sought to be given them by punishments, they will try to avoid the punishment, but have no sense of shame.

2 'If they be led by virtue, and uniformity sought to be given them by the rules of propriety, they will have the sense of shame, and moreover will become good.'

CHAPTER IV.

1 The Master said, 'At fifteen, I had my mind bent on learning.

2 'At thirty, I stood firm.

3 'At forty, I had no doubts.

4 'At fifty, I knew the decrees of Heaven.

5 'At sixty, my ear was an obedient organ for the reception of truth.

6 'At seventy, I could follow what my heart desired, without transgressing what was right.'

CHAPTER V.

1 Măng Î asked what filial piety was. The Master said, 'It is not being disobedient.'

2 Soon after, as Fan Ch'ih was driving him, the Master told him, saying, 'Măng-sun asked me what filial piety was, and I answered him,-- "not being disobedient."'

3 Fan Ch'ih said, 'What did you mean?' The Master replied, 'That parents, when alive, be served according to propriety; that when dead, they should be buried according to propriety; and that they should be sacrificed to according to propriety.'

CHAPTER VI.

Măng Wû asked what filial piety was. The Master said, 'Parents are anxious lest their children should be sick.'

CHAPTER VII.

Tsze-yû asked what filial piety was. The Master said, 'The filial piety of now-a-days means the support of one's parents. But dogs and horses likewise are able to do something in

the way of support;-- without reverence, what is there to distinguish the one support given from the other?'

CHAPTER VIII.

Tsze-hsiâ asked what filial piety was. The Master said, 'The difficulty is with the countenance. If, when their elders have any troublesome affairs, the young take the toil of them, and if, when the young have wine and food, they set them before their elders, is THIS to be considered filial piety?'

CHAPTER IX.

The Master said, 'I have talked with Hûi for a whole day, and he has not made any objection to *anything I said*;-- as if he were stupid. He has retired, and I have examined his conduct when away from me, and found him able to illustrate my *teachings*. Hûi!-- He is not stupid.'

CHAPTER X.

1 The Master said, 'See what a man does.

2 'Mark his motives.

3 'Examine in what things he rests

4 'How can a man conceal his character?

5 How can a man conceal his character?'

CHAPTER XI.

The Master said, 'If a man keeps cherishing his old knowledge, so as continually to be acquiring new, he may be a teacher of others.'

CHAPTER XII.

The Master said, 'The accomplished scholar is not a utensil.'

CHAPTER XIII.

Tsze-kung asked what constituted the superior man. The Master said, 'He acts before he speaks, and afterwards speaks according to his actions.'

CHAPTER XIV.

The Master said, 'The superior man is catholic and no partisan. The mean man is partisan and not catholic.'

CHAPTER XV.

The Master said, 'Learning without thought is labour lost; thought without learning is perilous.'

CHAPTER XVI.

The Master said, 'The study of strange doctrines is injurious indeed!'

CHAPTER XVII.

The Master said, 'Yû, shall I teach you what knowledge is? When you know a thing, to hold that you know it; and when you do not know a thing, to allow that you do not know it;-- this is knowledge.'

CHAPTER XVIII.

1 Tsze-chang was learning with a view to official emolument.

2 The Master said, 'Hear much and put aside the points of which you stand in doubt, while you speak cautiously at the same time of the others:-- then you will afford few occasions for blame. See much and put aside the things which seem perilous, while you are cautious at the same time in carrying the others into practice:--then you will have few occasions for repentance. When one gives few occasions for blame in his words, and few occasions for repentance in his conduct, he is in the way to get emolument.'

CHAPTER XIX.

The Duke Âi asked, saying, 'What should be done in order to secure the submission of the people?' Confucius replied, 'Advance the upright and set aside the crooked, then the people will submit. Advance the crooked and set aside the upright, then the people will not submit.'

CHAPTER XX.

Chi K'ang asked how to cause the people to reverence their ruler, to be faithful to him, and to go on to nerve themselves to virtue. The Master said, 'Let him preside over them with gravity;-- then they will reverence him. Let him be filial and kind to all;-- then they will be faithful to him. Let him advance the good and teach the incompetent;-- then they will eagerly seek to be virtuous.'

CHAPTER XXI.

1 Some one addressed Confucius, saying, 'Sir, why are you not engaged in the government?'

2 The Master said, 'What does the Shû-ching say of filial piety?-- "You are filial, you discharge your brotherly duties. These qualities are displayed in government." This then also constitutes the exercise of government. Why must there be THAT-- making one be in the government?'

CHAPTER XXII.

The Master said, 'I do not know how a man without truthfulness is to get on. How can a large carriage be made to go without the cross-bar for yoking the oxen to, or a small carriage without the arrangement for yoking the horses?'

CHAPTER XXIII.

1 Tsze-chang asked whether the affairs of ten ages after could be known.

2 Confucius said, 'The Yin dynasty followed the regulations of the Hsia: wherein it took from or added to them may be known. The Chau dynasty has followed the regulations of Yin: wherein it took from or added to them may be known. Some other may follow the Chau, but though it should be at the distance of a hundred ages, its affairs may be known.'

CHAPTER XXIV.

1 The Master said, 'For a man to sacrifice to a spirit which does not belong to him is flattery.

2 'To see what is right and not to do it is want of courage.'

BOOK III.
PA YIH.

CHAPTER I.

Confucius said of the head of the Chî family, who had eight rows of pantomimes in his area, 'If he can bear to do this, what may he not bear to do?'

CHAPTER II.

The three families used the YUNG ode, while the vessels were being removed, *at the conclusion of the sacrifice*. The Master said, '"Assisting are the princes;-- the son of heaven looks profound and grave:"-- what application can these words have in the hall of the three families?'

CHAPTER III.

The Master said, 'If a man be without the virtues proper to humanity, what has he to do with the rites of propriety? If a man be without the virtues proper to humanity, what has he to do with music?'

CHAPTER IV.

1 Lin Fang asked what was the first thing to be attended to in ceremonies.

2 The Master said, 'A great question indeed!

3 'In *festive* ceremonies, it is better to be sparing than extravagant. In the ceremonies of mourning, it is better that there be deep sorrow than a minute attention to observances.'

CHAPTER V.

The Master said, 'The rude tribes of the east and north have their princes, and are not like the States of our great land which are without them.'

CHAPTER VI.

The chief of the Chî family was about to sacrifice to the T'ai mountain. The Master said to Zan Yû, 'Can you not save him from this?' He answered, 'I cannot.' Confucius said, 'Alas! will you say that the T'ai mountain is not so discerning as Lin Fang?'

CHAPTER VII.

The Master said, 'The student of virtue has no contentions. If it be said he cannot avoid them, shall this be in archery? *But* he bows complaisantly *to his competitors*; thus he ascends *the hall*, descends, and exacts the forfeit of drinking. In his contention, he is still the Chün-tsze.'

CHAPTER VIII.

1 Tsze-hsiâ asked, saying, 'What is the meaning of the passage-- "The pretty dimples of her artful smile! The well-defined black and white of her eye! The plain ground for the colours?"'

2 The Master said, 'The business of laying on the colours follows (the preparation of) the plain ground.'

3 'Ceremonies then are a subsequent thing?' The Master said 'It is Shang who can bring out my meaning. Now I can begin to talk about the odes with him.'

CHAPTER IX.

The Master said, 'I could describe the ceremonies of the Hsiâ dynasty, but Chî cannot sufficiently attest my words. I could describe the ceremonies of the Yin dynasty, but Sung cannot sufficiently attest my words. (*They cannot do so*) because of the insufficiency of their records and wise men. If those were sufficient, I could adduce them in support of my words.'

CHAPTER X.

The Master said, 'At the great sacrifice, after the pouring out of the libation, I have no wish to look on.'

CHAPTER XI.

Some one asked the meaning of the great sacrifice. The Master said, 'I do not know. He who knew its meaning would find it as easy to govern the kingdom as to look on this;-- pointing to his palm.

CHAPTER XII.

1 He sacrificed *to the dead*, as if they were present. He sacrificed to the spirits, as if the spirits were present.

2 The Master said, 'I consider my not being present at the sacrifice, as if I did not sacrifice.'

CHAPTER XIII.

1 Wăng-sun Chiâ asked, saying, 'What is the meaning of the saying, "It is better to pay court to the furnace than to the south-west corner?"'

2 The Master said, 'Not so. He who offends against Heaven has none to whom he can pray.'

CHAPTER XIV.

The Master said, 'Châu had the advantage of viewing the two past dynasties. How complete and elegant are its regulations! I follow Châu.'

CHAPTER XV.

The Master, when he entered the grand temple, asked about everything. Some one said, 'Who will say that the son of the man of Tsâu knows the rules of propriety! He has entered the grand temple and asks about everything.' The Master heard the remark, and said, 'This is a rule of propriety.'

CHAPTER XVI.

The Master said, 'In archery it is not going *through* the leather which is the principal thing;-- because people's strength is not equal. This was the old way.'

CHAPTER XVII.

1 Tsze-kung wished to do away with the offering of a sheep connected with the inauguration of the first day of each month.

2 The Master said, 'Ts'ze, you love the sheep; I love the ceremony.'

CHAPTER XVIII.

The Master said, 'The full observance of the rules of propriety in serving one's prince is accounted by people to be flattery.'

CHAPTER XIX.

The Duke Ting asked how a prince should employ his ministers, and how ministers should serve their prince. Confucius replied, 'A prince should employ his minister according to according to the rules of propriety; ministers should serve their prince with faithfulness.'

CHAPTER XX.

The Master said, 'The Kwan Tsü is expressive of enjoyment without being licentious, and of grief without being hurtfully excessive.'

CHAPTER XXI.

1 The Duke Âi asked Tsâi Wo about the altars of the spirits of the land. Tsâi Wo replied, 'The Hsiâ sovereign planted the pine tree about them; the men of the Yin planted the cypress; and the men of the Châu planted the chestnut tree, meaning thereby to cause the people to be in awe.'

2 When the Master heard it, he said, 'Things that are done, it is needless to speak about; things that have had their course, it is needless to remonstrate about; things that are past, it is needless to blame.'

CHAPTER XXII.

1 The Master said, 'Small indeed was the capacity of Kwan Chung!'

2 Some one said, 'Was Kwan Chung parsimonious?' 'Kwan,' was the reply, 'had the *San Kwei*, and his officers performed no double duties; how can he be considered parsimonious?'

3 'Then, did Kwan Chung know the rules of propriety?' The Master said, 'The princes of States have a screen intercepting the view at their gates. Kwan had likewise a screen at his gate. The princes of States on any friendly meeting between two of them, had a stand on which to place their inverted cups. Kwan had also such a stand. If Kwan knew the rules of propriety, who does not know them?'

CHAPTER XXXII.

The Master instructing the grand music-master of Lü said, 'How to play music may be known. At the commencement of the piece, all the parts should sound together. As it proceeds, they should be in harmony *while* severally distinct and flowing without break, and thus on to the conclusion.'

CHAPTER XXIV.

The border warden at Yî requested to be introduced to the Master, saying, 'When men of superior virtue have come to this, I have never been denied the privilege of seeing them.' The followers of *the sage* introduced him, and when he came out from the interview, he said, 'My friends, why are you distressed by your master's loss of office? The kingdom has long been without the principles of truth and right; Heaven is going to use your master as a bell with its wooden tongue.'

CHAPTER XXV.

The Master said of the Shâo that it was perfectly beautiful and also perfectly good. He said of the Wû that it was perfectly beautiful but not perfectly good.

CHAPTER XXVI.

The Master said, 'High station filled without indulgent generosity; ceremonies performed without reverence; mourning conducted without sorrow;-- wherewith should I contemplate such ways?'

BOOK IV.
LE JIN.

CHAPTER I.

The Master said, 'It is virtuous manners which constitute the excellence of a neighborhood. If a man in selecting a residence, do not fix on one where such prevail, how can he be wise?'

CHAPTER II.

The Master said, 'Those who are without virtue cannot abide long either in a condition of poverty and hardship, or in a condition of enjoyment. The virtuous rest in virtue; the wise desire virtue.'

CHAPTER III.

The Master said, 'It is only the (*truly*) virtuous man, who can love, or who can hate, others.'

CHAPTER IV.

The Master said, 'If the will be set on virtue, there will be no practice of wickedness.'

CHAPTER V.

1 The Master said, 'Riches and honours are what men desire. If it cannot be obtained in the proper way, they should not be held. Poverty and meanness are what men dislike. If it cannot be avoided in the proper way, they should not be avoided.

2 'If a superior man abandon virtue, how can he fulfil the requirements of that name?

3 'The superior man does not, even for the space of a single meal, act contrary to virtue. In moments of haste, he cleaves to it. In seasons of danger, he cleaves to it.'

CHAPTER VI.

1 The Master said, 'I have not seen a person who loved virtue, or one who hated what was not virtuous. He who loved virtue, would esteem nothing above it. He who hated what is not virtuous, would practise virtue in such a way that he would not allow anything that is not virtuous to approach his person.

2 'Is any one able for one day to apply his strength to virtue? I have not seen the case in which his strength would be insufficient.

3 'Should there possibly be any such case, I have not seen it.'

CHAPTER VII.

The Master said, 'The faults of men are characteristic of the class to which they belong. By observing a man's faults, it may be known that he is virtuous.'

CHAPTER VIII.

The Master said, 'If a man in the morning hear the right way, he may die in the evening without regret.'

CHAPTER IX.

The Master said, 'A scholar, whose mind is set on truth, and who is ashamed of bad clothes and bad food, is not fit to be discoursed with.'

CHAPTER X.

The Master said, 'The superior man, in the world, does not set his mind either for anything, or against anything; what is right he will follow.'

CHAPTER XI.

The Master said, 'The superior man thinks of virtue; the small man thinks of comfort. The superior man thinks of the sanctions of law; the small man thinks of favours *which he may receive*.'

CHAPTER XII.

The Master said: 'He who acts with a constant view to his own advantage will be much murmured against.'

CHAPTER XIII.

The Master said, 'If a *prince* is able to govern his kingdom with the complaisance proper to the rules of propriety, what difficulty will he have? If he cannot govern it with that complaisance, what has he to do with the rules of propriety?'

CHAPTER XIV.

The Master said, '*A man should say*, I am not concerned that I have no place, I am concerned how I may fit myself for one. I am not concerned that I am not known, I seek to be worthy to be known.'

CHAPTER XV.

1 The Master said, 'Shan, my doctrine is that of an all-pervading unity.' The disciple Tsăng replied, 'Yes.'

2 The Master went out, and the other disciples asked, saying, 'What do his words mean?' Tsăng said, 'The doctrine of our master is to be true to the principles of our nature and the benevolent exercise of them to others,-- this and nothing more.'

CHAPTER XVI.

The Master said, 'The mind of the superior man is conversant with righteousness; the mind of the mean man is conversant with gain.'

CHAPTER XVII.

The Master said, 'When we see men of worth, we should think of equalling them; when we see men of a contrary character, we should turn inwards and examine ourselves.'

CHAPTER XVIII.

The Master said, 'In serving his parents, *a son* may remonstrate with them, but gently; when he sees that they do not incline to follow *his advice*, he shows an increased degree of reverence, but does not abandon *his purpose*; and should they punish him, he does not allow himself to murmur.'

CHAPTER XIX.

The Master said, 'While his parents are alive, *the son* may not go abroad to a distance. If he does go abroad, he must have a fixed place to which he goes.'

CHAPTER XX.

The Master said, 'If the son for three years does not alter from the way of his father, he may be called filial.'

CHAPTER XXI.

The Master said, 'The years of parents may by no means not be kept in the memory, as an occasion at once for joy and for fear.'

CHAPTER XXII.

The Master said, 'The reason why the ancients did not readily give utterance to their words, was that they feared lest their actions should not come up to them.'

CHAPTER XXIII.

The Master said, 'The cautious seldom err.'

CHAPTER XXIV.

The Master said, 'The superior man wishes to be slow in his speech and earnest in his conduct.'

CHAPTER XXV.

The Master said, 'Virtue is not left to stand alone. He who practises it will have neighbors.'

CHAPTER XXVI.

Tsze-yû said, 'In serving a prince, frequent remonstrances lead to disgrace. Between friends, frequent reproofs make the friendship distant.'

BOOK V.
KUNG-YE CH'ĂNG.

CHAPTER I.

1 The Master said of Kung-ye Ch'ăng that he might be wived; although he was put in bonds, he had not been guilty of any crime. *Accordingly*, he gave him his own daughter to wife.

2 Of Nan Yung he said that if the country were well governed he would not be out of office, and if it were ill-governed, he would escape punishment and disgrace. He gave him the daughter of his own elder brother to wife.

CHAPTER II.

The Master said of Tsze-chien, 'Of superior virtue indeed is such a man! If there were not virtuous men in Lû, how could this man have acquired this character?'

CHAPTER III.

Tsze-kung asked, 'What do you say of me, Ts'ze? The Master said, 'You are a utensil.' 'What utensil?' 'A gemmed sacrificial utensil.'

CHAPTER IV.

1 Some one said, 'Yung is truly virtuous, but he is not ready with his tongue.'

2 The Master said, 'What is the good of being ready with the tongue? They who encounter men with smartnesses of speech for the most part procure themselves hatred. I know not whether he be truly virtuous, but why should he show readiness of the tongue?'

CHAPTER V.

The Master was wishing Ch'î-tiâo K'âi to enter on official employment. He replied, 'I am not yet able to rest in the assurance of THIS.' The Master was pleased.

CHAPTER VI.

The Master said, 'My doctrines make no way. I will get upon a raft, and float about on the sea. He that will accompany me will be Yû, I dare say.' Tsze-lû hearing this was glad, upon which the Master said, 'Yû is fonder of daring than I am. He does not exercise his judgment upon matters.'

CHAPTER VII.

1 Măng Wû asked about Tsze-lû, whether he was perfectly virtuous. The Master said, 'I do not know.'

2 He asked again, when the Master replied, 'In a kingdom of a thousand chariots, Yu might be employed to manage the military levies, but I do not know whether he be perfectly virtuous.'

3 'And what do you say of Ch'iû?' The Master replied, 'In a city of a thousand families, or a clan of a hundred chariots, Ch'iû might be employed as governor, but I do not know whether he is perfectly virtuous.'

4 'What do you say of Ch'ih?' The Master replied, 'With his sash girt and standing in a court, Ch'ih might be employed to converse with the visitors and guests, but I do not know whether he is perfectly virtuous.'

CHAPTER VIII.

1 The Master said to Tsze-kung, 'Which do you consider superior, yourself or Hûi?'

2 Tsze-kung replied, 'How dare I compare myself with Hûi? Hûi hears one point and knows all about a subject; I hear one point, and know a second.

3 The Master said, 'You are not equal to him. I grant you, you are not equal to him.'

CHAPTER IX.

1 Tsâi Yü being asleep during the daytime, the Master said, 'Rotten wood cannot be carved; a wall of dirty earth will not receive the trowel. This Yü!-- what is the use of my reproving him?'

2 The Master said, 'At first, my way with men was to hear their words, and give them credit for their conduct. Now my way is to hear their words, and look at their conduct. It is from Yü that I have learned to make this change.'

CHAPTER X.

The Master said, 'I have not seen a firm and unbending man.' Some one replied, 'There is Shăn Ch'ang.' 'Ch'ang,' said the Master, 'is under the influence of his passions; how can he be pronounced firm and unbending?'

CHAPTER XI.

Tsze-kung said, 'What I do not wish men to do to me, I also wish not to do to men.' The Master said, 'Ts'ze, you have not attained to that.'

CHAPTER XII.

Tsze-kung said, 'The Master's *personal* displays *of his principles* and *ordinary* descriptions of them may be heard. His discourses about *man's* nature, and the way of Heaven, cannot be heard.'

CHAPTER XIII.

When Tsze-lû heard anything, if he had not yet succeeded in carrying it into practice, he was only afraid lest he should hear something else.

CHAPTER XIV.

Tsze-kung asked, saying, 'On what ground did Kung-wăn get that title of Wăn?' The Master said, 'He was of an active nature and yet fond of learning, and he was not ashamed to ask *and learn* of his inferiors!-- On these grounds he has been styled Wăn.'

CHAPTER XV.

The Master said of Tsze-ch'an that he had four of the characteristics of a superior man:-- in his conduct of himself, he was humble; in serving his superiors, he was respectful; in nourishing the people, he was kind; in ordering the people, he was just.'

CHAPTER XVI.

The Master said, 'Yen P'ing knew well how to maintain friendly intercourse. The acquaintance might be long, but he showed the *same* respect *as at first*.'

CHAPTER XVII.

The Master said, 'Tsang Wăn kept a large tortoise in a house, on the capitals of the pillars of which he had hills made, and with representations of duckweed on the small pillars *above the beams supporting the rafters*.-- Of what sort was his wisdom?'

CHAPTER XVIII.

1 Tsze-chang asked, saying, 'The minister Tsze-wăn thrice took office, and manifested no joy in his countenance. Thrice he retired from office, and manifested no displeasure. He made it a point to inform the new minister of the way in which he had conducted the government;-- what do you say of him?' The Master replied. 'He was loyal.' 'Was he perfectly virtuous?' 'I do not know. How can he be pronounced perfectly virtuous?'

2 *Tsze-chang* proceeded, 'When the officer Ch'ûi killed the prince of Ch'î, Ch'ăn Wăn, though he was the owner of forty horses, abandoned them and left the country. Coming to another State, he said, "They are here like our great officer, Ch'ûi," and left it. He came to a second State, and with the same observation left it also;-- what do you say of him?' The Master replied, 'He was pure.' 'Was he perfectly virtuous?' 'I do not know. How can he be pronounced perfectly virtuous?'

CHAPTER XIX.

Chî Wân thought thrice, and then acted. When the Master was informed of it, he said, 'Twice may do.'

CHAPTER XX.

The Master said, 'When good order prevailed in his country, Ning Wû acted the part of a wise man. When his country was in disorder, he acted the part of a stupid man. Others may equal his wisdom, but they cannot equal his stupidity.'

CHAPTER XXI.

When the Master was in Ch'ăn, he said, 'Let me return! Let me return! The little children of my school are ambitious and too hasty.

They are accomplished and complete so far, but they do not know how to restrict and shape themselves.'

CHAPTER XXII.

The Master said, 'Po-î and Shû-ch' î did not keep the former wickednesses of men in mind, and hence the resentments directed towards them were few.'

CHAPTER XXIII.

The Master said, 'Who says of Wei-shăng Kao that he is upright? One begged some vinegar of him, and he begged it of a neighbor and gave it to the man.'

CHAPTER XXIV.

The Master said, 'Fine words, an insinuating appearance, and excessive respect;-- Tso Ch'iû-ming was ashamed of them. I also am ashamed of them. To conceal resentment against a person, and appear friendly with him;-- Tso Ch'iû-ming was ashamed of such conduct. I also am ashamed of it.'

CHAPTER XXV.

1 Yen Yüan and Chi Lû being by his side, the Master said to them, 'Come, let each of you tell his wishes.'

2 Tsze-lû said, 'I should like, having chariots and horses, and light fur dresses, to share them with my friends, and though they should spoil them, I would not be displeased.'

3 Yen Yüan said, 'I should like not to boast of my excellence, nor to make a display of my meritorious deeds.'

4 Tsze-lû then said, 'I should like, sir, to hear your wishes.' The Master said, 'They are, in regard to the aged, to give them rest;

in regard to friends, to show them sincerity; in regard to the young, to treat them tenderly.'

CHAPTER XXVI.

The Master said, 'It is all over! I have not yet seen one who could perceive his faults, and inwardly accuse himself.'

CHAPTER XXVII.

The Master said, 'In a hamlet of ten families, there may be found one honourable and sincere as I am, but not so fond of learning.'

BOOK VI.
YUNG YÊY.

CHAPTER I.

1 The Master said, 'There is Yung!-- He might occupy the place of a prince.'

2 Chung-kung asked about Tsze-sang Po-tsze. The Master said, 'He may pass. He does not mind small matters.'

3 Chung-kung said, 'If a man cherish in himself a reverential feeling of the *necessity of attention to business*, though he may be easy in small matters in his government of the people, that may be allowed. But if he cherish in himself that easy feeling, and also carry it out in his practice, is not such an easy mode of procedure excessive?

4 The Master said, 'Yung's words are right.'

CHAPTER II.

The Duke Âi asked which of the disciples loved to learn. Confucius replied to him, 'There was Yen Hûi; HE loved to learn. He did not transfer his anger; he did not repeat a fault. Unfortunately, his appointed time was short and he died; and now there is not *such another*. I have not yet heard of any one who loves to learn as *he did*.'

CHAPTER III.

1 Tsze-hwâ being employed on a mission to Ch'î, the disciple Zan requested grain for his mother. The Master said, 'Give her a *fû*.' Yen requested more. 'Give her an *yü*,' said the Master. Yen gave her five ping.

2 The Master said, 'When Ch'ih was proceeding to Ch'î, he had fat horses to his carriage, and wore light furs. I have heard that a superior man helps the distressed, but does not add to the wealth of the rich.'

3 Yüan Sze being made governor of his town by the Master, he gave him nine hundred measures of grain, but Sze declined them.

4 The Master said, 'Do not decline them. May you not give them away in the neighborhoods, hamlets, towns, and villages?'

CHAPTER IV.

The Master, speaking of Chung-kung, said, 'If the calf of a brindled cow be red and horned, although men may not wish to use it, would *the spirits of* the mountains and rivers put it aside?'

CHAPTER V.

The Master said, 'Such was Hûi that for three months there would be nothing in his mind contrary to perfect virtue. The others may attain to this on some days or in some months, but nothing more.'

CHAPTER VI.

Chi K'ang asked about Chung-yû, whether he was fit to be employed as an officer of government. The Master said, 'Yû is a man of decision; what difficulty would he find in being an officer of government?' K'ang asked, 'Is Ts'ze fit to be employed as an officer of government?' and was answered, 'Ts'ze is a man of intelligence; what difficulty would he find in being an officer of government?' And to the same question about Ch'iû the Master gave the same reply, saying, 'Ch'iû is a man of various ability.'

CHAPTER VII.

The chief of the Chi family sent to ask Min Tsze-ch'ien to be governor of Pî. Min Tsze-ch'ien said, 'Decline the offer for me politely. If any one come again to me with a second invitation, I shall be *obliged to go and live* on the banks of the Wăn.'

CHAPTER VIII.

Po-niû being ill, the Master went to ask for him. He took hold of his hand through the window, and said, 'It is killing him. It is the appointment *of Heaven*, alas! That such a man should have such a sickness! That such a man should have such a sickness!'

CHAPTER IX.

The Master said, 'Admirable indeed was the virtue of Hûi! With a single bamboo dish of rice, a single gourd dish of drink, and living in his mean narrow lane, while others could not have endured the distress, he did not allow his joy to be affected by it. Admirable indeed was the virtue of Hûi!'

CHAPTER X.

Yen Ch'iû said, 'It is not that I do not delight in your doctrines, but my strength is insufficient.' The Master said, 'Those whose strength is insufficient give over in the middle of the way but now you limit yourself.'

CHAPTER XI.

The Master said to Tsze-hsiâ, 'Do you be a scholar after the style of the superior man, and not after that of the mean man.'

CHAPTER XII.

Tsze-yû being governor of Wu-ch'ăng, the Master said to him, 'Have you got good men *there*?' He answered, 'There is Tan-t'âi Mieh-ming, who never in walking takes a short cut, and never comes to my office, excepting on public business.'

CHAPTER XIII.

The Master said, 'Măng Chih-fan does not boast of his merit. Being in the rear on an occasion of flight, when they were about to enter the gate, he whipped up his horse, saying, "It is not that I dare to be last. My horse would not advance."'

CHAPTER XIV.

The Master said, 'Without the specious speech of the litanist T'o and the beauty of *the prince* Châo of Sung, it is difficult to escape in the present age.'

CHAPTER XV.

The Master said, 'Who can go out but by the door? How is it that men will not walk according to these ways?'

CHAPTER XVI.

The Master said, 'Where the solid qualities are in excess of accomplishments, we have rusticity; where the accomplishments are in excess of the solid qualities, we have the manners of a clerk. When the accomplishments and solid qualities are equally blended, we then have the man of virtue.'

CHAPTER XVII.

The Master said, 'Man is born for uprightness. If a man lose his uprightness, and yet live, his escape *from death* is the effect of mere good fortune.'

CHAPTER XVIII.

The Master said, 'They who know *the truth* are not equal to those who love it, and they who love it are not equal to those who delight in it.'

CHAPTER XIX.

The Master said, 'To those whose talents are above mediocrity, the highest subjects may be announced. To those who are below mediocrity, the highest subjects may not be announced.'

CHAPTER XX.

Fan Ch'ih asked what constituted wisdom. The Master said, 'To give one's self earnestly to the duties due to men, and, while respecting spiritual beings, to keep aloof from them, may be called wisdom.' He asked about perfect virtue. The Master said, 'The man of virtue makes the difficulty *to be overcome* his first business, and success only a subsequent consideration;-- this may be called perfect virtue.'

CHAPTER XXI.

The Master said, 'The wise find pleasure in water; the virtuous find pleasure in hills. The wise are active; the virtuous are tranquil. The wise are joyful; the virtuous are long-lived.'

CHAPTER XXII.

The Master said, 'Ch'î, by one change, would come to the State of Lû. Lû, by one change, would come to a State where true principles predominated.'

CHAPTER XXIII.

The Master said, 'A cornered vessel without corners.-- A strange cornered vessel! A strange cornered vessel!'

CHAPTER XXIV.

Tsâi Wo asked, saying, 'A benevolent man, though it be told him,-- 'There is a man in the well' will go in after him, I suppose.' Confucius said, 'Why should he do so?' A superior man may be made to *go to the well*, but he cannot be made to go down into it. He may be imposed upon, but he cannot be fooled.'

CHAPTER XXV.

The Master said, 'The superior man, extensively studying all learning, and keeping himself under the restraint of the rules of propriety, may thus likewise not overstep what is right.'

CHAPTER XXVI.

The Master having visited Nan-tsze, Tsze-lû was displeased, on which the Master swore, saying, 'Wherein I have done improperly, may Heaven reject me, may Heaven reject me!'

CHAPTER XXVII.

The Master said, 'Perfect is the virtue which is according to the Constant Mean! Rare for a long time has been its practise among the people.'

CHAPTER XXVIII.

1 Tsze-kung said, 'Suppose the case of a man extensively conferring benefits on the people, and able to assist all, what would you say of him? Might he be called perfectly virtuous? The Master said, 'Why speak only of virtue in connexion with him? Must he not have the qualities of a sage? Even Yâo and Shun were still solicitous about this.

2 'Now the man of perfect virtue, wishing to be established himself, seeks also to establish others; wishing to be enlarged himself, he seeks also to enlarge others.

3 'To be able to judge *of others* by what is nigh *in ourselves*;--this may be called the art of virtue.'

BOOK VII.
SHÛ R.

CHAPTER I.

The Master said, 'A transmitter and not a maker, believing in and loving the ancients, I venture to compare myself with our old P'ang.'

CHAPTER II.

The Master said, 'The silent treasuring up of knowledge; learning without satiety; and instructing others without being wearied:-- which one of these things belongs to me?'

CHAPTER III.

The Master said, 'The leaving virtue without proper cultivation; the not thoroughly discussing what is learned; not being able to move towards righteousness of which a knowledge is gained; and not being able to change what is not good:-- these are the things which occasion me solicitude.'

CHAPTER IV.

When the Master was unoccupied with business, his manner was easy, and he looked pleased.

CHAPTER V.

The Master said, 'Extreme is my decay. For a long time, I have not dreamed, as I was wont to do, that I saw the duke of Châu.'

CHAPTER VI.

1 The Master said, 'Let the will be set on the path of duty.

2 'Let every attainment in what is good be firmly grasped.

3 'Let perfect virtue be accorded with.

4 'Let relaxation and enjoyment be found in the polite arts.'

CHAPTER VII.

The Master said, 'From the man bringing his bundle of dried flesh for my teaching upwards, I have never refused instruction to any one.'

CHAPTER VIII.

The Master said, 'I do not open up the truth to one who is not eager *to get knowledge*, nor help out any one who is not anxious to explain himself. When I have presented one corner of a subject to any one, and he cannot from it learn the other three, I do not repeat my lesson.'

CHAPTER IX.

1 When the Master was eating by the side of a mourner, he never ate to the full.

2 He did not sing on the same day in which he had been weeping.

CHAPTER X.

1 The Master said to Yen Yüan, 'When called to office, to undertake its duties; when not so called, to lie retired;-- it is only I and you who have attained to this.'

2 Tsze-lû said, 'If you had the conduct of the armies of a great State, whom would you have to act with you?'

3 The Master said, 'I would not have him to act with me, who will unarmed attack a tiger, or cross a river without a boat, dying without any regret. My associate must be the man who proceeds to action full of solicitude, who is fond of adjusting his plans, and then carries them into execution.'

CHAPTER XI.

The Master said, 'If the search for riches is sure to be successful, though I should become a groom with whip in hand to get them, I will do so. As the search may not be successful, I will follow after that which I love.'

CHAPTER XII.

The things in reference to which the Master exercised the greatest caution were -- fasting, war, and sickness.

CHAPTER XIII.

When the Master was in Ch'i, he heard the Shâo, and for three months did not know the taste of flesh. 'I did not think" he said, 'that music could have been made so excellent as this.'

CHAPTER XIV.

1 Yen Yû said, 'Is our Master for the ruler of Wei?' Tsze-kung said, 'Oh! I will ask him.'

2 He went in accordingly, and said, 'What sort of men were Po-î and Shû-ch' î?' 'They were ancient worthies,' said the Master. 'Did they have any repinings *because of their course*?' The Master again replied, 'They sought to act virtuously, and they did so; what was there for them to repine about?' On this, Tsze-kung went out and said, 'Our Master is not for him.'

CHAPTER XV.

The Master said, 'With coarse rice to eat, with water to drink, and my bended arm for a pillow;-- I have still joy in the midst of these things. Riches and honours acquired by unrighteousness, are to me as a floating cloud.'

CHAPTER XVI.

The Master said, 'If some years were added to my life, I would give fifty to the study of the Yî, and then I might come to be without great faults.'

CHAPTER XVII

The Master's frequent themes of discourse were--the Odes, the History, and the maintenance of the Rules of Propriety. On all these he frequently discoursed.

CHAPTER XVIII.

1 The Duke of Sheh asked Tsze-lû about Confucius, and Tsze-lû did not answer him.

2 The Master said, 'Why did you not say to him,-- He is simply a man, who in his eager pursuit (of knowledge) forgets his food, who in the joy *of its attainment* forgets his sorrows, and who does not perceive that old age is coming on?'

CHAPTER XIX.

The Master said, 'I am not one who was born in the possession of knowledge; I am one who is fond of antiquity, and earnest in seeking it *there*.'

CHAPTER XX.

The subjects on which the Master did not talk, were-- extraordinary things, feats of strength, disorder, and spiritual beings.

CHAPTER XXI.

The Master said, 'When I walk along with two others, they may serve me as my teachers. I will select their good qualities and follow them, their bad qualities and avoid them.'

CHAPTER XXII.

The Master said, 'Heaven produced the virtue that is in me. Hwan T'ui-- what can he do to me?'

CHAPTER XXIII.

The Master said, 'Do you think, my disciples, that I have any concealments? I conceal nothing from you. There is nothing which I do that is not shown to you, my disciples;-- that is my way.'

CHAPTER XXIV.

There were four things which the Master taught,-- letters, ethics, devotion of soul, and truthfulness.

CHAPTER XXV.

1 The Master said, 'A sage it is not mine to see; could I see a man of real talent and virtue, that would satisfy me.'

2 The Master said, 'A good man it is not mine to see; could I see a man possessed of constancy, that would satisfy me.

3 'Having not and yet affecting to have, empty and yet affecting to be full, straitened and yet affecting to be at ease:-- it is difficult with such characteristics to have constancy.'

CHAPTER XXVI.

The Master angled,-- but did not use a net. He shot,-- but not at birds perching.

CHAPTER XXVII.

The Master said, 'There may be those who act without knowing why. I do not do so. Hearing much and selecting what is good and following it; seeing much and keeping it in memory:-- this is the second style of knowledge.'

CHAPTER XXVIII.

1 It was difficult to talk (profitably and reputably) with the people of Hû-hsiang, and a lad of that place having had an interview with the Master, the disciples doubted.

2 The Master said, 'I admit people's approach to me without committing myself *as to what they may do* when they have retired. Why must one be so severe? If a man purify himself to wait upon me, I receive him so purified, without guaranteeing his past conduct.'

CHAPTER XXIX.

The Master said, 'Is virtue a thing remote? I wish to be virtuous, and lo! virtue is at hand.'

CHAPTER XXX.

1 The minister of crime of Ch'ăn asked whether the duke Châo knew propriety, and Confucius said, 'He knew propriety.

2 Confucius having retired, the minister bowed to Wû-mâ Ch'î to come forward, and said, 'I have heard that the superior man is not a partisan. May the superior man be a partisan also? The prince married a daughter of the house of Wû, of the same surname with himself, and called her,-- "The elder Tsze of Wû." If the prince knew propriety, who does not know it?'

3 Wû-mâ Ch'î reported these remarks, and the Master said, 'I am fortunate! If I have any errors, people are sure to know them.'

CHAPTER XXXI.

When the Master was in company with a person who was singing, if he sang well, he would make him repeat the song, while he accompanied it with his own voice.

CHAPTER XXXII.

The Master said, 'In letters I am perhaps equal to other men, but *the character of* the superior man, carrying out in his conduct what he professes, is what I have not yet attained to.'

CHAPTER XXXIII.

The Master said, 'The sage and the man of perfect virtue;-- how dare I *rank myself with them*? It may simply be said of me, that I strive to become such without satiety, and teach others without weariness.' Kung-hsî Hwâ said, 'This is just what we, the disciples, cannot imitate you in.'

CHAPTER XXXIV.

The Master being very sick, Tsze- lû asked leave to pray for him. He said, 'May such a thing be done?' Tsze-lû replied, 'It may. In the Eulogies it is said, "Prayer has been made for thee to the spirits of the upper and lower worlds '" The Master said, 'My praying has been for a long time.'

CHAPTER XXXV.

The Master said, 'Extravagance leads to insubordination, and parsimony to meanness. It is better to be mean than to be insubordinate.'

CHAPTER XXXVI.

The Master said, 'The superior man is satisfied and composed; the mean man is always full of distress.'

CHAPTER XXXVII.

The Master was mild, and yet dignified; majestic, and yet not fierce; respectful, and yet easy.

BOOK VIII.
T'ÂI-PO.

CHAPTER I.

The Master said, 'T'âi-po may be said to have reached the highest point of virtuous action. Thrice he declined the kingdom, and the people in ignorance of his motives could not express their approbation of his conduct.'

CHAPTER II.

1 The Master said, 'Respectfulness, without the rules of propriety, becomes laborious bustle; carefulness, without the rules of propriety, becomes timidity; boldness, without the rules of propriety, becomes insubordination; straightforwardness, without the rules of propriety, becomes rudeness.

2 'When those who are in high stations perform well all their duties to their relations, the people are aroused to virtue. When old friends are not neglected by them, the people are preserved from meanness.'

CHAPTER III.

The philosopher Tsăng being ill, he called to him the disciples of his school, and said, 'Uncover my feet, uncover my hands. It is said in the Book of Poetry, "We should be apprehensive and cautious, as if on the brink of a deep gulf, as if treading on thin ice," *and so have I been*. Now and hereafter, I know my escape *from all injury to my person*, O ye, my little children.'

CHAPTER IV.

1 The philosopher Tsăng being ill, Meng Chăng went to ask how he was.

2 Tsăng said to him, 'When a bird is about to die, its notes are mournful; when a man is about to die, his words are good.

3 'There are three principles of conduct which the man of high rank should consider specially important:-- that in his deportment and manner he keep from violence and heedlessness; that in regulating his countenance he keep near to sincerity; and that in his words and tones he keep far from lowness and impropriety. As to such matters as attending to the sacrificial vessels, there are the proper officers for them.'

CHAPTER V.

The philosopher Tsăng said, 'Gifted with ability, and yet putting questions to those who were not so; possessed of much, and yet putting questions to those possessed of little; having, as though he had not; full, and yet counting himself as empty; offended against, and yet entering into no altercation; formerly I had a friend who pursued this style of conduct.'

CHAPTER VI.

The philosopher Tsăng said, 'Suppose that there is an individual who can be entrusted with the charge of a young orphan *prince*, and can be commissioned with authority over *a state of* a hundred *lî*, and whom no emergency however great can drive from his principles:-- is such a man a superior man? He is a superior man indeed.'

CHAPTER VII.

1 The philosopher Tsăng said, 'The officer may not be without breadth of mind and vigorous endurance. His burden is heavy and his course is long.

2 'Perfect virtue is the burden which he considers it is his to sustain;-- is it not heavy? Only with death does his course stop;-- is it not long?

CHAPTER VIII.

1 The Master said, 'It is by the Odes that the mind is aroused.

2 'It is by the Rules of Propriety that the character is established.

3 'It is from Music that the finish is received.'

CHAPTER IX.

The Master said, 'The people may be made to follow a path of action, but they may not be made to understand it.'

CHAPTER X.

The Master said, 'The man who is fond of daring and is dissatisfied with poverty, will proceed to insubordination. So will the man who is not virtuous, when you carry your dislike of him to an extreme.'

CHAPTER XI.

The Master said, 'Though a man have abilities as admirable as those of the Duke of Châu, yet if he be proud and niggardly, those other things are really not worth being looked at.'

CHAPTER XII.

The Master said, 'It is not easy to find a man who has learned for three years without coming to be good.'

CHAPTER XIII.

1 The Master said, 'With sincere faith he unites the love of learning; holding firm to death, he is perfecting the excellence of his course.

2 '*Such an one* will not enter a tottering State, nor dwell in a disorganized one. When right principles of government prevail in the kingdom, he will show himself; when they are prostrated, he will keep concealed.

3 'When a country is well-governed, poverty and a mean condition are things to be ashamed of. When a country is ill-governed, riches and honour are things to be ashamed of.'

CHAPTER XIV.

The Master said, 'He who is not in any particular office, has nothing to do with plans for the administration of its duties.'

CHAPTER XV.

The Master said, 'When the music master Chih first entered on his office, the finish of the Kwan Tsü was magnificent;--how it filled the ears!'

CHAPTER XVI.

The Master said, 'Ardent and yet not upright; stupid and yet not attentive; simple and yet not sincere:-- such persons I do not understand.'

CHAPTER XVII.

The Master said, 'Learn as if you could not reach your object, and were always fearing also lest you should lose it.'

CHAPTER XVIII.

The Master said, 'How majestic was the manner in which Shun and Yu held possession of the empire, as if it were nothing to them!'

CHAPTER XIX.

1 The Master said, 'Great indeed was Yâo as a sovereign! How majestic was he! It is only Heaven that is grand, and only Yâo corresponded to it. How vast *was his virtue*! The people could find no name for it.

2 'How majestic was he in the works which he accomplished! How glorious in the elegant regulations which he instituted!'

CHAPTER XX.

1 Shun had five ministers, and the empire was well-governed.

2 King Wû said, 'I have ten able ministers.'

3 Confucius said, 'Is not *the saying* that talents are difficult to find, true? Only when the dynasties of T'ang and Yû met, were they more abundant than in this of *Châu, yet* there was a woman among them. *The able ministers* were no more than nine men.

4 '*King Wăn* possessed two of the three parts of the empire, and with those he served the dynasty of Yin. The virtue of the house of Châu may be said to have reached the highest point indeed.'

CHAPTER XXI.

The Master said, 'I can find no flaw in the character of Yü. He used himself coarse food and drink, but displayed the utmost filial piety towards the spirits. His ordinary garments were poor, but he displayed the utmost elegance in his sacrificial cap and apron. He lived in a low mean house, but expended all his strength on the ditches and water-channels. I can find nothing like a flaw in Yü.'

BOOK IX.
TSZE HAN.

CHAPTER I.

The subjects of which the Master seldom spoke were-- profitableness, and also the appointments *of Heaven*, and perfect virtue.

CHAPTER II.

1 A man of the village of Tâ-hsiang said, 'Great indeed is the philosopher K'ung! His learning is extensive, and yet he does not render his name famous by any *particular* thing.

2 The Master heard the observation, and said to his disciples, 'What shall I practise? Shall I practise charioteering, or shall I practise archery? I will practise charioteering.'

CHAPTER III.

1 The Master said, 'The linen cap is that prescribed by the rules of ceremony, but now a silk one is worn. It is economical, and I follow the common practice.

2 'The rules of ceremony prescribe the bowing below *the hall*, but now the practice is to bow *only* after ascending it. That is arrogant. I *continue* to bow below the hall, though I oppose the common practice.'

CHAPTER IV.

There were four things from which the Master was entirely free. He had no foregone conclusions, no arbitrary predeterminations, no obstinacy, and no egoism.

CHAPTER V.

1 The Master was put in fear in K'wang.

2 He said, 'After the death of King Wăn, was not the cause of truth lodged here in me?

3 'If Heaven had wished to let this cause of truth perish, then I, a future mortal, should not have got such a relation to that cause. While Heaven does not let the cause of truth perish, what can the people of K'wang do to me?'

CHAPTER VI.

1 A high officer asked Tsze-kung, saying, 'May we not say that your Master is a sage? How various is his ability!'

2 Tsze-kung said, 'Certainly Heaven has endowed him unlimitedly. He is about a sage. And, moreover, his ability is various.

3 The Master heard of the conversation and said, 'Does the high officer know me? When I was young, my condition was low, and therefore I acquired my ability in many things, but they were mean matters. Must the superior man have such variety of ability? He does not need variety of ability.'

4 Lâo said, 'The Master said, "Having no official employment, I acquired many arts."'

CHAPTER VII.

The Master said, 'Am I indeed possessed of knowledge? I am not knowing. But if a mean person, who appears quite empty-like, ask anything of me, I set it forth from one end to the other, and exhaust it.'

CHAPTER VIII.

The Master said, 'The FĂNG bird does not come; the river sends forth no map:-- it is all over with me!'

CHAPTER IX.

When the Master saw a person in a mourning dress, or any one with the cap and upper and lower garments of full dress, or a blind person, on observing them *approaching*, though they were younger than himself, he would rise up, and if he had to pass by them, he would do so hastily.

CHAPTER X.

1 Yen Yüan, *in admiration of the Master's doctrines*, sighed and said, 'I looked up to them, and they *seemed to become* more high; I tried to penetrate them, and they *seemed to become* more firm; I looked at them before me, and suddenly they *seemed to be* behind.

2 'The Master, by orderly method, skilfully leads men on. He enlarged my mind with learning, and taught me the restraints of propriety.

3 'When I wish to give over the *study of his doctrines*, I cannot do so, and having exerted all my ability, there seems something to stand right up before me; but though I wish to follow *and lay hold of it*, I really find no way to do so.'

CHAPTER XI.

1 The Master being very ill, Tsze-lû wished the disciples to act as ministers to him.

2 During a remission of his illness, he said, 'Long has the conduct of Yû been deceitful! By pretending to have ministers when I have them not, whom should I impose upon? Should I impose upon Heaven?

3 'Moreover, than that I should die in the hands of ministers, is it not better that I should die in the hands of you, my disciples? And though I may not get a great burial, shall I die upon the road?'

CHAPTER XII.

Tsze-kung said, 'There is a beautiful gem here. Should I lay it up in a case and keep it? or should I seek for a good price and sell it?' The Master said, 'Sell it! Sell it! But I would wait for one to offer the price.'

CHAPTER XIII.

1 The Master was wishing to go and live among the nine wild tribes of the east.

2 Some one said, 'They are rude. How can you do such a thing?' The Master said, 'If a superior man dwelt among them, what rudeness would there be?'

CHAPTER XIV.

The Master said, 'I returned from Wei to Lû, and then the music was reformed, and the pieces in the Royal songs and Praise songs all found their proper places.'

CHAPTER XV.

The Master said, 'Abroad, to serve the high ministers and nobles; at home, to serve one's father and elder brothers; in all duties to the dead, not to dare not to exert one's self; and not to be overcome of wine:-- which one of these things do I attain to?'

CHAPTER XVI.

The Master standing by a stream, said, 'It passes on just like this, not ceasing day or night!'

CHAPTER XVII.

The Master said, 'I have not seen one who loves virtue as he loves beauty.'

CHAPTER XVIII.

The Master said, '*The prosecution of learning* may be compared to what may happen in raising a mound. If there want but one basket *of earth* to complete the work, and I stop, the stopping is my own work. It may be compared *to throwing down the earth* on the level ground. Though *but* one basketful is thrown *at a time*, the advancing with it is my own going forward.'

CHAPTER XIX.

The Master said, 'Never flagging when I set forth anything to him;--ah! that is Hui.'

CHAPTER XX.

The Master said of Yen Yuan, 'Alas! I saw his constant advance. I never saw him stop in his progress.'

CHAPTER XXI.

The Master said, 'There are cases in which the blade springs, but the plant does not go on to flower! There are cases where it flowers, but no fruit is subsequently produced!'

CHAPTER XXII.

The Master said, 'A youth is to be regarded with respect. How do we know that his future will not be equal to our present? If he reach the age of forty or fifty, and has not made himself heard of, then indeed he will not be worth being regarded with respect.'

CHAPTER XXIII.

The Master said, 'Can men refuse to assent to the words of strict admonition? But it is reforming the conduct because of them which is valuable. Can men refuse to be pleased with words of gentle advice? But it is unfolding their aim which is valuable. If a man be pleased with these words, but does not unfold their aim, and assents to those, but does not reform his conduct, I can really do nothing with him.'

CHAPTER XXIV

The Master said, 'Hold faithfulness and sincerity as first principles. Have no friends not equal to yourself. When you have faults, do not fear to abandon them.'

CHAPTER XXV.

The Master said, 'The commander of the forces of a large state may be carried off, but the will of even a common man cannot be taken from him.'

CHAPTER XXVI.

1 The Master said, 'Dressed himself in a tattered robe quilted with hemp, yet standing by the side of men dressed in furs, and not ashamed;-- ah! it is Yû who is equal to this!

2 '"He dislikes none, he covets nothing;-- what can he do but what is good!"'

3 Tsze-lû kept continually repeating these words of the ode, when the Master said, 'Those things are by no means sufficient to constitute (perfect) excellence.'

CHAPTER XXVII.

The Master said, 'When the year becomes cold, then we know how the pine and the cypress are the last to lose their leaves.'

CHAPTER XXVIII.

The Master said, 'The wise are free from perplexities; the virtuous from anxiety; and the bold from fear.'

CHAPTER XXIX.

The Master said, 'There are some with whom we may study in common, but we shall find them unable to go along with us to principles. Perhaps we may go on with them to principles, but we shall find them unable to get established in those along with us. Or if we may get so established along with them, we shall find them unable to weigh occurring events along with us.'

CHAPTER XXX.

1 How the flowers of the aspen-plum flutter and turn! Do I not think of you? But your house is distant.

2 The Master said, 'It is the want of thought about it. How is it distant?'

BOOK X.
HEANG TANG.

CHAPTER I.

1 Confucius, in his village, looked simple and sincere, and as if he were not able to speak.

2 When he was in the *prince's* ancestorial temple, or in the court, he spoke minutely on every point, but cautiously.

CHAPTER II.

1 When he was waiting at court, in speaking with the great officers of the lower grade, he spake freely, but in a straightforward manner; in speaking with those of the higher grade, he did so blandly, but precisely.

2 When the ruler was present, his manner displayed respectful uneasiness; it was grave, but self-possessed.

CHAPTER III.

1 When the prince called him to employ him in the reception of a visitor, his countenance appeared to change, and his legs to move forward with difficulty.

2 He inclined himself to the *other officers* among whom he stood, moving his left or right arm, *as their position required*, but keeping the skirts of his robe before and behind evenly adjusted.

3 He hastened forward, with *his arms* like the wings of a bird.

4 When the guest had retired, he would report to the prince, 'The visitor is not turning round any more.'

CHAPTER IV.

1 When he entered the palace gate, he seemed to bend his body, as if it were not sufficient to admit him.

2 When he was standing, he did not occupy the middle of the gate-way; when he passed in or out, he did not tread upon the threshold.

3 When he was passing the *vacant* place *of the prince*, his countenance appeared to change, and his legs to bend under him, and his words came as if he hardly had breath to utter them

4 He ascended the reception hall, holding up his robe with both his hands, and his body bent; holding in his breath also, as if he dared not breathe.

5 When he came out *from the audience*, as soon as he had descended one step, he began to relax his countenance, and had a satisfied look. When he had got to the bottom of the steps, he advanced rapidly to his place, *with his arms* like wings, and on occupying it, his manner still showed respectful uneasiness.

CHAPTER V.

1 When he was carrying the scepter *of his ruler*, he seemed to bend his body, as if he were not able to bear its weight. He did not hold it higher than the position of the hands in making a bow, nor lower than their position in giving anything to another. His countenance seemed to change, and look apprehensive, and he dragged his feet along as if they were held by something to the ground.

2 In presenting the presents *with which he was charged*, he wore a placid appearance.

3 At his private audience, he looked highly pleased.

CHAPTER VI.

1 The superior man did not use a deep purple, or a puce colour, in the ornaments of his dress.

2 Even in his undress, he did not wear anything of a red or reddish colour.

3 In warm weather, he had a single garment either of coarse or fine texture, but he wore it displayed over an inner garment.

4 Over lamb's fur he wore a garment of black; over fawn's fur one of white; and over fox's fur one of yellow.

5 The fur robe of his undress was long, with the right sleeve short.

6 He required his sleeping dress to be half as long again as his body.

7 When staying at home, he used thick furs of the fox or the badger.

8 When he put off mourning, he wore all the appendages of the girdle.

9 His under-garment, except when it was required to be of the curtain shape, was made of silk cut narrow above and wide below.

10 He did not wear lamb's fur or a black cap, on a visit of condolence.

11 On the first day of the month he put on his court robes, and presented himself at court.

CHAPTER VII.

1 When fasting, he thought it necessary to have his clothes brightly clean and made of linen cloth.

2 When fasting, he thought it necessary to change his food, and also to change the place where he commonly sat in the apartment.

CHAPTER VIII.

1 He did not dislike to have his rice finely cleaned, nor to have his minced meat cut quite small.

2 He did not eat rice which had been injured by heat or damp and turned sour, nor fish or flesh which was gone. He did not eat what was discoloured, or what was of a bad flavour, nor anything which was ill-cooked, or was not in season.

3 He did not eat meat which was not cut properly, nor what was served without its proper sauce.

4 Though there might be a large quantity of meat, he would not allow what he took to exceed the due proportion for the rice. It was only in wine that he laid down no limit for himself, but he did not allow himself to be confused by it.

5 He did not partake of wine and dried meat bought in the market.

6 He was never without ginger when he ate.

7 He did not eat much.

8 When he had been assisting at the prince's sacrifice, he did not keep the flesh which he received overnight. The flesh of his family sacrifice he did not keep over three days. If kept over three days, people could not eat it.

9 When eating, he did not converse. When in bed, he did not speak.

10 Although his food might be coarse rice and vegetable soup, he would offer a little of it in sacrifice with a grave, respectful air.

CHAPTER IX.

If his mat was not straight, he did not sit on it.

CHAPTER X.

1 When the villagers were drinking together, on those who carried staffs going out, he went out immediately after.

2 When the villagers were going through their ceremonies to drive away pestilential influences, he put on his court robes and stood on the eastern steps.

CHAPTER XI.

1 When he was sending complimentary inquiries to any one in another State, he bowed twice as he escorted the messenger away.

2 Chi K'ang having sent him a present of physic, he bowed and received it, saying, 'I do not know it. I dare not taste it.'

CHAPTER XII.

The stable being burned down, when he was at court, on his return he said, 'Has any man been hurt?' He did not ask about the horses.

CHAPTER XIII.

1 When the prince sent him a gift of *cooked* meat, he would adjust his mat, *first* taste it, *and then give it away to others*. When the prince sent him a gift of undressed meat, he would have it cooked, and offer it *to the spirits of his ancestors*. When the prince sent him a gift of a living animal, he would keep it alive.

2 When he was in attendance on the prince and joining in the entertainment, the prince only sacrificed. He first tasted everything.

3 When he was ill and the prince came to visit him, he had his head to the east, made his court robes be spread over him, and drew his girdle across them.

4 When the prince's order called him, without waiting for his carriage to be yoked, he went at once.

CHAPTER XIV.

When he entered the ancestral temple of the State, he asked about everything.

CHAPTER XV.

1 When any of his friends died, if he had no relations who could be depended on for the necessary offices, he would say, 'I will bury him.'

2 When a friend sent him a present, though it might be a carriage and horses, he did not bow.

3 The only present for which he bowed was that of the flesh of sacrifice.

CHAPTER XVI.

1 In bed, he did not lie like a corpse. At home, he did not put on any formal deportment.

2 When he saw any one in a mourning dress, though it might be an acquaintance, he would change countenance; when he saw any one wearing the cap of full dress, or a blind person, though he might be in his undress, he would salute them in a ceremonious manner.

3 To any person in mourning he bowed forward to the crossbar of his carriage; he bowed in the same way to any one bearing the tables of population.

4 When he was at an entertainment where there was an abundance of provisions set before him, he would change countenance and rise up.

5 On a sudden clap of thunder, or a violent wind, he would change countenance.

CHAPTER XVII.

1 When he was about to mount his carriage, he would stand straight, holding the cord.

2 When he was in the carriage, he did not turn his head quite round, he did not talk hastily, he did not point with his hands.

CHAPTER XVIII.

1 Seeing the countenance, it instantly rises. It flies round, and by and by settles.

2 *The Master* said, 'There is the hen-pheasant on the hill bridge. At its season! At its season!' Tsze-lû made a motion to it. Thrice it smelt him and then rose.

BOOK XI.
HSIEN TSIN.

CHAPTER I.

1 The Master said, 'The men of former times, in the matters of ceremonies and music were rustics, *it is said*, while the men of these latter times, in ceremonies and music, are accomplished gentlemen.

2 'If I have occasion to use those things, I follow the men of former times.'

CHAPTER II.

1 The Master said, 'Of those who were with me in Ch'ăn and Ts'âi, there are none to be found to enter my door.'

2 Distinguished for their virtuous principles and practice, there were Yen Yûan, Min Tsze-ch'ien, Zan Po-niû, and Chung-kung; for their ability in speech, Tsâi Wo and Tsze-kung; for their administrative talents, Zan Yû and Chî Lû; for their literary acquirements, Tsze-yû and Tsze-hsiâ.

CHAPTER III.

The Master said, 'Hûi gives me no assistance. There is nothing that I say in which he does not delight.'

CHAPTER IV.

The Master said, 'Filial indeed is Min Tsze-ch'ien! Other people say nothing of him different from the report of his parents and brothers.'

CHAPTER V.

Nan Yung was frequently repeating the *lines* about a white scepter stone. Confucius gave him the daughter of his elder brother to wife.

CHAPTER VI.

Chi K'ang asked which of the disciples loved to learn. Confucius replied to him, 'There was Yen Hûi; he loved to learn. Unfortunately his appointed time was short, and he died. Now there is no one *who loves to learn, as he did.*'

CHAPTER VII.

1 When Yen Yüan died, Yen Lû begged the carriage of the Master to *sell* and get an outer shell for his *son's* coffin.

2 The Master said, 'Every one calls his son his son, whether he has talents or has not talents. There was Lî; when he died, he had a coffin but no outer shell. I would not walk on foot to get a shell for him, because, having followed in the rear of the great officers, it was not proper that I should walk on foot.'

CHAPTER VIII.

When Yen Yüan died, the Master said, 'Alas! Heaven is destroying me! Heaven is destroying me!'

CHAPTER IX.

1 When Yen Yüan died, the Master bewailed him exceedingly, and the disciples who were with him said, 'Master, your grief is excessive?'

2 'Is it excessive?' said he.

3 'If I am not to mourn bitterly for this man, for whom should I mourn?'

CHAPTER X.

1 When Yen Yüan died, the disciples wished to give him a great funeral, and the Master said, 'You may not do so.'

2 The disciples did bury him in great style.

3 The Master said, 'Hûi behaved towards me as his father. I have not been able to treat him as my son. The fault is not mine; it belongs to you, O disciples.'

CHAPTER XI.

Chî Lû asked about serving the spirits of *the dead*. The Master said, 'While you are not able to serve men, how can you serve *their spirits*?' *Chî Lû added*, 'I venture to ask about death?' He was answered, 'While you do not know life, how can you know about death?'

CHAPTER XII.

1 The disciple Min was standing by his side, looking bland and precise; Tsze-lû, looking bold and soldierly; Zan Yû and Tsze-kung, with a free and straightforward manner. The Master was pleased.

2 He said, 'Yû, there!-- he will not die a natural death.'

CHAPTER XIII.

1 Some parties in Lû were going to take down and rebuild the Long Treasury.

2 Min Tsze-ch'ien said, 'Suppose it were to be repaired after its old style;-- why must it be altered and made anew?'

3 The Master said, 'This man seldom speaks; when he does, he is sure to hit the point.'

CHAPTER XIV.

1 The Master said, 'What has the lute of Yû to do in my door?'

2 The other disciples *began* not to respect Tsze-lû. The Master said, 'Yu has ascended to the hall, though he has not yet passed into the inner apartments.'

CHAPTER XV.

1 Tsze-kung asked which of the two, Shih or Shang, was the superior. The Master said, 'Shih goes *beyond the due mean*, and Shang does not come up to it.'

2 'Then,' said Tsze-kung, 'the superiority is with Shih, I suppose.'

3 The Master said, 'To go beyond is as wrong as to fall short.'

CHAPTER XVI.

1 The head of the Chî family was richer than the duke of Châu had been, and yet Ch'iû collected his imposts for him, and increased his wealth.

2 The Master said, 'He is no disciple of mine. My little children, beat the drum and assail him.'

CHAPTER XVII.

1 Ch'âi is simple.

2 Shăn is dull.

3 Shih is specious.

4 Yû is coarse.

CHAPTER XVIII.

1 The Master said, 'There is Hûi! He has nearly attained to *perfect virtue*. He is often in want.

2 'Ts'ze does not acquiesce in the appointments *of Heaven*, and his goods are increased by him. Yet his judgments are often correct.'

CHAPTER XIX.

Tsze-chang asked what were the characteristics of the GOOD man. The Master said, 'He does not tread in the footsteps of others, but moreover, he does not enter the chamber *of the sage*.'

CHAPTER XX.

The Master said, 'If, because a man's discourse appears solid and sincere, we allow him *to be a good man*, is he *really* a superior man? or is his gravity only in appearance?'

CHAPTER XXI.

Tsze-lû asked whether he should immediately carry into practice what he heard. The Master said, 'There are your father and elder brothers *to be consulted*;-- why should you act on that principle of immediately carrying into practice what you hear?' Zan Yû asked the same, whether he should immediately carry into practice what he heard, and the Master answered, 'Immediately carry into practice what you hear.' Kung-hsî Hwâ said, 'Yû asked whether he should carry immediately into practice what he heard, and you said, "There are your father and elder brothers *to be consulted*." Ch'iû asked whether he should immediately carry into practice what he heard, and you said, "Carry it immediately into practice." I, Ch'ih, am perplexed, and venture to ask you for an explanation.' The Master said, 'Ch'iû is retiring and slow; therefore, I urged him forward. Yû has more than his own share of energy; therefore I kept him back.'

CHAPTER XXII.

The Master was put in fear in K'wang and Yen Yüan fell behind. The Master, *on his rejoining him*, said, 'I thought you had died.' Hûi replied, 'While you were alive, how should I presume to die?'

CHAPTER XXIII.

1 Chî Tsze-zan asked whether Chung Yû and Zan Ch'iû could be called great ministers.

2 The Master said, 'I thought you would ask about some extraordinary individuals, and you only ask about Yû and Ch'iû!

3 'What is called a great minister, is one who serves his prince according to what is right, and when he finds he cannot do so, retires.

4 'Now, as to Yû and Ch'iû, they may be called ordinary ministers.'

5 Tsze-zan said, 'Then they will always follow their chief;--will they?'

6 The Master said, 'In an act of parricide or regicide, they would not follow him.'

CHAPTER XXIV.

1 Tsze-lû got Tsze-kâo appointed governor of Pî.

2 The Master said, 'You are injuring a man's son.

3 Tsze-lû said, 'There are (there) common people and officers; there are the altars of the spirits of the land and grain. Why must one read books before he can be considered to have learned?

4 The Master said, 'It is on this account that I hate your glib-tongued people.'

CHAPTER XXV.

1 Tsze-lû, Tsăng Hsî, Zan Yû, and Kung-hsî Hwâ were sitting by the Master.

2 He said to them, 'Though I am a day or so older than you, do not think of that.

3 'From day to day you are saying,-"We are not known." If some *ruler* were to know you, what would you like to do?'

4 Tsze-lû hastily and lightly replied, 'Suppose the case of a State of ten thousand chariots; let it be straitened between *other* large States; let it be suffering from invading armies; and to this let there be added a famine in corn and in all vegetables:-- if I were intrusted with the government of it, in three years' time I could make the people to be bold, and to recognise the rules of righteous conduct.' The Master smiled at him.

5 *Turning to Yen Yû*, he said, 'Ch'iû, what are your wishes?' Ch'iû replied, 'Suppose a state of sixty or seventy li square, or one of fifty or sixty, and let me have the government of it;-- in three years' time, I could make plenty to abound among the people. As to *teaching them* the principles of propriety, and music, I must wait for the rise of a superior man *to do that*.'

6 'What are your wishes, Ch'ih,' *said the Master next to Kung-hsî Hwâ. Ch'ih* replied, 'I do not say that my ability extends to these things, but I should wish to learn them. At the services of the ancestral temple, and at the audiences of the princes with the sovereign, I should like, dressed in the dark square-made robe and the black linen cap, to act as a small assistant.'

7 *Last of all, the Master asked Tsăng Hsî*, 'Tien, what are your wishes?' *Tien*, pausing as he was playing on his lute, while it was yet twanging, laid the instrument aside, and rose. 'My wishes,' he said, 'are different from the cherished purposes of

these three gentlemen.' 'What harm is there in that?' said the Master; 'do you also, as well as they, speak out your wishes.' *Tien* then said, 'In *this*, the last month of spring, with the dress of the season all complete, along with five or six young men who have assumed the cap, and six or seven boys, I would wash in the Î, enjoy the breeze among the rain altars, and return home singing.' The Master heaved a sigh and said, 'I give my approval to Tien.'

8 The three others having gone out, Tsăng Hsî remained behind, and said, 'What do you think of the words of these three friends?' The Master replied, 'They simply told each one his wishes.'

9 *Hsî* pursued, 'Master, why did you smile at Yû?'

10 He was answered, 'The management of a State demands the rules of propriety. His words were not humble; therefore I smiled at him.'

11 *Hsî again said*, 'But was it not a State which Ch'iû proposed for himself?' *The reply was*, 'Yes; did you ever see a territory of sixty or seventy li or one of fifty or sixty, which was not a State?'

12 *Once more, Hsî inquired*, 'And was it not a State which Ch'ih proposed for himself?' *The Master again replied*, 'Yes; who but princes have to do with ancestral temples, and with audiences but the sovereign? If Ch'ih were to be a small *assistant* in these *services*, who could be a great one?

BOOK XII.
YEN YUAN.

CHAPTER I.

1 Yen Yüan asked about perfect virtue. The Master said, 'To subdue one's self and return to propriety, is perfect virtue. If a man can for one day subdue himself and return to propriety, all under heaven will ascribe perfect virtue to him. Is the practice of perfect virtue from a man himself, or is it from others?'

2 Yen Yüan said, 'I beg to ask the steps of that process.' The Master replied, 'Look not at what is contrary to propriety; listen not to what is contrary to propriety; speak not what is contrary to propriety; make no movement which is contrary to propriety.' Yen Yüan *then* said, 'Though I am deficient in intelligence and vigour, I will make it my business to practise this lesson.'

CHAPTER II.

Chung-kung asked about perfect virtue. The Master said, '*It is*, when you go abroad, *to behave to every one* as if you were receiving a great guest; to employ the people as if you were assisting at a great sacrifice; not to do to others as you would not wish done to yourself; to have no murmuring against you in the country, and none in the family.' Chung-kung said, 'Though I am deficient in intelligence and vigour, I will make it my business to practise this lesson.'

CHAPTER III.

1 Sze-mâ Niû asked about perfect virtue.

2 The Master said, 'The man of perfect virtue is cautious and slow in his speech.'

3 'Cautious and slow in his speech!' said Niû;-- 'is this what is meant by perfect virtue?' The Master said, 'When a man feels the difficulty of doing, can he be other than cautious and slow in speaking?'

CHAPTER IV.

1 Sze-mâ Niû asked about the superior man. The Master said, 'The superior man has neither anxiety nor fear.'

2 'Being without anxiety or fear!' said Niû;-- 'does this constitute what we call the superior man?'

3 The Master said, 'When internal examination discovers nothing wrong, what is there to be anxious about, what is there to fear?'

CHAPTER V.

1 Sze-mâ Niû, full of anxiety, said, '*Other* men all have their brothers, I only have not.'

2 Tsze-hsiâ said to him, 'There is the following saying which I have heard:–

3 '"Death and life have their determined appointment; riches and honours depend upon Heaven."

4 'Let the superior man never fail reverentially to order his own conduct, and let him be respectful to others and observant of propriety:-- then all within the four seas will be his brothers. What has the superior man to do with being distressed because he has no brothers?'

CHAPTER VI.

Tsze-chang asked what constituted intelligence. The Master said, 'He with whom neither slander that gradually soaks *into the mind*, nor statements that startle like a wound in the flesh, are successful, may be called intelligent indeed. Yea, he with whom neither soaking slander, nor startling statements, are successful, may be called farseeing.'

CHAPTER VII.

1 Tsze-kung asked about government. The Master said, '*The requisites of government are* that there be sufficiency of food, sufficiency of military equipment, and the confidence of the people in their ruler.'

2 Tsze-kung said, 'If it cannot be helped, and one of these must be dispensed with, which of the three should be foregone first?' 'The military equipment,' said the Master.

3 Tsze-kung *again* asked, 'If it cannot be helped, and one of the remaining two must be dispensed with, which of them should be foregone?' The Master answered, 'Part with the food. From of old, death has been the lot of all men; but if the people have no faith *in their rulers*, there is no standing *for the state*.'

CHAPTER VIII.

1 Chî Tsze-ch'ăng said, 'In a superior man it is only the substantial qualities which are wanted;-- why should we seek for ornamental accomplishments?

2 Tsze-kung said, 'Alas! Your words, sir, show you to be a superior man, but four horses cannot overtake the tongue.

3 Ornament is as substance; substance is as ornament. The hide of a tiger or a leopard stripped of its hair, is like the hide of a dog or a goat stripped of its hair.'

CHAPTER IX.

1 The Duke Aî inquired of Yû Zo, saying, 'The year is one of scarcity, and *the returns for* expenditure are not sufficient;-- what is to be done?

2 Yû Zo replied to him, 'Why not *simply* tithe the people?

3 'With two tenths, said the duke, 'I find it not enough;-- how could I do with that system of one tenth?

4 Yû Zo answered, 'If the people have plenty, their prince will not be left to want alone. If the people are in want, their prince cannot enjoy plenty alone.'

CHAPTER X.

1 Tsze-chang having asked how virtue was to be exalted, and delusions to be discovered, the Master said, 'Hold faithfulness and sincerity as first principles, and be moving continually to what is right;-- this is the way to exalt one's virtue.

2 'You love a man and wish him to live; you hate him and wish him to die. Having wished him to live, you also wish him to die. This is a case of delusion.

3 '"It may not be on account of her being rich, yet you come to make a difference."'

CHAPTER XI.

1 The Duke Ching, of Ch'î, asked Confucius about government.

2 Confucius replied, *'There is government*, when the prince is prince, and the minister is minister; when the father is father, and the son is son.'

3 'Good!' said the duke; 'if, indeed; the prince be not prince, the minister not minister, the father not father, and the son not son, although I have my revenue, can I enjoy it?'

CHAPTER XII.

1 The Master said, 'Ah! it is Yû, who could with half a word settle litigations!'

2 Tsze-lû never slept over a promise.

CHAPTER XIII.

The Master said, 'In hearing litigations, I am like any other body. What is necessary, *however*, is to cause *the people* to have no litigations.'

CHAPTER XIV.

Tsze-chang asked about government. The Master said, '*The art of governing* is to keep *its affairs* before the mind without weariness, and to practise them with undeviating consistency.'

CHAPTER XV.

The Master said, 'By extensively studying all learning, and keeping himself under the restraint of the rules of propriety, *one* may thus likewise not err from what is right.'

CHAPTER XVI.

The Master said, 'The superior man *seeks* to perfect the admirable qualities of men, and does not *seek* to perfect their bad qualities. The mean man does the opposite of this.'

CHAPTER XVII.

Chi K'ang asked Confucius about government. Confucius replied, 'To govern means to rectify. If you lead on *the people* with correctness, who will dare not to be correct?'

CHAPTER XVIII.

Chi K'ang, distressed about the number of thieves *in the State*, inquired of Confucius *how to do away with them*. Confucius said, 'If you, sir, were not covetous, although you should reward them to do it, they would not steal.'

CHAPTER XIX.

Chi K'ang asked Confucius about government, saying, 'What do you say to killing the unprincipled for the good of the principled?' Confucius replied, 'Sir, in carrying on your government, why should you use killing at all? Let your evinced desires be for what is good, and the people will be good. The relation between superiors and inferiors, is like that between the wind and the grass. The grass must bend, when the wind blows across it.'

CHAPTER XX.

1 Tsze-chang asked, 'What must the officer be, who may be said to be distinguished?'

2 The Master said, 'What is it you call being distinguished?'

3 Tsze-chang replied, 'It is to be heard of through the State, to be heard of throughout his clan.'

4 The Master said, 'That is notoriety, not distinction.

5 'Now the man of distinction is solid and straightforward, and loves righteousness. He examines people's words, and looks at their countenances. He is anxious to humble himself to others. Such a man will be distinguished in the country; he will be distinguished in his clan.

6 'As to the man of notoriety, he assumes the appearance of virtue, but his actions are opposed to it, and he rests in this character without any doubts about himself. Such a man will be heard of in the country; he will be heard of in the clan.'

CHAPTER XXI.

1 Fan Ch'ih rambling with the Master under the trees about the rain altars, said, 'I venture to ask how to exalt virtue, to correct cherished evil, and to discover delusions.'

2 The Master said, 'Truly a good question!

3 'If doing what is to be done be made the first business, and success a secondary consideration;-- is not this the way to exalt virtue? To assail one's own wickedness and not assail that of others;-- is not this the way to correct cherished evil? For a morning's anger to disregard one's own life, and involve that of his parents;-- is not this a case of delusion?'

CHAPTER XXII.

1 Fan Ch'ih asked about benevolence. The Master said, 'It is to love *all* men.' He asked about knowledge. The Master said, 'It is to know *all* men.'

2 Fan Ch'ih did not immediately understand *these answers*.

3 The Master said, 'Employ the upright and put aside all the crooked;-- in this way the crooked can be made to be upright.'

4 Fan Ch'ih retired, and, seeing Tsze-hsiâ, he said to him, 'A little while ago, I had an interview with our Master, and asked him about knowledge. He said, 'Employ the upright, and put aside all the crooked;-- in this way, the crooked will be made to be upright.' What did he mean?'

5 Tsze-hsiâ said, 'Truly rich is his saying!

6 'Shun, being in possession of the kingdom, selected from among all the people, and employed Kâo-yâo, on which all who were devoid of virtue disappeared. T'ang, being in possession of the kingdom, selected from among all the people, and employed Î Yin, and all who were devoid of virtue disappeared.'

CHAPTER XXIII.

Tsze-kung asked about friendship. The Master said, 'Faithfully admonish your *friend*, and skillfully lead him on. If you find him impracticable, stop. Do not disgrace yourself.'

CHAPTER XXIV.

The philosopher Tsăng said, 'The superior man on grounds of culture meets with his friends, and by their friendship helps his virtue.'

BOOK XIII.
TSZE-LÛ.

CHAPTER I.

1 Tsze-lû asked about government. The Master said, 'Go before the people with *your example*, and be laborious in their affairs.'

2 He requested further instruction, and was answered, 'Be not weary (in these things).'

CHAPTER II.

1 Chung-kung, being chief minister to the Head of the Chi family, asked about government. The Master said, 'Employ first the services of your various officers, pardon small faults, and raise to office men of virtue and talents.'

2 *Chung-kung* said, 'How shall I know the men of virtue and talent, so that I may raise them to office?' He was answered, 'Raise to office those whom you know. As to those whom you do not know, will others neglect them?'

CHAPTER III.

1 Tsze-lû said, 'The ruler of Wei has been waiting for you, in order with you to administer the government. What will you consider the first thing to be done?'

2 The Master replied, 'What is necessary is to rectify names.'

3 'So, indeed!' said Tsze-lû. 'You are wide of the mark! Why must there be such rectification?'

4 The Master said, 'How uncultivated you are, Yû! A superior man, in regard to what he does not know, shows a cautious reserve.

5 'If names be not correct, language is not in accordance with the truth of things. If language be not in accordance with the truth of things, affairs cannot be carried on to success.

6 'When affairs cannot be carried on to success, proprieties and music will not flourish. When proprieties and music do not flourish, punishments will not be properly awarded. When punishments are not properly awarded, the people do not know how to move hand or foot.

7 'Therefore a superior man considers it necessary that the names he uses may be spoken *appropriately*, and also that what he speaks may be carried out *appropriately*. What the superior man requires, is just that in his words there may be nothing incorrect.'

CHAPTER IV.

1 Fan Ch'ih requested to be taught husbandry. The Master said, 'I am not so good for that as an old husbandman.' He requested also to be taught gardening, and was answered, 'I am not so good for that as an old gardener.'

2 Fan Ch'ih having gone out, the Master said, 'A small man, indeed, is Fan Hsü!

3 If a superior love propriety, the people will not dare not to be reverent. If he love righteousness, the people will not dare not to submit to *his example*. If he love good faith, the people will not dare not to be sincere. Now, when these things obtain, the people from all quarters will come to him, bearing their children on their backs;-- what need has he of a knowledge of husbandry?'

CHAPTER V.

The Master said, 'Though a man may be able to recite the three hundred odes, yet if, when intrusted with a governmental charge, he knows not how to act, or if, when sent to any quarter on a mission, he cannot give his replies unassisted, notwithstanding the extent *of his learning*, of what practical use is it?'

CHAPTER VI.

The Master said, 'When a prince's personal conduct is correct, his government is effective without the issuing of orders. If his personal conduct is not correct, he may issue orders, but they will not be followed.'

CHAPTER VII.

The Master said, 'The governments of Lû and Wei are brothers.'

CHAPTER VIII.

The Master said of Ching, a scion of the ducal family of Wei, that he knew the economy of a family well. When he began to have means, he said, 'Ha! here is a collection!' When they were a little increased, he said, 'Ha! this is complete!' When he had become rich, he said, 'Ha! this is admirable!'

CHAPTER IX.

1 When the Master went to Wei, Zan Yû acted as driver of his carriage.

2 The Master observed, 'How numerous are the people!'

3 Yû said, 'Since they are thus numerous, what more shall be done for them?' 'Enrich them,' was the reply.

4 'And when they have been enriched, what more shall be done?' The Master said, 'Teach them.'

CHAPTER X.

The Master said, 'If there were (any of the princes) who would employ me, in the course of twelve months, I should have done something considerable. In three years, *the government* would be perfected.'

CHAPTER XI.

The Master said, '"If good men were to govern a country *in succession* for a hundred years, they would be able to transform the violently bad, and dispense with capital punishments." True indeed is this saying!'

CHAPTER XII.

The Master said, 'If a truly royal ruler were to arise, it would *still* require a generation, and then virtue would prevail.'

CHAPTER XIII.

The Master said, 'If a minister make his own conduct correct, what difficulty will he have in assisting in government? If he cannot rectify himself, what has he to do with rectifying others?'

CHAPTER XIV.

The disciple Zan returning from the court, the Master said to him, 'How are you so late?' He replied, 'We had government business.' The Master said, 'It must have been *family* affairs. If there had been government business, though I am not now in office, I should have been consulted about it.'

CHAPTER XV.

1 The Duke Ting asked whether there was a single sentence which could make a country prosperous. Confucius replied, 'Such an effect cannot be expected from one sentence.

2 'There is a saying, however, which people have-- "To be a prince is difficult; to be a minister is not easy."

3 'If a *ruler* knows this,-- the difficulty of being a prince,-- may there not be expected from this one sentence the prosperity of his country?'

4 *The duke then* said, 'Is there a single sentence which can ruin a country?' Confucius replied, 'Such an effect as that cannot be expected from one sentence. There is, *however*, the saying which people have-- "I have no pleasure in being a prince, but only in that no one can offer any opposition to what I say!"

5 'If a *ruler's* words be good, is it not also good that no one oppose them? But if they are not good, and no one opposes them, may there not be expected from this one sentence the ruin of his country?'

CHAPTER XVI.

1 The Duke of Sheh asked about government.

2 The Master said, '*Good government obtains*, when those who are near are made happy, and those who are far off are attracted.'

CHAPTER XVII.

Tsze-hsiâ, being governor of Chü-fû, asked about government. The Master said, 'Do not be desirous to have things done quickly; do not look at small advantages. Desire to have things done quickly prevents their being done thoroughly. Looking at small advantages prevents great affairs from being accomplished.'

CHAPTER XVIII.

1 The Duke of Sheh informed Confucius, saying, 'Among us here there are those who may be styled upright in their conduct. If their father have stolen a sheep, they will bear witness to the fact.'

2 Confucius said, 'Among us, in our part of the country, those who are upright are different from this. The father conceals the misconduct of the son, and the son conceals the misconduct of the father. Uprightness is to be found in this.'

CHAPTER XIX.

Fan Ch'ih asked about perfect virtue. The Master said, 'It is, in retirement, to be sedately grave; in the management of business, to be reverently attentive; in intercourse with others, to be strictly sincere. Though a man go among rude, uncultivated tribes, these *qualities* may not be neglected.'

CHAPTER XX.

1 Tsze-kung asked, saying, 'What qualities must a man possess to entitle him to be called an officer? The Master said, 'He who in his conduct of himself maintains a sense of shame, and when sent to any quarter will not disgrace his prince's commission, deserves to be called an officer.'

2 *Tsze-kung* pursued, 'I venture to ask who may be placed in the next lower rank?' And he was told, 'He whom the circle of his relatives pronounce to be filial, whom his fellow-villagers and neighbours pronounce to be fraternal.'

3 *Again the disciple asked*, 'I venture to ask about the class still next in order.' *The Master* said, 'They are determined to be sincere in what they say, and to carry out what they do. They are obstinate little men. Yet perhaps they may make the next class.'

4 *Tsze-kung finally* inquired, 'Of what sort are those of the present day, who engage in government?' The Master said 'Pooh! they are so many pecks and hampers, not worth being taken into account.'

CHAPTER XXI.

The Master said, 'Since I cannot get men pursuing the due medium, to whom I might communicate *my instructions*, I must find the ardent and the cautiously-decided. The ardent will advance and lay hold *of truth*; the cautiously-decided will keep themselves from what is wrong.'

CHAPTER XXII.

1 The Master said, 'The people of the south have a saying-- "A man without constancy cannot be either a wizard or a doctor." Good!

2 'Inconstant in his virtue, he will be visited with disgrace.'

3 The Master said, 'This arises simply from not attending to the prognostication.'

CHAPTER XXIII.

The Master said, 'The superior man is affable, but not adulatory; the mean man is adulatory, but not affable.'

CHAPTER XXIV.

Tsze-kung asked, saying, 'What do you say of a man who is loved by all the people of his neighborhood?' The Master replied, 'We may not for that accord our approval of him.' 'And what do you say of him who is hated by all the people of his neighborhood?' The Master said, 'We may not for that conclude that he is bad. It is better than either of these cases that the good in the neighborhood love him, and the bad hate him.'

CHAPTER XXV.

The Master said, 'The superior man is easy to serve and difficult to please. If you try to please him in any way which is not accordant with right, he will not be pleased. But in his employment of men, he uses them according to their capacity. The mean man is difficult to serve, and easy to please. If you try to please him, though it be in a way which is not accordant with right, he may be pleased. But in his employment of men, he wishes them to be equal to everything.'

CHAPTER XXVI.

The Master said, 'The superior man has a dignified ease without pride. The mean man has pride without a dignified ease.'

CHAPTER XXVII.

The Master said, 'The firm, the enduring, the simple, and the modest are near to virtue.'

CHAPTER XXVIII.

Tsze-lû asked, saying, 'What qualities must a man possess to entitle him to be called a scholar?' The Master said, 'He must be thus,-- earnest, urgent, and bland:-- among his friends, earnest and urgent; among his brethren, bland.'

CHAPTER XXIX.

The Master said, 'Let a good man teach the people seven years, and they may then likewise be employed in war.'

CHAPTER XXX.

The Master said, 'To lead an uninstructed people to war, is to throw them away.'

BOOK XIV.
HSIEN WAN.

CHAPTER I.

Hsien asked what was shameful. The Master said, 'When good government prevails in a state, *to be thinking only of* salary; and, when bad government prevails, *to be thinking, in the same way, only of* salary;-- this is shameful.'

CHAPTER II.

1 'When the love of superiority, boasting, resentments, and covetousness are repressed, this may be deemed perfect virtue.'

2 The Master said, 'This may be regarded as the achievement of what is difficult. But I do not know that it is to be deemed perfect virtue.'

CHAPTER III.

The Master said, 'The scholar who cherishes the love of comfort is not fit to be deemed a scholar.'

CHAPTER IV.

The Master said, 'When good government prevails in a state, language may be lofty and bold, and actions the same. When bad government prevails, the actions may be lofty and bold, but the language may be with some reserve.'

CHAPTER V.

The Master said, 'The virtuous will be sure to speak *correctly*, but those whose speech is good may not always be virtuous. Men of principle are sure to be bold, but those who are bold may not always be men of principle.'

CHAPTER VI.

Nan-kung Kwo, submitting an inquiry to Confucius, said, 'I was skillful at archery, and Âo could move a boat along upon the land, but neither of them died a natural death. Yü and Chî personally wrought at the toils of husbandry, and they became possessors of the kingdom.' The Master made no reply; but when Nan-kung Kwo went out, he said, 'A superior man indeed is this! An esteemer of virtue indeed is this!'

CHAPTER VII.

The Master said, 'Superior men, and yet not *always* virtuous, there have been, alas! But there never has been a mean man, and, *at the same time*, virtuous.'

CHAPTER VIII.

The Master said, 'Can there be love which does not lead to strictness with its object? Can there be loyalty which does not lead to the instruction of its object?'

CHAPTER IX.

The Master said, 'In preparing the governmental notifications, P'î Shăn first made the rough draft; Shî-shû examined and discussed its contents; Tsze-yü, the manager of Foreign intercourse, then polished the style; and, finally, Tsze-ch'ân of Tung-lî gave it the proper elegance and finish.'

CHAPTER X.

1 Some one asked about Tsze-ch'ân. The Master said, 'He was a kind man.

2 He asked about Tsze-hsî. The Master said, 'That man! That man!'

3 He asked about Kwan Chung. 'For him,' said the Master, 'the city of Pien, with three hundred families, was taken from the chief of the Po family, who did not utter a murmuring word, though, to the end of his life, he had only coarse rice to eat.'

CHAPTER XI.

The Master said, 'To be poor without murmuring is difficult. To be rich without being proud is easy.'

CHAPTER XII.

The Master said, 'Măng Kung-ch'o is more than fit to be chief officer in the families of Châo and Wei, but he is not fit to be great officer to either of *the States* Tang or Hsieh.'

CHAPTER XIII.

1 Tsze-lû asked what constituted a COMPLETE man. The Master said, 'Suppose a man with the knowledge of Tsăng Wû-chung, the freedom from covetousness of Kung-ch'o, the bravery of Chwang of Pien, and the varied talents of Zan Ch'iû; add to these the accomplishments of the rules of propriety and music:--such a one might be reckoned a COMPLETE man.'

2 *He then* added, 'But what is the necessity for a complete man of the present day to have all these things? The man, who in the view of gain, thinks of righteousness; who in the view of danger is prepared to give up his life; and who does not forget

an old agreement however far back it extends:-- such a man may be reckoned a COMPLETE man.'

CHAPTER XIV.

1 The Master asked Kung-ming Chiâ about Kung-shû Wăn, saying, 'Is it true that your master speaks not, laughs not, and takes not?'

2 Kung-ming Chiâ replied, 'This has arisen from the reporters going beyond the *truth*.-- My master speaks when it is the time to speak, and so men do not get tired of his speaking. He laughs when there is occasion to be joyful, and so men do not get tired of his laughing. He takes when it is consistent with righteousness to do so, and so men do not get tired of his taking.' The Master said, 'So! But is it so with him?'

CHAPTER XV.

The Master said, 'Tsang Wû-chung, keeping possession of Fang, asked of *the duke of* Lû to appoint a successor to him *in his family*. Although it may be said that he was not using force with his sovereign, I believe he was.'

CHAPTER XVI.

The Master said, 'The duke Wăn of Tsin was crafty and not upright. The duke Hwan of Ch'î was upright and not crafty.'

CHAPTER XVII.

1 Tsze-lû said, 'The Duke Hwan caused his brother Chiû to be killed, when Shâo Hû died *with his master*, but Kwan Chung did not die. May not I say that he was wanting in virtue?'

2 The Master said, 'The Duke Hwan assembled all the princes together, and that not with weapons of war and chariots:-- it

was all through the influence of Kwan Chung. Whose beneficence was like his? Whose beneficence was like his?'

CHAPTER XVIII.

1 Tsze-kung said, 'Kwan Chung, I apprehend, was wanting in virtue. When the Duke Hwan caused his brother Chiû to be killed, Kwan Chung was not able to die with him. Moreover, he became prime minister to Hwan.'

2 The Master said, 'Kwan Chung acted as prime minister to the Duke Hwan, made him leader of all the princes, and united and rectified the whole kingdom. Down to the present day, the people enjoy the gifts which he conferred. But for Kwan Chung, we should now be wearing our hair unbound, and the lappets of our coats buttoning on the left side.

3 'Will you require from him the small fidelity of common men and common women, who would commit suicide in a stream or ditch, no one knowing anything about them?'

CHAPTER XIX.

1 The great officer, Hsien, who had been *family* minister to Kung-shu Wăn, ascended to the prince's *court* in company with Wăn.

2 The Master, having heard of it, said, 'He deserved to be considered WĂN (the accomplished).'

CHAPTER XX.

1 The Master was speaking about the unprincipled course of the duke Ling of Wei, when Ch'î K'ang said, 'Since he is of such a character, how is it he does not lose his State?'

2 Confucius said, 'The Chung-shû Yü has the superintendence of his guests and of strangers; the litanist, T'o, has the

management of his ancestral temple; and Wang-sun Chia has the direction of the army and forces:-- with such officers as these, how should he lose his State?'

CHAPTER XXI.

The Master said, 'He who speaks without modesty will find it difficult to make his words good.'

CHAPTER XXII.

1 Chăn Ch'ăng murdered the Duke Chien *of* Ch'î.

2 Confucius bathed, went to court, and informed the duke Âi, saying, 'Chan Hang has slain his sovereign. I beg that you will undertake to punish him.'

3 The duke said, 'Inform the chiefs of the three families of it."

4 Confucius *retired, and* said, 'Following in the rear of the great officers, I did not dare not to represent such a matter, and my prince says, "Inform the chiefs of the three families of it."'

5 He went to the chiefs, and informed them, but they would not act. Confucius *then* said, 'Following in the rear of the great officers, I did not dare not to represent such a matter.'

CHAPTER XXIII.

Tsze-lû asked how a ruler should be served. The Master said, 'Do not impose on him, and, moreover, withstand him to his face.'

CHAPTER XXIV.

The Master said, 'The progress of the superior man is upwards; the progress of the mean man is downwards.'

CHAPTER XXV.

The Master said, 'In ancient times, men learned with a view to their own improvement. Now-a-days men learn with a view to the approbation of others.'

CHAPTER XXVI.

1 Chü Po-yü sent a messenger with *friendly inquiries* to Confucius.

2 Confucius sat with him, and questioned him. 'What,' said he, 'is your master engaged in?' The messenger replied, 'My master is anxious to make his faults few, but he has not yet succeeded.' He then went out, and the Master said, 'A messenger indeed! A messenger indeed!'

CHAPTER XXVII.

The Master said, 'He who is not in any particular office, has nothing to do with plans for the administration of its duties.'

CHAPTER XXVIII.

The philosopher Tsăng said, 'The superior man, in his thoughts, does not go out of his place.'

CHAPTER XXIX.

The Master said, 'The superior man is modest in his speech, but exceeds in his actions.'

CHAPTER XXX.

1 The Master said, 'The way of the superior man is threefold, but I am not equal to it. Virtuous, he is free from anxieties; wise, he is free from perplexities; bold, he is free from fear.

2 Tsze-kung said, 'Master, that is what you yourself say.'

CHAPTER XXXI.

Tsze-kung was *in the habit* of comparing men together. The Master said, 'Tsze must have reached a high pitch of excellence! Now, I have not leisure *for this*.'

CHAPTER XXXII.

The Master said, 'I will not be concerned at men's not knowing me; I will be concerned at my own want of ability.'

CHAPTER XXXIII.

The Master said, 'He who does not anticipate attempts to deceive him, nor think beforehand of his not being believed, and yet apprehends these things readily (*when they occur*);-- is he not a man of superior worth?'

CHAPTER XXXIV.

1 Wei-shăng Mâu said to Confucius, 'Ch'iû, how is it that you keep roosting about? Is it not that you are an insinuating talker?

2 Confucius said, 'I do not dare to play the part of such a talker, but I hate obstinacy.'

CHAPTER XXXV.

The Master said, 'A horse is called a ch'î, not because of its strength, but because of its *other* good qualities.'

CHAPTER XXXVI.

1 Some one said, 'What do you say concerning the principle that injury should be recompensed with kindness?'

2 The Master said, 'With what then will you recompense kindness?

3 'Recompense injury with justice, and recompense kindness with kindness.'

CHAPTER XXXVII.

1 The Master said, 'Alas! there is no one that knows me.'

2 Tsze-kung said, 'What do you mean by thus saying—that no one knows you?' The Master replied, 'I do not murmur against Heaven. I do not grumble against men. My studies lie low, and my penetration rises high. But there is Heaven;-- that knows me!'

CHAPTER XXXVIII.

1 The Kung-po Liâo, having slandered Tsze-lû to Chî-sun, Tsze-fû Ching-po informed Confucius of it, saying, 'Our master is certainly being led astray by the Kung-po Liâo, but I have still power enough left to cut *Liâo* off, and expose his corpse in the market and in the court.'

2 The Master said, 'If *my* principles are to advance, it is so ordered. If they are to fall to the ground, it is so ordered. What can the Kung-po Liâo do where such ordering is concerned?'

CHAPTER XXXIX.

1 The Master said, 'Some men of worth retire from the world.

2 Some retire from *particular* States.

3 Some retire because of *disrespectful* looks.

4 Some retire because of *contradictory* language.'

CHAPTER XL.

The Master said, 'Those who have done this are seven men.'

CHAPTER XLI.

Tsze-lû happening to pass the night in Shih-măn, the gate-keeper said to him, 'Whom do you come from?' Tsze-lû said, 'From Mr. K'ung.' 'It is he,-- is it not?'-- said the other, 'who knows the impracticable nature of the times and yet will be doing in them.'

CHAPTER XLII.

1 The Master was playing, *one day*, on a musical stone in Wei, when a man, carrying a straw basket, passed the door of the house where Confucius was, and said, 'His heart is full who so beats the musical stone.'

2 A little while after, he added, 'How contemptible is the one-ideaed obstinacy *those sounds display*! When one is taken no notice of, he has simply at once to give over *his wish for public employment*. "Deep water must be crossed with the clothes on; shallow water may be crossed with the clothes held up."'

3 The Master said, 'How determined is he in his purpose! But this is not difficult!'

CHAPTER XLIII.

1 Tsze-chang said, 'What is meant when the Shû says that Kâo-tsung, while observing the usual imperial mourning, was for three years without speaking?'

2 The Master said, 'Why must Kâo-tsung *be referred to as an example of this*? The ancients all did so. When the sovereign died, the officers all attended to their several duties, taking instructions from the prime minister for three years.'

CHAPTER XLIV.

The Master said, 'When rulers love to *observe* the rules of propriety, the people respond readily to the calls on them for service.'

CHAPTER XLV.

Tsze-lû asked what constituted the superior man. The Master said, 'The cultivation of himself in reverential carefulness.' 'And is this all?' said Tsze-lû. 'He cultivates himself so as to give rest to others,' was the reply. 'And is this all?' again asked Tsze-lû. The Master said, 'He cultivates himself so as to give rest to all the people. He cultivates himself so as to give rest to all the people:-- even Yâo and Shun were still solicitous about this.'

CHAPTER XLVI.

Yüan Zang was squatting on his heels, and so waited *the approach* of the Master, who said to him, 'In youth not humble as befits a junior; in manhood, doing nothing worthy of being handed down; and living on to old age:-- this is to be a pest.' With this he hit him on the shank with his staff.

CHAPTER XLVI.

1 A youth of the village of Ch'üeh was employed by Confucius to carry the messages between him and his visitors. Some one asked about him, saying, 'I suppose he has made great progress.'

2 The Master said, 'I observe that he is fond of occupying the seat of *a full-grown man*; I observe that he walks shoulder to shoulder with his elders. He is not one who is seeking to make progress *in learning*. He wishes quickly to become a man.'

BOOK XV.
WEI LING KUNG.

CHAPTER I.

1 The Duke Ling of Wei asked Confucius about tactics. Confucius replied, 'I have heard all about sacrificial vessels, but I have not learned military matters.' On this, he took his departure the next day.

2 When he was in Chăn, their provisions were exhausted, and his followers became so ill that they were unable to rise.

3 Tsze-lû, with evident dissatisfaction, said, 'Has the superior man likewise to endure *in this way*?' The Master said, 'The superior man may indeed have to endure want, but the mean man, when he is in want, gives way to unbridled license.'

CHAPTER II.

1 The Master said, 'Ts'ze, you think, I suppose, that I am one who learns many things and keeps them in memory?'

2 Tsze-kung replied, 'Yes,-- but perhaps it is not so?'

3 'No,' was the answer; 'I seek a unity all-pervading.'

CHAPTER III.

The Master said. 'Yû, those who know virtue are few.'

CHAPTER IV.

The Master said, 'May not Shun be instanced as having governed efficiently without exertion? What did he do? He did nothing but gravely and reverently occupy his royal seat.'

CHAPTER V.

1 Tsze-chang asked how a man should conduct himself, so as to be *everywhere appreciated*.

2 The Master said, 'Let his words be sincere and truthful, and his actions honourable and careful;-- such conduct may be practiced among the rude tribes of the South or the North. If his words be not sincere and truthful and his actions not honourable and careful, will he, with such conduct, be appreciated, even in his neighborhood?

3 'When he is standing, let him see those two things, as it were, fronting him. When he is in a carriage, let him see them attached to the yoke. Then may he subsequently carry them into practice.'

4 Tsze-chang wrote these counsels on the end of his sash.

CHAPTER VI.

1 The Master said, 'Truly straightforward was the historiographer Yü. When good government prevailed in his State, he was like an arrow. When bad government prevailed, he was like an arrow.

2 A superior man indeed is Chü Po-yü! When good government prevails in his state, he is to be found in office. When bad government prevails, he can roll his principles up, and keep them in his breast.'

CHAPTER VII.

The Master said, 'When a man may be spoken with, not to speak to him is to err in reference to the man. When a man may not be spoken with, to speak to him is to err in reference to our words. The wise err neither in regard to their man nor to their words.'

CHAPTER VIII.

The Master said, 'The determined scholar and the man of virtue will not seek to live at the expense of injuring their virtue. They will even sacrifice their lives to preserve their virtue complete.'

CHAPTER IX.

Tsze-kung asked about the practice of virtue. The Master said, 'The mechanic, who wishes to do his work well, must first sharpen his tools. When you are living in any state, take service with the most worthy among its great officers, and make friends of the most virtuous among its scholars.'

CHAPTER X.

1 Yen Yüan asked how the government of a country should be administered.

2 The Master said, 'Follow the seasons of Hsiâ.

3 'Ride in the state carriage of Yin.

4 'Wear the ceremonial cap of Châu.

5 'Let the music be the Shâo with its pantomimes.

6 Banish the songs of Chăng, and keep far from specious talkers. The songs of Chăng are licentious; specious talkers are dangerous.'

CHAPTER XI.

The Master said, 'If a man take no thought about what is distant, he will find sorrow near at hand.'

CHAPTER XII.

The Master said, 'It is all over! I have not seen one who loves virtue as he loves beauty.'

CHAPTER XIII.

The Master said, 'Was not Tsang Wăn like one who had stolen his situation? He knew the virtue and the talents of Hûi of Liû-hsiâ, and yet did not *procure that he should* stand with him *in court*.'

CHAPTER XIV.

The Master said, 'He who requires much from himself and little from others, will keep himself from *being the object of* resentment.'

CHAPTER XV.

The Master said, 'When a man is *not in the habit of* saying-- "What shall I think of this? What shall I think of this?" I can indeed do nothing with him!'

CHAPTER XVI.

The Master said, 'When a number of people are together, for a whole day, without their conversation turning on righteousness, and when they are fond of carrying out *the suggestions of* a small shrewdness;-- theirs is indeed a hard case.'

CHAPTER XVII.

The Master said, 'The superior man *in everything* considers righteousness to be essential. He performs it according to the rules of propriety. He brings it forth in humility. He completes it with sincerity. This is indeed a superior man.'

CHAPTER XVIII.

The Master said, 'The superior man is distressed by his want of ability. He is not distressed by men's not knowing him.'

CHAPTER XIX.

The Master said, 'The superior man dislikes the thought of his name not being mentioned after his death.'

CHAPTER XX.

The Master said, 'What the superior man seeks, is in himself. What the mean man seeks, is in others.'

CHAPTER XXI.

The Master said, 'The superior man is dignified, but does not wrangle. He is sociable, but not a partizan.'

CHAPTER XXII.

The Master said, 'The superior man does not promote a man *simply* on account of his words, nor does he put aside *good* words because of the man.'

CHAPTER XXIII.

Tsze-kung asked, saying, 'Is there one word which may serve as a rule of practice for all one's life?' The Master said, 'Is not RECIPROCITY such a word? What you do not want done to yourself, do not do to others.'

CHAPTER XXIV.

1 The Master said, 'In my dealings with men, whose evil do I blame, whose goodness do I praise, beyond what is proper? If I do sometimes exceed in praise, there must be ground for it in my examination of the individual.

2 'This people supplied the ground why the three dynasties pursued the path of straightforwardness.'

CHAPTER XXV.

The Master said, 'Even in my *early* days, a historiographer would leave a blank in his text, and he who had a horse would lend him to another to ride. Now, alas! there are no such things.'

CHAPTER XXVI.

The Master said, 'Specious words confound virtue. Want of forbearance in small matters confounds great plans.'

CHAPTER XXVII.

The Master said, 'When the multitude hate a man, it is necessary to examine into the case. When the multitude like a man, it is necessary to examine into the case.'

CHAPTER XXVIII.

The Master said, 'A man can enlarge the principles *which he follows*; those principles do not enlarge the man.'

CHAPTER XXIX.

The Master said, 'To have faults and not to reform them,-- this, indeed, should be pronounced having faults.'

CHAPTER XXX.

The Master said, 'I have been the whole day without eating, and the whole night without sleeping:-- occupied with thinking. It was of no use. The better plan is to learn.'

CHAPTER XXXI.

The Master said, 'The object of the superior man is truth. Food is not his object. There is plowing;-- even in that there is *sometimes* want. So with learning;-- emolument may be found in it. The superior man is anxious lest he should not get truth; he is not anxious lest poverty should come upon him.'

CHAPTER XXXII.

1 The Master said, 'When a man's knowledge is sufficient to attain, and his virtue is not sufficient to enable him to hold, whatever he may have gained, he will lose again.

2 'When his knowledge is sufficient to attain, and he has virtue enough to hold fast, if he cannot govern with dignity, the people will not respect him.

3 'When his knowledge is sufficient to attain, and he has virtue enough to hold fast; when he governs also with dignity, yet if he try to move the people contrary to the rules of propriety: full excellence is not reached.'

CHAPTER XXXIII.

The Master said, 'The superior man cannot be known in little matters; but he may be intrusted with great concerns. The small man may not be intrusted with great concerns, but he may be known in little matters.'

CHAPTER XXXIV.

The Master said, 'Virtue is more to man than either water or fire. I have seen men die from treading on water and fire, but I have never seen a man die from treading the course of virtue.'

CHAPTER XXXV.

The Master said, 'Let every man consider virtue as what devolves on himself. He may not yield the performance of it *even* to his teacher.'

CHAPTER XXXVI.

The Master said, 'The superior man is correctly firm, and not firm merely.'

CHAPTER XXXVII.

The Master said, 'A minister, in serving his prince, reverently discharges his duties, and makes his emolument a secondary consideration.'

CHAPTER XXXVIII.

The Master said, 'In teaching there should be no distinction of classes.'

CHAPTER XXXIX.

The Master said, 'Those whose courses are different cannot lay plans for one another.'

CHAPTER XL.

The Master said, 'In language it is simply required that it convey the meaning.'

CHAPTER XLI.

1 The Music-master, Mien, having called upon him, when they came to the steps, the Master said, 'Here are the steps.' When they came to the mat *for the guest* to sit upon, he said, 'Here is the mat.' When all were seated, the Master informed him, saying, 'So and so is here; so and so is here.'

2 The Music-master, Mien, having gone out, Tsze-chan asked, saying. 'Is it the rule to tell those things to the Music-master?'

3 The Master said, 'Yes. This is certainly the rule for those who lead the blind.'

BOOK XVI.
KE SHE.

CHAPTER I.

1 The head of the Chî family was going to attack Chwan-yü.

2 Zan Yû and Chi-lû had an interview with Confucius, and said, '*Our chief*, Chî, is going to commence operations against Chwan-yü.'

3 Confucius said, 'Ch'iû, is it not you who are in fault here?'

4 'Now, in regard to Chwan-yü, long ago, a former king appointed its ruler to preside over *the sacrifices* to the eastern Măng; moreover, it is in the midst of the territory of our State; and its ruler is a minister in direct connexion with the sovereign:-- What has *your chief* to do with attacking it?'

5 Zan Yû said, 'Our master wishes the thing; neither of us two ministers wishes it.'

6 Confucius said, 'Ch'iû, there are the words of Châu Zan,-- "When he can put forth his ability, he takes his place in the ranks *of office*; when he finds himself unable to do so, he retires from it. How can he be used as a guide to a blind man, who does not support him when tottering, nor raise him up when fallen?"

7 'And further, you speak wrongly. When a tiger or rhinoceros escapes from his cage; when a tortoise or piece of jade is injured in its repository:-- whose is the fault?'

8 Zan Yû said, 'But at present, Chwan-yü is strong and near to Pî; if *our chief* do not now take it, it will hereafter be a sorrow to his descendants.'

9 Confucius said. ' Ch'iû, the superior man hates that declining to say-- "I want such and such a thing," and framing explanations *for the conduct*.'

10 'I have heard that rulers of States and chiefs of families are not troubled lest their people should be few, but are troubled lest they should not keep their several places; that they are not troubled with fears of poverty, but are troubled with fears of a want of contented repose *among the people in their several places*. For when the people keep their several places, there will be no poverty; when harmony prevails, there will be no scarcity of people; and when there is such a *contented* repose, there will be no rebellious upsettings.

11 'So it is.-- Therefore, if remoter people are not submissive, all the influences of civil culture and virtue are to be cultivated to attract them to be so; and when they have been so attracted, they must be made contented and tranquil.

12 'Now, here are you, Yû and Ch'iû, assisting your chief. Remoter people are not submissive, and, *with your help*, he cannot attract them to him. In his own territory there are divisions and downfalls, leavings and separations, and, *with your help*, he cannot preserve it.

13 'And yet he is planning these hostile movements within the State.-- I am afraid that the sorrow of the Chî-sun *family* will not be on account of Chwan-yü, but will be found within the screen of their own court.'

CHAPTER II.

1 Confucius said, 'When good government prevails in the empire, ceremonies, music, and punitive military expeditions proceed from the son of Heaven. When bad government prevails in the empire, ceremonies, music, and punitive military expeditions proceed from the princes. When these things proceed from the princes, as a rule, the cases will be few in which they do not lose their power in ten generations. When they proceed from the Great officers *of the princes, as a rule*, the cases will be few in which they do not lose their power in five generations. When

the subsidiary ministers *of the great officers* hold in their grasp the orders of the state, *as a rule*, the cases will be few in which they do not lose their power in three generations.

2 'When right principles prevail in the kingdom, government will not be in the hands of the Great officers.

3 'When right principles prevail in the kingdom, there will be no discussions among the common people.'

CHAPTER III.

Confucius said, 'The revenue *of the State* has left the ducal House now for five generations. The government has been in the hands of the Great officers for four generations. On this account, the descendants of the three Hwan are much reduced.'

CHAPTER IV.

Confucius said, 'There are three friendships which are advantageous, and three which are injurious. Friendship with the upright; friendship with the sincere; and friendship with the man of much observation:-- these are advantageous. Friendship with the man of specious airs; friendship with the insinuatingly soft; and friendship with the glib-tongued:-- these are injurious.'

CHAPTER V.

Confucius said, 'There are three things men find enjoyment in which are advantageous, and three things they find enjoyment in which are injurious. To find enjoyment in the discriminating study of ceremonies and music; to find enjoyment in speaking of the goodness of others; to find enjoyment in having many worthy friends:-- these are advantageous. To find enjoyment in extravagant pleasures; to find enjoyment in idleness and sauntering; to find enjoyment in the pleasures of feasting:-- these are injurious.'

CHAPTER VI.

Confucius said, 'There are three errors to which they who stand in the presence of a man of virtue and station are liable. They may speak when it does not come to them to speak;-- this is called rashness. They may not speak when it comes to them to speak;-- this is called concealment. They may speak without looking at the countenance *of their superior*;-- this is called blindness.'

CHAPTER VII.

Confucius said, 'There are three things which the superior man guards against. In youth, when the physical powers are not yet settled, he guards against lust. When he is strong and the physical powers are full of vigor, he guards against quarrelsomeness. When he is old, and the animal powers are decayed, he guards against covetousness.'

CHAPTER VIII.

1 Confucius said, 'There are three things of which the superior man stands in awe. He stands in awe of the ordinances of Heaven. He stands in awe of great men. He stands in awe of the words of sages.

2 'The mean man does not know the ordinances of Heaven, and *consequently* does not stand in awe of them. He is disrespectful to great men. He makes sport of the words of sages.'

CHAPTER IX.

Confucius said, 'Those who are born with the possession of knowledge are the highest class of men. Those who learn, and so, *readily*, get possession of knowledge, are the next. Those who are dull and stupid, and yet compass the learning, are another class next to these. As to those who are dull and stupid and yet do not learn;-- they are the lowest of the people.'

CHAPTER X.

Confucius said, 'The superior man has nine things which are subjects with him of thoughtful consideration. In regard to the use of his eyes, he is anxious to see clearly. In regard to the use of his ears, he is anxious to hear distinctly. In regard to his countenance, he is anxious that it should be benign. In regard to his demeanor, he is anxious that it should be respectful. In regard to his speech, he is anxious that it should be sincere. In regard to his doing of business, he is anxious that it should be reverently careful. In regard to what he doubts about, he is anxious to question others. When he is angry, he thinks of the difficulties (his anger may involve him in). When he sees gain to be got, he thinks of righteousness.'

CHAPTER XI.

1 Confucius said, 'Contemplating good, *and pursuing it*, as if they could not reach it; contemplating evil, *and shrinking from it*, as they would from thrusting the hand into boiling water:-- I have seen such men, as I have heard such words.

2 'Living in retirement to study their aims, and practicing righteousness to carry out their principles:-- I have heard these words, but I have not seen such men.'

CHAPTER XII.

1 The duke Ching of Ch'î had a thousand teams, each of four horses, but on the day of his death, the people did not praise him for a single virtue. Po-î and Shû-ch'i died of hunger at the foot of the Shâu-yang mountain, and the people, down to the present time, praise them.

2 'Is not that saying illustrated by this?'

CHAPTER XIII.

3 Ch'ăn K'ang asked Po-yü, saying, 'Have you heard any lessons *from your father* different *from what we have all heard*?'

4 Po-yü replied, 'No. He was standing alone once, when I passed below the hall with hasty steps, and said to me, "Have you learned the Odes?" On my replying "Not yet," *he added*, "If you do not learn the Odes, you will not be fit to converse with." I retired and studied the Odes.

5 'Another day, he was in the same way standing alone, when I passed by below the hall with hasty steps, and said to me, 'Have you learned the rules of Propriety?' On my replying 'Not yet,' *he added*, 'If you do not learn the rules of Propriety, your character cannot be established.' I then retired, and learned the rules of Propriety.

6 'I have heard only these two things from him.'

7 Ch'ăng K'ang retired, and, quite delighted, said, 'I asked one thing, and I have got three things. I have heard about the Odes. I have heard about the rules of Propriety. I have also heard that the superior man maintains a distant reserve towards his son.'

CHAPTER XIV.

The wife of the prince of a state is called by him FÛ ZAN. She calls herself HSIÂO T'UNG. The people of the State call her CHÜN FÛ ZAN, and, to the people of other States, they call her K'WA HSIÂO CHÜN. The people of other states also call her CHÜN FÛ ZAN.

BOOK XVII.
YANG HO.

CHAPTER I.

1 Yang Ho wished to see Confucius, but Confucius would not go to see him. *On this*, he sent a present of a pig to Confucius, who, having chosen a time when Ho was not at home, went to pay his respects *for the gift*. He met him, *however*, on the way.

2 *Ho* said to Confucius, 'Come, let me speak with you.' He then asked, 'Can he be called benevolent who keeps his jewel in his bosom, and leaves his country to confusion?' *Confucius* replied, 'No.' 'Can he be called wise, who is anxious to be engaged in public employment, and yet is constantly losing the opportunity of being so?' *Confucius* again said, 'No.' 'The days and months are passing away; the years do not wait for us.' Confucius said, 'Right; I will go into office.'

CHAPTER II.

The Master said, 'By nature, men are nearly alike; by practice, they get to be wide apart.'

CHAPTER III.

The Master said, 'There are only the wise of the highest class, and the stupid of the lowest class, who cannot be changed.'

CHAPTER IV.

1 The Master, having come to Wû-ch'ăng, heard *there* the sound of stringed instruments and singing.

2 Well pleased and smiling, he said, 'Why use an ox knife to kill a fowl?'

3 Tsze-yû replied, 'Formerly, Master, I heard you say,-- "When the man of high station is well instructed, he loves men; when the man of low station is well instructed, he is easily ruled."'

4 The Master said, 'My disciples, Yen's words are right. What I said was only in sport.'

CHAPTER V.

1 Kung-shăn Fû-zâo, when he was holding Pi, and in an attitude of rebellion, invited the Master to visit him, who was rather inclined to go.

2 Tsze-lû was displeased, and said, 'Indeed, you cannot go! Why must you think of going to see Kung-shan?'

3 The Master said, 'Can it be without some reason that he has invited ME? If any one employ me, may I not make an eastern Châu?'

CHAPTER VI.

Tsze-chang asked Confucius about perfect virtue. Confucius said, 'To be able to practise five things everywhere under heaven constitutes perfect virtue.' He begged to ask what they were, and was told, 'Gravity, generosity *of soul*, sincerity, earnestness, and kindness. If you are grave, you will not be treated with disrespect. If you are generous, you will win all. If you are sincere, people will repose trust in you. If you are earnest, you will accomplish much. If you are kind, this will enable you to employ the services of others.

CHAPTER VII.

1 Pî Hsî inviting him to visit him, the Master was inclined to go.

2 Tsze-lû said, 'Master, formerly I have heard you say, "When a man in his own person is guilty of doing evil, a superior man will not associate with him." Pî Hsî is in rebellion, holding possession of Chung-mâu; if you go to him, what shall be said?'

3 The Master said, 'Yes, I did use these words. But is it not said, that, if a thing be really hard, it may be ground without being made thin? Is it not said, that, if a thing be really white, it may be steeped in a dark fluid without being made black?

4 'Am I a bitter gourd! How can I be hung up out of the way of being eaten?'

CHAPTER VIII.

1 The Master said, 'Yû, have you heard the six words to which are attached six becloudings?' Yû replied, 'I have not.'

2 'Sit down, and I will tell them to you.

3 'There is the love of being benevolent without the love of learning;-- the beclouding here leads to a foolish simplicity. There is the love of knowing without the love of learning;-- the beclouding here leads to dissipation of mind. There is the love of being sincere without the love of learning;-- the beclouding here leads to an injurious disregard of consequences. There is the love of straightforwardness without the love of learning;-- the beclouding here leads to rudeness. There is the love of boldness without the love of learning;-- the beclouding here leads to insubordination. There is the love of firmness without the love of learning;-- the beclouding here leads to extravagant conduct.'

CHAPTER IX.

1 The Master said, 'My children, why do you not study the Book of Poetry?

2 '*The Odes* serve to stimulate the mind.

3 'They may be used for purposes of self-contemplation.

4 'They teach the art of sociability.

5 'They show how to regulate feelings of resentment.

6 'From them you learn the more immediate duty of serving one's father, and the remoter one of serving one's prince.

7 'From them we become largely acquainted with the names of birds, beasts, and plants.'

CHAPTER X.

The Master said to Po-yü, 'Do you give yourself to the Châu-nan and the Shâo-nan. The man who has not studied the Châu-nan and the Shâo-nan, is like one who stands with his face right against a wall. Is he not so?'

CHAPTER XI.

The Master said, '"It is according to the rules of propriety," they say.-- "It is according to the rules of propriety," they say. Are gems and silk all that is meant by propriety? "It is music," they say.-- "It is music," they say. Are bells and drums all that is meant by music?'

CHAPTER XII.

The Master said, 'He who puts on an appearance of stern firmness, while inwardly he is weak, is like one of the small, mean people;--yea, is he not like the thief who breaks through, or climbs over, a wall?'

CHAPTER XIII.

The Master said, 'Your good, careful people of the villages are the thieves of virtue.'

CHAPTER XIV

The Master said, 'To tell, as we go along, what we -have heard on the way, is to cast away our virtue.'

CHAPTER XV

1 The Master said, 'There are those mean creatures! How impossible it is along with them to serve one's prince!

2 'While they have not got their aims, their anxiety is how to get them. When they have got them, their anxiety is lest they should lose them.

3 'When they are anxious lest such things should be lost, there is nothing to which they will not proceed.'

CHAPTER XVI.

1 The Master said, 'Anciently, men had three failings, which now perhaps are not to be found.

2 'The high-mindedness of antiquity showed itself in a disregard of small things; the high-mindedness of the present day shows itself in wild license. The stern dignity of antiquity showed itself in grave reserve; the stern dignity of the present day shows itself in quarrelsome perverseness. The stupidity of antiquity showed itself in straightforwardness; the stupidity of the present day shows itself in sheer deceit.'

CHAPTER XVII.

The Master said, 'Fine words and an insinuating appearance are seldom associated with virtue.'

CHAPTER XVIII.

The Master said, 'I hate the manner in which purple takes away *the luster* of vermilion. I hate the way in which the songs of Chang confound the music of the Yâ. I hate those who with their sharp mouths overthrow kingdoms and families.'

CHAPTER XIX.

1 The Master said, 'I would prefer not speaking.'

2 Tsze-kung said, 'If you, Master, do not speak, what shall we, your disciples, have to record?

3 The Master said, 'Does Heaven speak? The four seasons pursue their courses, and all things are *continually* being produced, *but* does Heaven say anything?'

CHAPTER XX.

Zû Pei wished to see Confucius, but Confucius declined, on the ground of being sick, to see him. When the bearer of this message went out at the door, (the Master) took his lute and sang to it, in order that Pei might hear him.

CHAPTER XXI.

1 Tsâi Wo asked about the three years' mourning *for parents*, saying that one year was long enough.

2 'If the superior man,' said he, 'abstains for three years from the observances of propriety, those observances will be quite

lost. If for three years he abstains from music, music will be ruined.

3 '*Within a year* the old grain is exhausted, and the new grain has sprung up, and, in procuring fire by friction, we go through all the changes of wood for that purpose. After a complete year, the mourning may stop.'

4 The Master said, 'If you were, *after a year*, to eat good rice, and wear embroidered clothes, would you feel at ease?' 'I should,' replied Wo.

5 The Master said, 'If you can feel at ease, do it. But a superior man, during the whole period of mourning, does not enjoy pleasant food which he may eat, nor derive pleasure from music which he may hear. He also does not feel at ease, if he is comfortably lodged. Therefore he does not do *what you propose*. But now you feel at ease and may do it.'

6 Tsâi Wo then went out, and the Master said, 'This shows Yü's want of virtue. It is not till a child is three years old that it is allowed to leave the arms of its parents. And the three years' mourning is universally observed throughout the empire. Did Yü enjoy the three years' love of his parents?'

CHAPTER XXII.

The Master said, 'Hard is it to deal with him, who will stuff himself with food the whole day, without applying his mind to anything *good*! Are there not gamesters and chess players? To be one of these would still be better than doing nothing at all.'

CHAPTER XXIII.

Tsze-lü said, 'Does the superior man esteem valour?' The Master said, 'The superior man holds righteousness to be of highest importance. A man in a superior situation, having valour without righteousness, will be guilty of insubordination; one of the lower people having valour without righteousness, will commit robbery.'

CHAPTER XXIV.

1 Tsze-kung said, 'Has the superior man his hatreds also?' The Master said, 'He has his hatreds. He hates those who proclaim the evil of others. He hates the man who, being in a low station, slanders his superiors. He hates those who have *valour merely*, and are unobservant of propriety. He hates those who are forward and determined, and, *at the same time*, of contracted understanding.'

2 *The Master* then inquired, 'Ts'ze, have you also your hatreds?' *Tsze-kung replied*, 'I hate those who pry out matters, and ascribe the knowledge to their wisdom. I hate those who are *only* not modest, and think that they are valourous. I hate those who make known secrets, and think that they are straightforward.'

CHAPTER XXV.

The Master said, 'Of all people, girls and servants are the most difficult to behave to. If you are familiar with them, they lose their humility. If you maintain a reserve towards them, they are discontented.'

CHAPTER XXVI.

The Master said, 'When a man at forty is the object of dislike, he will always continue what he is.'

BOOK XVIII.
WEI TSZE.

CHAPTER I.

1 The Viscount of Wei withdrew *from the court*. The Viscount of Chî became a slave *to Châu*. Pî -kan remonstrated with him and died.

2 Confucius said, 'The Yin dynasty possessed *these* three men of virtue.'

CHAPTER II.

Hui of Liu-hsia being chief criminal judge, was thrice dismissed from his office. Some one said to him, 'Is it not yet time for you, sir, to leave this?' He replied, 'Serving men in an upright way, where shall I go to, and not experience such a thrice-repeated dismissal? If I choose to serve men in a crooked way, what necessity is there for me to leave the country of my parents?'

CHAPTER III.

The duke Ching of Ch'î, *with reference to the manner in which* he should treat Confucius, said, 'I cannot treat him as I would the chief of the Ch'î family. I will treat him in a manner between that accorded to the chief of the Ch'î, and that given to the chief of the Măng family.' He also said, 'I am *old*; I cannot use his *doctrines*.' Confucius took his departure.

CHAPTER IV.

The people of Ch'i sent to Lu a present of female musicians, which Chi Hwan received, and for three days no court was held. Confucius took his departure.

CHAPTER V.

1 The madman of Ch'û, Chieh-yü, passed by Confucius, singing and saying, 'O FĂNG! O FĂNG! How is your virtue degenerated! As to the past, reproof is useless; but the future may still be provided against. Give up *your vain pursuit*. Give up *your vain pursuit*. Peril awaits those who now engage in affairs of government.'

2 Confucius alighted and wished to converse with him, but Chieh-yü hastened away, so that he could not talk with him.

CHAPTER VI.

1 Ch'ang-tsü and Chieh-nî were at work in the field together, when Confucius passed by them, and sent Tsze-lû to inquire for the ford.

2 Ch'ang-tsü said, 'Who is he that holds the reins in the carriage there?' Tsze-lû told him, 'It is K'ung Ch'iû.' 'Is it not K'ung Ch'iû of Lû?' asked he. 'Yes,' was the reply, to which the other rejoined, 'He knows the ford.'

3 *Tsze-lû then* inquired of Chieh-nî, who said to him, 'Who are you, sir?' He answered, 'I am Chung Yû.' 'Are you not the disciple of K'ung Ch'iû of Lû?' asked the other. 'I am,' replied he, and then Chieh-nî said to him, 'Disorder, like a swelling flood, spreads over the whole empire, and who is he that will change its state *for you*? Than follow one who merely withdraws from this one and that one, had you not better follow those who have withdrawn from the world altogether?' *With this* he fell to covering up the seed, *and proceeded with his work*, without stopping.

4 Tsze-lû went and reported their remarks, when the Master observed with a sigh, 'It is impossible to associate with birds and beasts, as if they were the same with us. If I associate not with these people,-- with mankind,-- with whom shall I associate? If right principles prevailed through the empire, there would be no use for me to change its state.'

CHAPTER VII.

5 Tsze-lû, following the Master, happened to fall behind, when he met an old man, carrying across his shoulder on a staff a basket for weeds. Tsze-lû said to him, 'Have you seen my master, sir!' The old man replied, 'Your four limbs are unaccustomed to toil; you cannot distinguish the five kinds of grain:-- who is your master?' With this, he planted his staff in the ground, and proceeded to weed.

6 Tsze-lû joined his hands across his breast, and stood *before him*.

7 The old man kept Tsze-lû to pass the night in his house, killed a fowl, prepared millet, and feasted him. He also introduced to him his two sons.

8 Next day, Tsze-lû went on his way, and reported *his adventure*. The Master said, 'He is a recluse,' and sent Tsze-lû back to see him again, but when he got to the place, the old man was gone.

9 Tsze-lû then said *to the family*, 'Not to take office is not righteous. If the relations between old and young may not be neglected, how is it that he sets aside the duties that should be observed between sovereign and minister? Wishing to maintain his personal purity, he allows that great relation to come to confusion. A superior man takes office, and performs the righteous duties belonging to it. As to the failure of right principles to make progress, he is aware of that.'

CHAPTER VIII.

1 The men who have retired to privacy from the world have been Po-î, Shû-ch'î, Yü-chung, Î-yî, Chû-chang, Hûi of Lûi-hsîa, and Shâo-lien.

2 The Master said, 'Refusing to surrender their wills, or to submit to any taint in their persons;-- such, I think, were Po-î and Shû-ch'î.

3 'It may be said of Hûi of Lûi-hsîa, and of Shâo-lien, that they surrendered their wills, and submitted to taint in their persons, but their words corresponded with reason, and their actions were such as men are anxious to see. This is all that is to be remarked in them.

4 'It may be said of Yü-chung and Î-yî, that, while they hid themselves in their seclusion, they gave a license to their words; but, in their persons, they succeeded in preserving their purity, and, in their retirement, they acted according to the exigency of the times.

5 'I am different from all these. I have no course for which I am predetermined, and no course against which I am predetermined.'

CHAPTER IX.

1 The grand music master, Chih, went to Ch'î.

2 Kan, *the master of the band at* the second meal, went to Ch'û. Liâo, *the band master at* the third meal, went to Ts'âi. Chüêh, *the band master* at the fourth meal, went to Ch'in.

3 Fûng-shu, the drum master, withdrew to *the north of the river*.

4 Wû, the master of the hand drum, withdrew to the Han.

5 Yang, the assistant music master, and Hsiang, master of the musical stone, withdrew *to an island in* the sea.

CHAPTER X.

The duke of Châu addressed *his son*, the duke of Lû, saying, 'The virtuous prince does not neglect his relations. He does not cause the great ministers to repine at his not employing them. Without some great cause, he does not dismiss from their offices the members of old families. He does not seek in one man talents for every employment.'

CHAPTER XI.

To Châu belonged the eight officers, Po-tâ, Po-kwô, Chung-tû, Chung-hwû, Shû-yâ, Shû-hsiâ, Chî-sui, and Chî-kwa.

BOOK XIX.
TSZE-CHANG.

CHAPTER I.

Tsze-chang said, 'The scholar, *trained for public duty*, seeing threatening danger, is prepared to sacrifice his life. When the opportunity of gain is presented to him, he thinks of righteousness. In sacrificing, his thoughts are reverential. In mourning, his thoughts are about the grief *which he should feel*. Such a man commands our approbation indeed.'

CHAPTER II.

Tsze-chang said, 'When a man holds fast to virtue, but without seeking to enlarge it, and believes right principles, but without firm sincerity, what account can be made of his existence or non-existence?'

CHAPTER III.

The disciples of Tsze-hsiâ asked Tsze-chang about the principles that should characterize mutual intercourse. Tsze-chang asked, 'What does Tsze-hsiâ say on the subject?' They replied, 'Tsze-hsiâ says:-- "Associate with those who can *advantage you*. Put away from you those who cannot *do so*."' Tsze-chang observed, 'This is different from what I have learned. The superior man honours the talented and virtuous, and bears with all. He praises the good, and pities the incompetent. Am I possessed of great talents and virtue?-- who is there among men whom I will not bear with? Am I devoid of talents and virtue?-- men will put me away from them. What have we to do with the putting away of others?'

CHAPTER IV.

Tsze-hsiâ said, 'Even in inferior studies and employments there is something worth being looked at; but if it be attempted to carry them out to what is remote, there is a danger of their proving inapplicable. Therefore, the superior man does not practise them.'

CHAPTER V.

Tsze-hsiâ said, 'He, who from day to day recognizes what he has not yet, and from month to month does not forget what he has attained to, may be said indeed to love to learn.'

CHAPTER VI.

Tsze-hsiâ said, 'There are learning extensively, and having a firm and sincere aim; inquiring with earnestness, and reflecting with self-application:-- virtue is in such a course.'

CHAPTER VII.

Tsze-hsiâ said, 'Mechanics have their shops to dwell in, in order to accomplish their works. The superior man learns, in order to reach to the utmost of his principles.'

CHAPTER VIII.

Tsze-hsiâ said, 'The mean man is sure to gloss his faults.'

CHAPTER IX.

Tsze-hsiâ said, 'The superior man undergoes three changes. Looked at from a distance, he appears stern; when approached, he is mild; when he is heard to speak, his language is firm and decided.'

CHAPTER X.

Tsze-hsiâ said, 'The superior man, having obtained their confidence, may then impose labours on his people. If he have not gained their confidence, they will think that he is oppressing them. Having obtained the confidence *of his prince*, one may then remonstrate with him. If he have not gained his confidence, *the prince* will think that he is vilifying him.'

CHAPTER XI.

Tsze-hsiâ said, 'When a person does not transgress the boundary line in the great virtues, he may pass and repass it in the small virtues.'

CHAPTER XII.

1 Tsze-yû said, 'The disciples and followers of Tsze-hsiâ, in sprinkling and sweeping the ground, in answering and replying, in advancing and receding, are sufficiently accomplished. But these are only the branches *of learning*, and they are left ignorant of what is essential.-- How can they be acknowledged as sufficiently taught?'

2 Tsze-hsiâ heard of the remark and said, 'Alas! Yen Yû is wrong. According to the way of the superior man in teaching, what departments are there which he considers of prime importance, and delivers? what are there which he considers of secondary importance, and allows himself to be idle about? But as in the case of plants, which are assorted according to their classes, so he deals with his disciples. How can the way of a superior man be such as to make fools of any of them? Is it not the sage alone, who can unite in one the beginning and the consummation of learning?'

CHAPTER XIII.

Tsze-hsiâ said, 'The officer, having discharged all his duties, should devote his leisure to learning. The student, having completed his learning, should apply himself to be an officer.'

CHAPTER XIV.

Tsze-hsiâ said, 'Mourning, having been carried to the utmost degree of grief, should stop with that.'

CHAPTER XV.

Tsze-hsiâ said, 'My friend Chang can do things which are hard to be done, but yet he is not perfectly virtuous.'

CHAPTER XVI.

The philosopher Tsăng said, 'How imposing is the manner of Chang! It is difficult along with him to practise virtue.'

CHAPTER XVII.

The philosopher Tsăng said, 'I heard this from our Master:-- "Men may not have shown what is in them to the full extent, and yet they will be found to do so, on occasion of mourning for their parents."'

CHAPTER XVIII.

The philosopher Tsăng said, 'I have heard this from our Master:-- "The filial piety of Măng Chwang, in other matters, was what other men are competent to, but, as seen in his not changing the ministers of his father, nor his father's mode of government, it is difficult to be attained to."'

CHAPTER XIX.

The chief of the Măng family having appointed Yang Fû to be chief criminal judge, the latter consulted the philosopher Tsăng. Tsăng said, 'The rulers have failed in their duties, and the people consequently have been disorganised, for a long time. When you have found out the truth of any accusation, be grieved for and pity them, and do not feel joy at your own ability.'

CHAPTER XX.

Tsze-kung said, 'Châu's wickedness was not so great *as that name implies*. Therefore, the superior man hates to dwell in a low-lying situation, where all the evil of the world will flow in upon him.'

CHAPTER XXI.

Tsze-kung said, 'The faults of the superior man are like the eclipses of the sun and moon. He has his faults, and all men see them; he changes again, and all men look up to him.'

CHAPTER XXII.

1 Kung-sun Ch'âo of Wei asked Tsze-kung, saying, 'From whom did Chung-nî get his learning?'

2 Tsze-kung replied, 'The doctrines of Wăn and Wu have not yet fallen to the ground. They are to be found among men. Men of talents and virtue remember the greater principles of them, and others, not possessing such talents and virtue, remember the smaller. *Thus*, all possess the doctrines of Wăn and Wu. Where could our Master go that he should not have an opportunity of learning them? And yet what necessity was there for his having a regular master?'

CHAPTER XXIII.

1 Shû-sun Wû-shû observed to the great officers in the court, saying, 'Tsze-kung is superior to Chung-nî.'

2 Tsze-fû Ching-po reported the observation to Tsze-kung, who said, 'Let me use the comparison of a house and its *encompassing* wall. My wall *only* reaches to the shoulders. One may peep over it, and see whatever is valuable in the apartments.

3 'The wall of my Master is several fathoms high. If one do not find the door and enter by it, he cannot see the ancestral temple with its beauties, nor all the officers in their rich array.

4 'But I may assume that they are few who find the door. Was not the observation of the chief only what might have been expected?'

CHAPTER XXIV.

Shû-sun Wû-shû having spoken revilingly of Chung-nî, Tsze-kung said, 'It is of no use doing so. Chung-nî cannot be reviled. The talents and virtue of other men are hillocks and mounds which may be stepped over. Chung-ni is the sun or moon, which it is not possible to step over. Although a man may wish to cut himself off *from the sage*, what harm can he do to the sun or moon? He only shows that he does not know his own capacity.

CHAPTER XXV.

1 Ch'ăn Tsze-ch'in, addressing Tsze-kung, said, 'You are too modest. How can Chung-nî be said to be superior to you?'

2 Tsze-kung said to him, 'For one word a man is *often* deemed to be wise, and for one word he is *often* deemed to be foolish. We ought to be careful indeed in what we say.

3 'Our Master cannot be attained to, just in the same way as the heavens cannot be gone up to by the steps of a stair.

4 'Were our Master in the position of the ruler of a State or the chief of a Family, we should find verified the description *which has been given of a sage's rule*:-- he would plant the people, and forthwith they would be established; he would lead them on, and forthwith they would follow him; he would make them happy, and forthwith *multitudes* would resort to *his dominions*; he would stimulate them, and forthwith they would be harmonious. While he lived, he would be glorious. When he died, he would be bitterly lamented. How is it possible for him to be attained to?'

BOOK XX.
YÂO YÜEH.

CHAPTER I.

1 Yâo said, 'Oh! you, Shun, the Heaven-determined order of succession now rests in your person. Sincerely hold fast the due Mean. If there shall be distress and want within the four seas, the Heavenly revenue will come to a perpetual end.'

2 Shun also used the same language in giving charge to Yü.

3 *T'ang* said, 'I the child Lî, presume to use a dark-coloured victim, and presume to announce to Thee, O most great and sovereign God, that the sinner I dare not pardon, and thy ministers, O God, I do not keep in obscurity. The examination of them is by thy mind, O God. If, in my person, I commit offences, they are not to be attributed to you, *the people of* the myriad regions. If you in the myriad regions commit offences, these offences must rest on my person.'

4 Châu conferred great gifts, and the good were enriched.

5 'Although he has his near relatives, they are not equal to *my* virtuous men. The people are throwing blame upon me, the One man.'

6 He carefully attended to the weights and measures, examined the body of the laws, restored the discarded officers, and the good government of the kingdom took its course.

7 He revived States that had been extinguished, restored families whose line of succession had been broken, and called to office those who had retired into obscurity, so that throughout the kingdom the hearts of the people turned towards him.

8 What he attached chief importance to, were the food of the people, the duties of mourning, and sacrifices.

9 By his generosity, he won all. By his sincerity, he made the people repose trust in him. By his earnest activity, his achievements were great. By his justice, all were delighted.

CHAPTER II.

1 Tsze-chang asked Confucius, saying, 'In what way should *a person in authority* act in order that he may conduct government properly?' The Master replied, 'Let him honour the five excellent, and banish away the four bad, things;-- then may he conduct government properly.' Tsze-chang said, 'What are meant by the five excellent things?' The Master said, 'When the person in authority is beneficent without great expenditure; when he lays tasks on the people without their repining; when *he pursues what he* desires without being covetous; when he maintains a dignified ease without being proud; when he is majestic without being fierce.'

2 Tsze-chang said, 'What is meant by being beneficent without great expenditure?' The Master replied, 'When *the person in authority* makes more beneficial to the people the things from which they naturally derive benefit;-- is not this being beneficent without *great* expenditure? When he chooses the labours which are proper, and makes them labour on them, who will repine? When his desires are set on benevolent *government*, and he secures it, who will accuse him of covetousness? Whether he has to do with many people or few, or with things great or small, he does not dare to indicate any disrespect;-- is not this to maintain a dignified ease without any pride? He adjusts his clothes and cap, and throws a dignity into his looks, so that, thus dignified, he is looked at with awe;-- is not this to be majestic without being fierce?'

3 Tsze-chang then asked, 'What are meant by the four bad things?' The Master said, 'To put the people to death without

having instructed them;-- this is called cruelty. To require from them, *suddenly*, the full tale of work, without having given them warning;-- this is called oppression. To issue orders as if without urgency, *at first*, and, when the time comes, *to insist on them with severity*;-- this is called injury. And, generally, in the giving *pay or rewards to men*, to do it in a stingy way;-- this is called acting the part of a mere official.'

CHAPTER III.

1 The Master said, 'Without recognising the ordinances of Heaven, it is impossible to be a superior man.

2 'Without an acquaintance with the rules of Propriety, it is impossible for the character to be established.

3 'Without knowing the force of words, it is impossible to know men.'